W9-BCU-208

A PHILOSOPHICAL APPROACH
TO RELIGION

A Philosophical Approach to Religion

W. Donald Hudson
Reader in Moral Philosophy
University of Exeter

First edition 1974
Reprinted 1976

Published by
THE MACMILLAN PRESS LTD
London and Basingstoke
Associated companies in New York
Dublin Melbourne Johannesburg and Madras

SBN 333 15559 9

Printed in Great Britain by
UNWIN BROTHERS LIMITED
Woking and London

TO MURIEL AND ARTHUR

with gratitude and affection

Contents

Preface   ix
Introduction   xi

1 THE LOGICAL STRUCTURE
  OF RELIGIOUS BELIEF   1

  Questions *within* Religious Belief   1
  Questions *about* Religious Belief   1
  Philosophical Questions *about* Religious Belief   3
  Mapping the Frontiers of Religious Belief   8
  Exposing the Presuppositions of Religious Belief   13
  The Concept of god   14
  The Concept of god as Constitutive of Religious Belief   16
  Conclusion   22

2 THE PROBLEM OF OBJECTIVITY:
  (i) CONCEPTUAL ANALYSIS   26

  Anselm's Ontological 'Proof'   27
  Anselm's First Line of Argument   29
  Anselm's Second Line of Argument and Recent
    Philosophy   31
  Conclusion   39

3 THE PROBLEM OF OBJECTIVITY:
  (ii) THE APPEAL TO EMPIRICAL EVIDENCE   41

  The Cosmological Argument   41
  The Argument from Design   56
  Religious Experience   67
  The Moral Argument   74
  Conclusion   88

4   THE PROBLEM OF OBJECTIVITY:
    (iii) THE REJECTION OF THE QUESTION   89

    Belief In and Belief That   90
    God and Love   94
    The Question Elusive to an Affirmative Answer 97

5   THE CHALLENGE OF SECULARIZATION   106

    (i) *The Nature of the Challenge*   107
    The Decline of Belief   107
    The Prevalence of a Secular World View   110
    The Philosophical Grounding of Secularization 116

    (ii) *The Response to the Challenge*   119
    Bonhoeffer   120
    Braithwaite   127
    Van Buren   131
    Tillich and Cox   133

    (iii) *The Levels of Secularization Reconsidered* 137
    The Decline of Belief   138
    The Secular World View   138
    The Philosophical Grounding   140

6   THE QUESTION OF RATIONALITY   143

    Proportioning Belief to the Evidence   144
    Avoiding Self-Contradiction   150
    Using Language Intelligibly   161
    Pascal's Wager   177
    Open-Mindedness   179
    Conclusion   186

    Conclusion   188
    Notes   192
    Index of Names   199

Preface

The main arguments of this book were presented in the Whitley Lectures which I gave during the autumn and winter of 1970-1 in London and Manchester.

I should like to express my appreciation of the honour which the Trustees did me in inviting me to lecture on their foundation.

Dr George Beasley-Murray and Mr Michael Taylor entertained me most cordially in their respective colleges whilst I was giving the lectures and I am grateful to them for many kindnesses. The audiences consisted of academics and students and I learned much from their questions and comments in the discussions which followed each lecture.

In preparing this book for publication I have as ever been most efficiently served in secretarial ways by Mrs Eugénie Ridgeon and my thanks are due to her.

Perhaps the most enjoyable aspect of the lectureship for me was the fact that it gave me the opportunity to spend a few days in Manchester as a guest in the home of my old friends Stanley and Agnes Ward and to relish once again their kindly hospitality.

W. D. HUDSON
University of Exeter

Acknowledgements

The author and publishers wish to thank the following, who have kindly given permission for the use of copyright material: Basil Blackwell & Mott Ltd for the extract from *Philosophical Investigations* by L. Wittgenstein; J. N. Findlay, 'Can God's Existence be Disproved?', from *Mind* (1948); The Independent Broadcasting Authority for the extract from *Religion in Britain and N. Ireland*; N. Malcolm, 'Is it a religious belief that God exists?', in J. Hick (ed.), *Faith and the Philosophers*; James Nisbet & Co Ltd and Yale University Press Ltd for the extract from *The Courage to Be* by Paul Tillich; Oliver & Boyd for the extract from P. Edwards, 'Some notes on anthropomorphic theology', in S. Hook (ed.), *Religious Experience and Truth: A Symposium* (London, 1959); Routledge & Kegan Paul Ltd and Schocken Books Inc. for the extract from *The Five Ways* by A. Kenny; The Royal Institute of Philosophy for 'Wittgensteinian Fideism' by K. Nielsen from *Philosophy* (1967); S.C.M. Press Ltd and Macmillan Publishing Co. Inc. for the extracts from *Letters and Papers from Prison* by Dietrich Bonhoeffer, revised edition (copyright © 1953, 1967, 1971 by S.C.M. Press Ltd); S.C.M. Press Ltd and Macmillan Publishing Co. Inc. for the extracts from *The Secular Meaning of the Gospel* by Paul van Buren; C. A. Watts & Co Ltd for the extract from *Christianity and Paradox* by R. W. Hepburn.

The publishers have made every effort to trace the copyright-holders, but if they have inadvertently overlooked any they will be pleased to make the necessary arrangement at the first opportunity.

Introduction

There are two main objectives which, I think, the philosophy of religion should enable us to attain. The first is an *understanding* of religion : philosophy should help one to clear one's head as to what religious belief is. The second objective is an *evaluation* of religion : philosophical study should assist one to appreciate what precisely is at issue so far as the intellectual respectability of religious belief is concerned and to form a judgment on that issue.

I offer this book as an attempt to say something useful in the pursuit of both these objectives.

To begin with, I shall try to define religious belief in the light of contemporary analytical philosophy. Such belief is expressed in language which is used in certain specific ways, on certain characteristic kinds of occasion, and for certain definitive purposes. I shall invoke Wittgenstein's notion of a 'language-game' or 'form of life' in my attempt to define religion. This notion seems to me to provide the best way in to a philosophical understanding of religion. The kind of question to which it gives rise is 'What are the tacit presuppositions of the religious "language-game"?', 'How does this "language-game" resemble, and how does it differ from, the uses to which language is put in other main concerns of *homo loquens*?', and so on. It is by answering such questions that we discover the logical structure of religious belief. We come to see what makes sense within religion and what does not. We perceive how words are woven with actions to constitute the religious 'form of life'. This is what I mean by defining religion or by understanding what it is.

It is not enough, however, simply to define religion or to show what does, and what does not, make sense within it. As soon as we are clear about that, the question confronts us : but does religion itself make sense? The religious 'language-game' is played, certainly; but is it intellectually respectable to play it? The philosopher of religion has not only to define religion, but to consider whether or not it is rationally defensible.

In a small book called *Ludwig Wittgenstein : The Bearing of His Philosophy on Religious Belief* (Lutterworth, 1968), which I published a year or two ago, I posed at the end, but did not attempt to answer, three questions which, I said, are inescapable, if religious belief is conceived as a Wittgensteinian 'language-game' or 'form of life'. I still think that these three questions taken together constitute the criterion of intellectual respectability so far as religion is concerned. In the present book I intend to discuss them as carefully and honestly as I can. They are as follows.

(i) The first is : does religion make sense in that it is *about something which really or objectively exists*? When one talks about God is one talking about anything which exists outside one's imagination? This looks like a straightforward question but of course it is an exceedingly complex one which has given rise to much intricate philosophizing from earliest times and still does so. Below I shall deal with three lines of approach to this question in Chapters 2, 3 and 4 respectively. Firstly, can it be answered merely by conceptual analysis as Anselm in ancient times and Professor Malcolm in modern, have held? Secondly, is there evidence in the world about us, or within our own experience, which supports belief in God in logically the same way as belief in the objective existence and character of the physical world is supported by scientific evidence? Or, thirdly, is something wrong with the whole idea that we can discover what really exists, so that the only way to deal with this present issue is, in the last analysis, to make a choice – an ultimate ontological choice? These are the three lines of approach which I shall pursue in my attempt to solve what I call 'the problem of objectivity'.

(ii) The second main question concerning the intellectual respectability of religious belief as I define the latter is : does religion make sense in that its basic concepts and processes of thought are *intelligible to modern man*? With this I shall try to deal in Chapter 5. The prevailing intellectual climate of our time is deeply secular, the presuppositions of our culture and civilization, largely atheistic. The last thing which could be said of this age, many would affirm, is that it is an age of faith. So complete has been the process of intellectual secularization, some hold, that religion can only be made sense of when its characteristic explanations and experiences are seen as departures from the norm. That is to say, we can understand religious accounts of what goes on only when we see what they leave out of, or add to, our more intellectually respectable ways of explaining things. We can see some point in religious experiences or activities only when we recognize the abnormal condition of those whom they visit, or occupy. Against this background, then, I shall try to clarify what is properly meant by 'intellectual secularization'; to determine the extent of it in our world; to outline the response to it which has in fact taken place within the Christian religion; and to propose a way, or ways, in which what I call 'the challenge of secularization' can be met by defenders of religion.

(iii) The third of my three main questions about religious belief is this: does religion make sense in that it is, or can be, *rational*? In Chapter 6, I shall consider five possible meanings of the word 'rational', which seem to me, singly or in combination, to define that word as it is commonly used. Then I shall ask how religion stands when tested against each of them. What I call 'the question of rationality' is, it goes without saying, absolutely fundamental to any attempt to evaluate religious belief philosophically; and so I shall try, within the space available and the limits of my own ability, to make the purport of that question clear and to answer it fairly.

I have no wish to conceal the fact that I count myself a religious believer. In that larger part of this book which is concerned with the defence of religion, however, I hope it will be apparent that I am motivated by philosophical interest rather than proselytizing fervour. It is, no doubt, to be expected that I shall reach the conclusion that religious belief is intellectually respectable; but I hope that I shall do so with a degree of impartiality which will render the exercise itself intellectually respectable.

1 The Logical Structure of Religious Belief

There are questions which arise *within* religious belief and questions which can be asked *about* it. I shall begin by briefly differentiating these two kinds of question in order to make it clear what I propose to discuss in this book.

Questions within Religious Belief

Questions *within* religious belief are those of the kind which preachers or prophets are expected to be able to answer. When the faithful ask, for example, 'Why has God done this to us?' or 'What does God expect of us?', it is the preacher or prophet who normally provides, or purports to provide, the answer. The philosopher as such may sometimes be of some small use where such questions within religious belief are concerned. For instance, when consistency is at issue. Take the classic answer to the question 'What doth the Lord require of thee?' – namely, 'To do justly, to love mercy and to walk humbly'.[1] Suppose someone asked within religious belief how we could be sure that this is the right answer. One way would be by being shown that this answer is consistent with beliefs which we already hold about God. It may be possible to show that if he is the God he is believed to be, he must (logically) require this of men. Thus a philosopher, because his job is logical analysis, could conceivably sometimes help the faithful to see where their beliefs are consistent with one another and where they are not and thereby show them how questions within belief should be answered. However, in this book I shall not be concerned with questions which arise within religious belief but with a certain kind of question which arises about it and which it is the peculiar concern of philosophy to answer.

Questions about Religious Belief

There are many different kinds of question which can be asked *about* religious belief and it may be useful for a start to differentiate the philosophical kind from others. Questions about religious belief may concern its psychology or its sociology, the history of its varied development in different ages or cultures, the comparative study of its manifold expressions in the many faiths to which men have adhered, and so on. A psychologist, for example, will describe the working of the religious mind and will assess how far, if at all, it is neurotic; a historian will describe the emergence of a corpus of religious beliefs and assess how far, if at all, it has influenced an age or culture for good or ill. And so on. It should be noted that each discipline – psychology, history, sociology, or whatever – from its own distinctive standpoint offers a *description* and an *assessment* of religion.

Philosophy is another such discipline. But in an important respect it differs from those to which I have just referred. Its *differentia* lies in the fact that it is concerned with the *logical analysis* of religious belief. Not, that is, with the *empirical* concerns of psychology, sociology, or history, but rather with the *logical* matter of what it does or does not make sense to *say* in religion and why. In a word, philosophy is concerned with *meaning.* What does religious language purport to mean; and can it logically mean what it purports to mean? Like other disciplines which answer questions *about* religious belief, philosophy from its own point of view offers both a *description* and an *assessment* of its subject matter. That is to say : (i) it furnishes us with an *analytical description* of the logical structure of religious belief and thereby discovers for us how, in respect of its logical structure, religious belief is like, and how unlike, other universes of discourse such as science or morality; (ii) it provides a *critical assessment* of particular moves which have been made in the expression, definition or defence of religious belief thereby discovering whether such moves were valid or not.

In the remainder of the present chapter I shall confine myself to philosophical *description* and attempt an account of the logical structure of religious belief. In the remaining chapters I shall turn to philosophical *assessment* and discuss certain critical questions which arise, given my account of the logical structure of religious belief.

Philosophical Questions about Religious Belief

I said that philosophy is concerned with meaning. It is modern analytical philosophy, of course, to which I am referring : and that is the viewpoint from which my whole attempt at a philosophical definition and defence of religion will be written. The question : what constitutes meaning? is fundamental in contemporary analytical philosophy. One conception which has emerged in response to that question is Wittgenstein's conception of a language-game. This is the conception upon which I shall base my account in this chapter of the logical structure of religious belief. Wittgenstein developed the notion of a language-game in his later writings and he explicitly regarded what he had to say about it as correcting another theory of meaning to which he had mistakenly subscribed in his earlier writings.

This earlier theory is expounded in his *Tractatus Logico-Philosophicus* (German edition 1921; with English translation, London, 1922). It is commonly called the 'picture theory' of meaning. His earliest recorded remark embodying this theory occurs in the *Notebooks* (Oxford, 1961), which he kept whilst serving in the trenches as a member of the Austrian Army. It is as follows : 'In the proposition a world is, as it were, put together experimentally. (As when in the law-courts in Paris a motor accident is represented by means of dolls, etc.)' (Entry dated September 29, 1914). Wittgenstein had evidently been reading in a magazine about a case in which some such model of an accident had been constructed in a French courtroom and it occurred to him that propositions model reality in a somewhat similar way. The elements of propositions and of reality, of course, differ – they are, according to the *Tractatus*, respectively 'names' and 'objects'. By 'names' Wittgenstein meant logically proper names which do not describe but denote or designate that of which they are the name. By 'objects' he meant the ultimate constituents of the world, which cannot be analysed into any other elements and can be referred to only by being named. Propositions – or at any rate the elementary propositions into which all other propositions can ultimately be analysed – are according to the *Tractatus* 'concatenations of *names*'.[2] Reality is correspondingly a concatenation of objects:'*Objects* make up the substance of the world'.[3] 'Name' and 'object' are, of course, both technical terms in the *Tractatus*.

Wittgenstein was here working fundamentally with the notion that the meaning of language is that to which it *refers*. He made no claim to have discovered names or objects empirically by his analysis of language or his investigation of reality respectively. His 'picture theory' was an exercise in arm-chair logic. If asked to give examples of a name or an object, he might well have shrugged off the demand as no concern of his. However hard it may be to offer examples of the 'simples' of either language or reality respectively, Wittgenstein would have said, they *must* exist for if they did not then it would be logically impossible for language to have precise, determinate meaning. Irreducible elements of language are arranged in propositions according to configurations which by convention picture the configurations of the irreducible elements of reality. This configuration of elements within the proposition, matching the configuration of objects in reality, Wittgenstein called 'logical form' and he said : 'What any picture, of whatever form, must have in common with reality, in order to be able to depict it – correctly or incorrectly – in any way at all, is logical form, i.e. the form of reality'.[4]

Why did Wittgenstein reject this 'picture theory' of meaning? He is said to have done so initially as the result of a question put to him by his Cambridge friend, the economist, Sraffa. Wittgenstein was insisting that a proposition and what it describes must have the same 'logical form' when Sraffa made a gesture – said by Professor Norman Malcolm who recounts this story to be 'familiar to Neapolitans as meaning something like dislike or contempt'[5] – of brushing the underneath of his chin with an outward sweep of the fingertips of one hand and asked Wittgenstein 'What is the logical form of *that*?'. Wittgenstein had no answer and this made him think that it was absurd to insist as he did that a proposition and what it describes must have the same 'logical form'.

Amongst reasons against the 'picture theory' which Wittgenstein worked out in his later writings are the following. To say that a word has no meaning when nothing corresponds to it in reality is to confuse the *meaning* of a name with the *bearer* of the name. 'When Mr N. N. dies, one says the bearer of the name dies, not that the meaning dies'.[6] Again : it will not do to speak as if an *absolute* one-one correspondence between the 'simples' of language and of reality is possible, because the question 'What *are* the "simples" of reality?' is always an open one. What, for instance, are the simple constituent parts of a tree – the different colours of the tree, or the infinite number of short straight lines into which its outline can be broken down, or what? 'We use the world "composite" (and therefore the word "simple")' said Wittgenstein 'in an enormous number of different and differently related ways'.[7] Yet again: the 'picture theory' assumes that a proposition is meaningless if it does not have an absolutely determinate sense. *But*, said Wittgenstein 'If I tell someone "Stand roughly here" – may not this explanation work perfectly – And cannot every other one fail too?'[8] I take Wittgenstein's point here to be that 'roughly' is a refusal to say exactly where to stand, yet we understand what is meant; and every other explanation could 'fail' in the sense that none would be so exact that it would be impossible to ask for more exact directions where to stand. I will not illustrate any further here Wittgenstein's detailed criticisms of the 'picture theory'. What is more important from our present point of view is the theory with which he replaced it.

Wittgenstein recognised that in the 'picture theory' he had imposed a certain conception of meaning *upon* language rather than 'looked' at language to see what in fact constitutes its meaning. He had simply prejudged the issue. He came to see the importance of overcoming prejudice and looking at the *uses* to which language is put. If one does so, he discovered, one will immediately see that naming is only one of them. 'Look at the sentence as an instrument and at its sense as its employment'[9] said Wittgenstein. He noted that the employment of language is multifarious and multifunctional in the following passage from his *Philosophical Investigations, 23* :

> But how many kinds of sentence are there? Say, assertion, question, and command? – There are *countless* kinds : countless different kinds of use of what we call 'symbols', 'words', 'sentences'. And this multiplicity is not something fixed, given once for all; but new types of language, new language-games, as we may say, come into existence, and others become obsolete and get forgotten. (We can get a rough picture of this from the changes in mathematics.)
>
> Here the term 'language-game' is meant to bring into prominence the fact that the *speaking* of language is part of an

activity, or of a form of life. Review the multiplicity of language-games in the following examples, and in others :
Giving orders, and obeying them –
Describing the appearance of an object, or giving its measurements –
Constructing an object from a description (a drawing) –
Reporting an event –
Speculating about an event –
Forming and testing a hypothesis–
Presenting the results of an experiment in tables and diagrams –
Making up a story; and reading it –
Play-acting –
Singing catches –
Guessing riddles –
Making a joke; telling it –
Solving a problem in practical arithmetic –
Translating from one language into another –
Asking, thanking, cursing, greeting, praying.

It is interesting to compare the multiplicity of the tools in language and of the ways they are used, the multiplicity of kinds of word and sentence, with what logicians have said about the structure of language. (Including the author of the *Tractatus Logico-Philosophicus*.)

Wittgenstein thought of a 'language-game' as a 'whole, consisting of language *and* the activities with which it is woven.'[10] The expression 'language-game' was intended, as just quoted, to 'bring into prominence the fact that the *speaking* of language is part of an activity or form of life'. Wittgenstein offered the following example of an elemental language-game :

A is building with building stones : there are blocks, pillars, slabs and beams. B has to pass the stones, and that in the order in which A needs them. For this purpose they use a language consisting of the words 'block', 'pillar', 'slab', 'beam'. A calls them out; – B brings the stone which he has learnt to bring at such-and-such a call. – Conceive this as a complete primitive language.[11]

The language-games in which man engages have of course become much more complicated than this but the essential point to take is that, in order to understand any piece of language one must set it within its appropriate language-game. The force of this point may be illustrated from Wittgenstein's cryptic remark, 'If a lion could talk, we could not understand him',[12] upon which Professor G. Pitcher makes this illuminating comment :

> . . . suppose a lion says 'It is now three o'clock' but without looking at a clock or his wristwatch – and we may imagine that it would be merely a stroke of luck if he should say this when it actually *is* three o'clock. Or suppose he says 'Goodness, it is three o'clock; I must hurry to make that appointment', but that he continues to lie there, yawning, making no effort to move, as lions are wont to do. In these circumstances – assuming that the lion's general behaviour is in every respect like that of an ordinary lion, save for his amazing ability to utter English sentences – we could not say that he has *asserted* or *stated* that it is three o'clock, even though he has uttered suitable words. We could not tell what, if anything, he has asserted, for the modes of behaviour into which his use of words is woven are too radically different from our own. We would not understand him, since he does not share the relevant forms of life with us.[13]

The supposed lion's remarks were not woven into the activities which normally go with such remarks when uttered in a human context. It is true that in children's books there are animals which talk and we do understand them. But the whole point about Tiger Tim or Yogi Bear is that they are not animals but human beings who happen to look like animals.

Language is not a mirror held up to reality as Wittgenstein supposed in the *Tractatus* – or, at least, not all meaningful language is. The question to ask in order to get at the meaning of language is : what is this piece of language being used for? What are men doing or purporting to do when they say such things? Words, said Wittgenstein, are like pieces in chess and 'the meaning of a piece is its role in the game'.[14]

In the light of all this, I suggest that religious belief should be thought of as one such language-game. Understanding a language-game philosophically involves at least two things : (i) mapping its *logical frontiers,* and (ii) exposing its *logical presuppositions.* I shall discuss these two matters in turn with particular reference to religious belief.

Mapping the Frontiers of Religious Belief

By mapping logical frontiers I mean differentiating a language-game clearly from other language-games. Wittgenstein spoke in one place of philosophy as 'a battle against bewitchment of our intelligence by means of language'.[15] Such bewitchment arises when one language-game gets confused with another; and it is just such confusion which philosophy exists to dispel by mapping clearly the frontiers between language-games.

As an example of the bewitchment of intelligence by means of language Wittgenstein offered St Augustine's puzzlement about time.[16] In effect, Augustine pictured time as a stream flowing past us. If that is what it is, then how can we measure it? was the puzzle. If we were to lay a measuring rod against this stream in order to measure time the task would be impossible for the following reasons. We should be measuring of necessity in the present. We could not therefore measure an interval of time in the past because it is no longer there in the present to be measured. For the same reason, neither could we measure an interval of time in the future. Moreover the present in which we did our measuring could not itself be measured because it would be no more than a point in time. We could not, therefore, measure past, present or future. So we could not measure time at all. This is a logical 'could not'. But as a matter of fact we *do* measure time – we say 'It lasts half an hour', 'I'll be in Scotland in a week's time', 'It was a week ago today', and so on. So there must be something wrong with a concept of measuring which makes it logically impossible to do what as a matter of empirical fact we can do.

Augustine's puzzlement arose, as Wittgenstein rightly said, because he drew 'a misleading analogy'.[17] Augustine thought of events as flowing through time as the water of a stream flows through space. But the language-games in which we speak of spatial and temporal streams respectively, though they may overlap, do not coincide. Movements in a spatial stream are measured against an agreed scale which is laid alongside the stream. But movements in time are measured by agreement that certain natural events (e.g. the rising or setting of the sun) or certain contrived events (e.g. the point by point unwinding of a spring) shall constitute *termini a quo* and *ad quem*. Units in the time span are marked off by the occurrence of such events, not by laying a measuring-rod against something called time. Augustine was held captive by a picture embedded in language.[18] His intelligence was bewitched by the deceptive word 'stream'.

The bewitchment of intelligence by means of language has to be resisted in the case of religious belief as firmly as elsewhere by careful logical mapwork. Anticipating briefly matters which will be more fully discussed in the sequel, let me give some indication of what I have in mind. Take, as a simple example of religious belief, the claim that God always cares for us when we are in need. Compare this with the belief, say, that the social services of this country always care for us when we are in – at any rate certain sorts of – need. If we look at the way in which these respective beliefs function – if, to recall Wittgenstein's remark, we see their sense as their employment – then differences begin to appear. The claim about the social services functions normally as a belief which is falsifiable by empirical evidence. If, for example, we discovered by taking random samples that half the unemployed do not in fact receive unemployment benefits, then *ceteris paribus* we should abandon the claim that the social services always care for us when we are in need. But it is not normal for a religious believer, when confronted by, say, the fact that half the population of the world is underfed, to disclaim his belief that God always cares for us when we are in need. Further reflection on how such a religious belief is used will show that it has a kind of ultimacy which the belief about the social services lacks. If, as I have supposed, *prima facie* evidence came to light that the State may not care for us, should we become unemployed, then normally we would abandon our belief that it always does so without hesitation and without beating about for ways of reconciling the fact that many unemployed receive no benefits with our belief that the social services always care for the unemployed. We should not, for instance, hazard the hypothesis that, although the State denies certain unemployed people free health services, weekly financial payments, etc., it is *really* caring for them by throwing them back on their own resources. But this is just the kind of thing which happens in the case of a religious belief. The belief that God always cares for us functions in religion in a way not unlike that in which the belief that every event has a cause functions in natural science. If a scientist cannot find the cause of an event, he does not conclude that it has none; he tries to find the cause and even if he never does find it he refuses to believe that this event had no cause. Similarly in theism the belief that God always cares for us functions as a kind of end-point to inquiry. It determines what the believer is looking for in the world about him, and goes on looking for however hard it may be to find, namely signs of the goodness and mercy of a God who cares for us.

Wittgenstein pointed out in his *Lectures on Religious Belief* (Oxford, 1966) that so far as empirical evidence for a religious belief in, say, the Last Judgment is concerned, it is logically possible (a) that a man should think that there are very strong grounds for believing that there will be a Last Judgment of the quick and the dead at such-and-such a date in future without this belief making any difference at all to anything else which he says or does; and (b) that a man should think the evidence for expecting such a dénouement to history very slender indeed and yet hold the idea of it always in the foreground of his mind so that it dominates his thought and action over a very wide range.

Surely Wittgenstein was right to insist that these characteristics – being held in the foreground of one's mind and regulating everything in one's life – are necessary conditions of a belief's being a *religious* belief.[19] By contrast, whether one believed that the social services will or will not care for one when one is in need could conceivably make no scrap of difference to anything else one thought, said or did. One's belief would be no less genuine a belief about the social services because it existed, so to speak, in isolation. But it is not the same with a religious belief. If a man said that he believed that God would care for him if he were in need but that this made no difference at all to him and that everything else in his life would be just the same if he did not believe it, then surely we would say that his belief was not a genuinely religious one. This brings out what has been called the 'commissive' character of religious beliefs. In saying that God always cares for me when I am in need, I am, as a religious believer, not simply stating an objective fact; I am expressing an attitude of trust in God. Notice that it is part of the point of my belief that I should go on holding it even when evidence appears to falsify it. It is part of the concept of trust that it goes beyond what can be conclusively established about the object of the trust from the available evidence; and trust is an integral aspect of any belief which can properly be called religious. (I have more to say about this when I write on belief-in and belief-that in Chapter 4.)

These, then, are examples of the kind of thing which I have in mind when I speak of careful logical mapwork where religious belief is concerned.

It is important to map the frontiers of religious belief carefully so that it is not confused with other kinds of belief. Some philosophers might offer as one example of such confusion the logical positivists' critique of religious belief. It was based, they would say, on a radical misconception as to what religious belief is. The positivists' insistence that religious beliefs must be either empirically verifiable or meaningless confuses statements of faith in God with beliefs about the nature of history or the physical world. So far from discrediting religion, it is argued, such 'category mistakes'[20] as they are sometimes called simply reveal misunderstanding of what religious belief is. (I shall discuss Logical Positivism further in Chapter 5.)

In the logical mapwork of which I have been speaking, however, it is essential to notice where the frontiers of the language-game we call religious belief *unite* it with other linguistic territories as well as where they mark it off from these. Religious discourse is not cut off from every other sort of discourse. Some, at least, of the language used in it is also widely used in non-religious contexts. This fact gives rise to the most difficult philosophical problems concerning religious belief. A common philosophical criticism of religion is that the language used to express belief in God 'dies by a thousand qualifications'.[21] For example, theists speak of God as 'good'. The question arises : how can 'good' be used here in anything like its normal sense when it describes a Being who, though able to prevent the pain and misery so rife in the world, refrains from doing so? To suggest, as some apologists for theism do, that God's goodness is *infinite* goodness and therefore the word 'good' does not have to fulfil the same conditions for meaningful use with reference to him as it does when used of men is surely to concede, in effect, that God is *not* good. At the very least, it is to evacuate the belief that God is good of the meaning which it is commonly taken to have. There *is* a problem of evil for those who believe in the goodness of God and the core of it is just this fact that the normal conditions for the use of 'good' do not appear to be fulfilled in the case of God. It is no solution to try and turn the tables on those who question the belief that God is good by pretending that this belief both is and is not the belief that God is good. If the meaning of 'good' with reference to God has to be stated in a contradiction then the belief that God is good is tantamount to a belief in nothing at all. Language needs to retain some of the significance which it has in other contexts in order to be meaningful in a religious context; and at times the fear arises that, in the religious context, it has been so eroded by qualification that it has lost all its significance and is in fact meaningless.

Wittgenstein in his *Lectures on Religious Belief* suggested that it is helpful to think of the religious believer as 'using a picture'; and as having to be trained in the technique of using the picture. Take his example of such a picture, namely, 'the eye of God'. It is perfectly in order for a Christian theist to ask 'Does God's eye see everything?' The answer is: yes. Eyes see, whether human or divine. God's eye sees everything, unlike human eyes which only see some things. But it would not be in order for a Christian theist to ask 'What shape are God's eyebrows?' There is no answer to this question because that is not how the picture 'the eye of God' is used. God's eye does not have any eyebrows.

A moment's reflection on this will show that an initiate into Christian belief needs to have learned two things: how the use of the word 'eye' in 'the eye of God' is (i) like and (ii) unlike its use in non-religious contexts. In raising questions such as 'Does God's eye see everything?', he needs to know that eyes in general see. In avoiding questions such as 'What shape are God's eyebrows?' he needs to know that God's eye, unlike human eyes, has no eyebrows. Learning what questions arise, and what questions do not, with regard to 'the eye of God' is learning the technique of using the picture. But it will be seen that *both* these learning processes are parasitic upon the meaning of the word 'eye' in *non*-religious contexts. You cannot know how God's eye is like, and how unlike, human eyes unless you know the use of the word 'eye' in contexts such as human biology or common sense discourse.

Whilst God's eye may be very unusual – in that it has no eyebrows – if it becomes so unusual that it would be odd to speak in any of the ways in which one would speak about a human eye with reference to the divine eye – odd, let us suppose, to speak of God's eye as *seeing* at all – then the question has to be faced 'Why speak at all of God's *eye?*' and it is hard to resist the conclusion that no answer can be given. With regard to God words must not be used in such a special sense that they have no sense at all. (I return to this subject in Chapter 6.)

Mapping the frontier of the religious language-game is, it will be apparent from all that I have been saying, not the easiest thing in the world. If the meaning of religious discourse is to be discovered and preserved, then : (i) its frontier has to be defined firmly enough to avoid that bewitchment of intelligence which arises from the confusion of language-games with one another; but (ii) at the same time it does not have to be marked off so sharply that religious language is cut off completely from other language-games and thus evacuated of significance.

Exposing the Presuppositions of Religious Belief

The second thing which I said that we must do, if we are to understand religious belief philosophically, is to expose its presuppositions. Wittgenstein remarked: '. . . what we do in our language-games always rests on a tacit presupposition'.[22] In line with this, I want to say that, in the case of every language-game, there is, in the last analysis, a concept or set of concepts, which is 'tacitly presupposed' in the sense that it is always implied in what is said within that language-game. And, in particular, I want to say that religious belief is no exception to this rule. The concept, or set of concepts, which is presuppposed in any language-game I shall call the *constitutive concept* of that language-game or form of life.

Let me try to show more clearly what I mean by a constitutive concept here from two examples other than religious belief. The language-game or form of life which we call morality is constituted by the concept of moral obligation. Everything which is said in moral discourse tacitly presupposes that there is such a thing as moral obligation. Within the language-game of morality people ask, and are told, what they *ought* to do. It may be relevant in deciding what ought to be done, to ask whether a given action will maximise happiness, fulfil the will of God, or whatever; but the notion of what ought to be done cannot be reduced to any of these notions. (For a modern discussion of this point see my *The Is-Ought Question* (London, 1969), or my *Modern Moral Philosophy* (London, 1970)). It is the consideration of what ought to be done, and this alone, which makes an issue a moral one.

Again, the language-game or form of life which we call physical science is constituted in its turn by the concept of a physical object. The subject matter of science, that is to say, is physical objects and nothing else. The objects may be of the smallest magnitude and their existence of the briefest duration, but if anything is not a physical, i.e. a spatio-temporally identifiable, object, then science has nothing to say about it.

The irreducible concepts of moral obligation and of physical objectivity are thus constitutive of morality and physical science respectively.

Now the important question for our present purpose is : what concept, or set of concepts, constitutes religious belief? I want to say that it is the concept of *god*. I write 'god' here with a small 'g' to make it clear that I am not thinking only of theism but of religious belief in the widest sense. There is, I am claiming, a concept, or set of concepts, *god,* which is implicit in all religious discourse in just the way that the concept of moral obligation is implicit in all moral discourse and the concept of a physical object, in all scientific.

Two questions then arise : (i) what precisely is meant by *god* here?, and (ii) what precisely is meant by saying that the concept of god is the *constitutive* concept of religious belief.

The Concept of god

By 'god' I mean the divine however it is conceived in a given religion. I think it true to say that god is invariably conceived as conscious and active in ways which are transcendent. This of course requires further explanation. God, or the divine, is conceived in many differing forms within religious belief as a whole and even at different stages of development within a given religious tradition. Think of the difference between the concept of divine consciousness or agency implicit in animism and that implicit in monotheism for example. But despite all such variations and degrees of development, whatever is god is, I think, conceived to be *conscious,* in the sense that god participates with understanding in the communication which invariably goes on between god and men; and god is conceived also to be *active,* in the sense that god wills certain ends and can at least under certain circumstances carry them into effect. By saying that divine consciousness and agency are *transcendent,* I mean, to put it in a nutshell, that there is always more to god's consciousness or activity than to man's.

God's understanding is more acute than man's or, at least, more guileful; god's activity is more powerful, or at least more effective. But not only is there, so to speak, more of the same kind of thing to god. Transcendence, as I am thinking of it here, is the special (let us say supernatural) character, which whatever is god is always conceived to have whereby god does not have to conform to all the (logical) conditions to which men have to conform in order to be conscious or active. For instance, the stick or stone within which the animist's god dwells does not need any physical sense, such as sight, hearing, touch, etc., in order to be communicated with; and again, the god of theism does not need a body in order to be active in the world.

I realise that two related criticisms may be brought against what I have said so briefly here about the concept of god. (i) One is that I have not taken full enough account of the wide diversity about the nature of the divine within what is commonly called religion and that my definition of 'god' needs to be far more comprehensive if it is fully to describe the logical grounding of religious belief. For instance, how is the transcendence of the spirit in whom the animist believes like, and how unlike, that of the god in whom the ethical monotheist believes? (ii) The other criticism is that, in claiming that the concept of god, as I define it, is always implicit in religious belief, I have imposed my own stipulative definition on religion. What, for instance, about certain forms of Buddhism which seem to attribute neither consciousness nor agency to the divine?

I am not unduly dismayed by either of these criticisms. As for the former, I readily admit that in a full-scale account of the logical structure of religious belief the concept of god would require comprehensive definition. It is important that none of its defining characteristics should be overlooked. A comprehensive definition would require a knowledge of comparative religion far beyond any to which I can lay claim. Like the concept of moral obligation, or the concept of a physical object, the concept of god is complex. And, just as moral philosophers may debate the correct analysis of the concept of moral obligation, or philosophers of science may debate that of the concept of a physical object, so philosophers of religion may disagree as to how precisely the concept of god should be defined. But I am not daunted by all this. It is not necessary to present an exhaustive analysis of the concept of god in order to make the point that there *is* such a concept and that it is *constitutive* of religious belief. It is simply that point which I am attempting to make.

As for the accusation that I have placed my own stipulative definition on religious belief by saying that it is constituted by the concept of god, I concede that there may be some forms of what is commonly called religion which do not tacitly presuppose transcendent consciousness and agency. But I am not concerned if there are. If all I have done is to mark off for consideration one area within what is normally called religious belief, and if all I have been saying and shall say applies only to that area, so be it. All I would observe is that words are often loose in their habits and one has sometimes to bring them into some sort of line in order to give any account of their use. That is what I am doing. There is a language-game or form of life which is constituted by the concept of god and much of that phenomenon which we call religion – from the crudest animism to the most ethically exalted monotheism – falls within it. It is the logical structure of this language-game which I am trying to clarify. If things which fall outside it sometimes get labelled 'religion', I think it can be shown that this is either (a) a metaphorical use of the word (e.g. when Communism is called a religion) or (b) a distinct use of 'religion' which is equivalent in meaning to what we would normally call metaphysics rather than to what we would normally call religion (e.g. some forms of Buddhism).

So much then for the first of the two questions which I said that I would try to answer concerning the concept of god, namely what precisely is meant by *god*? Now I turn to the second question.

The Concept of god as Constitutive of Religious Belief
This second question was : what precisely is meant by saying that the concept of god is the *constitutive* concept of religious belief? The best way I can think of to answer this briefly is as follows. The concept of god determines what in religious belief constitutes (a) an *explanation* and (b) an *experience*. Explanation and experience in religion as indeed anywhere else are, so to say, conceptually loaded.

It may shed some light on what I mean by this – and substantiate my point that religious belief is not logically dissimilar to any other language-game in being constituted in this sense by a concept, or set of concepts – if I quote some words from Professor K. R. Popper's, *The Logic of Scientific Discovery* (London, 1959, English translation of *Logik der Forschung,* Vienna, 1934) p. 280, with reference to explanation and experience in general :

> ...We do not stumble upon our experiences, nor do we let them flow over us like a stream. Rather, we have to be active : we have to '*make*' our experiences. It is we who always formu- late the questions put to nature; it is we who try again and again to put these questions so as to elicit a clear-cut 'yes' or 'no' (for nature does not give an answer unless pressed for it). And in the end, it is again we who give the answer; it is we ourselves who, after severe scrutiny, decide upon the answer to the question which we put to nature....

The important point which is being made in this quotation is that which I expressed a moment ago by saying that explanation and experience are 'conceptually loaded'. It applies to explanation and experience of any kind. In scientific explanation, for instance, the question which the scientist puts to nature is loaded most funda- mentally with the concept of physical, i.e. spatio-temporally identifiable, objectivity; and that is why the answer which the scientist gets – his explanation – is most fundamentally about physical objects and their movements in space and time. And as to experience, that of the scientist, *qua* scientist, is exclusively experience of physical objects and their spatio-temporal charac- teristics. He does not observe anything unless it is extended in space and time.

Similarly, the explanation and experience of the moralist *qua* moralist are determined by the concept of moral obligation. The question he puts to nature – or rather to human nature – concerns what ought to be done. The only explanation of human behaviour in which *qua* moralist he is interested is one which explains what ought to be, or to have been, done. The experiences which *qua* moralist he has are feelings of guilt, remorse, responsibility, etc. which no one could conceivably have who was not thinking in terms of the concept of moral obligation.

I wish to say that the explanations and experiences which occur within religious belief are constituted by the concept of god. I spoke of the latter as the concept of transcendent consciousness and agency. True, the forms which this concept assumes within religious belief are multifarious. But whatever is recognizable as religious belief, in the sense in which I take that expression, has the concept of god at its core. The question which the religious believer as such puts to nature, and the answer which he receives – i.e. his way of *explaining* things – has to do with god. And the *experiences* which *qua* religious believer he has are those which are 'made' by his entertainment of the concept of god.

Take an example of which Wittgenstein made much in his *Lectures on Religious Belief,* namely, the belief that we live under God's judgment. Wittgenstein represents this belief in a form which sophisticated Christians would consider naïve, if not crude. But this is not a serious defect. By taking a starkly simple instance of religious belief Wittgenstein has not falsified or misrepresented the nature of the latter. The simplicity of the example enables him to make his points cogently and clearly and without qualifications which might confuse the issue. However sophisticated an example of religious belief we were to take – god as the ground of Being, the principle of concretion, the life force, etc. – Wittgenstein's analysis in terms of 'using a picture' which determines explanation and makes experience could be applied to it. The core of belief in divine judgment – to return to Wittgenstein's example – is transcendent consciousness and agency, i.e. god. God is thought of here as conscious of what men do, or have done, and as active in rewarding or punishing them accordingly. In the lectures to which I have just referred Wittgenstein was interested in what constitutes the *difference* between religious believers and unbelievers as such, and he used his example of divine judgment to illustrate this difference. He said, in effect, that the difference between believers and unbelievers is fundamentally a difference in what constitutes for them respectively explanation and experience.

As to *explanation,* here is one example of the kind of thing which Wittgenstein said. He was speaking in the role of an unbeliever confronted by belief :

Take two people, one of whom talks of his behaviour and of what happens to him in terms of retribution, the other one does not. These people think entirely differently. . . .
Suppose someone is ill and he says : 'This is a punishment.' And I say : 'If I'm ill, I don't think of punishment at all.'
If you say : 'Do you believe the opposite?' – you can call it

believing the opposite, but it is entirely different from what you would normally call believing the opposite.

I think differently, in a different way. I say different things to myself. I have different pictures.[23]

Confronted by illness, Wittgenstein's believer asks a radically different question about it from his unbeliever and so gets a different explanation. He sets the illness, so to say, within the picture of divine judgment and it is explained for him when he recognizes it as a punishment. The picture he uses determines what constitutes for him an explanation of the illness.

As to *experience*. Let me again quote some cryptic words of Wittgenstein :

... (sc. in religious belief) a number of ways of thinking and acting crystallize and come together ...

A man would fight for his life not to be dragged into the fire. No induction. Terror. That is, as it were part of the substance of the belief.[24]

'Part of the substance of the belief'. Part, that is, of the difference between believer and unbeliever. Wittgenstein's words just quoted put one in mind of the story by Sartre about Monsieur de Rollebon. The Curé had tried to convert a dying man who was an unbeliever but in vain. De Rollebon, who was himself an atheist, bet the Curé that he, de Rollebon, would convert the unbeliever to Christianity within two hours. The Curé took the bet and lost. De Rollebon began the task at 3 p.m. By 5 p.m. the unbeliever confessed and at 7 o'clock he died. 'Are you so forceful in argument?' asked the Curé. 'You outdo even us'. 'I did not argue', answered de Rollebon. 'I made him fear Hell'. In so far as the fear of Hell is an example of a religious experience it is an example of an experience 'made', to use Popper's word, by a certain question put to nature or a certain picture used. This question and picture are constituted by the concept of god, i.e. of transcendent consciousness and agency expressed in judgment. Monsieur de Rollebon may not have argued with his convert but he could (logically) not have made him fear Hell without making him think in terms of god as judge.

These remarks about how religious explanations and experiences are constituted by the concept of god show how the religious

believer and the unbeliever differ from one another. The difference
between them is that they have what Wittgenstein calls 'different
pictures'. One important point which he brings out is that this
kind of disagreement – having different pictures – cannot be
resolved in any ordinary way.

If I say that I believe that there is going to be an eclipse of the
sun on such-and-such a date and someone else says that he does
not, we know how to settle our disagreement. There is a kind of
empirical evidence which shows whether an eclipse of the sun can
be predicted for the time in question or not. But when we turn to
religious beliefs like that in a divine judgment, the case is otherwise. There are many problems, e.g. What sort of evidence counts
here? What would render it probable that there will be a divine
judgment and what not? Even if such questions could be settled,
you might, as I noted above (p. 10) following Wittgenstein, still
have someone who thought the evidence good but was not a
religious believer and someone else who thought it flimsy but was.
Why? Because, said Wittgenstein, the 'indubitability' of such
evidence would not necessarily 'make me change my whole life'.[25]
Religious belief shows itself 'not by reasoning or by appeal to
ordinary grounds for belief, but rather by regulating for all in his
(the believer's) life'.[26]

When we ask just how it 'regulates' there are at least two
possible answers. The former reiterates a point which I made above
(p. 10). It is not important to us at the moment but I will note it in
passing. Statements such as 'We live under divine judgment' have,
to use J. L. Austin's expression, an illocutionary force which is
commissive. That is to say, *in* uttering them, the speaker commits
himself not just to a statement of fact but to a norm of conduct.
We see this if we think how very odd it would be for a believer to
say 'I believe that we live under divine judgment but I never let
that make the slightest difference to anything I do'. It may be that
some believers don't let it make much difference but it would still
be odd for them to *say* that they did not.

More important at the moment is this point. The proposition
'We live under divine judgment' 'regulates' the believer in the
sense which I have been trying to explain in this section, namely
that it *determines* what constitutes for him an *explanation* and
what does not and it *makes* his distinctive *experiences qua* believer
what they are. 'This is a punishment', says the believer; and that

explains it and gives the experience its 'feel' for him *qua* believer as 'This is pneumonia' would not. The point is that, this being so, the proposition 'We live under divine judgment' is not, for the believer, an ordinary assertion which he is ready to agree may be true or false as other kinds of assertion may. To use a picture, in Wittgenstein's sense, is not to make one assertion amongst others within a given language-game. The picture determines what it makes sense to say or feel and what, not. In the last analysis religious belief consists of some such picture or pictures, but it must not be thought odd in this respect since the same is true of other language-games. The fundamental pictures in the case of religion are, if I am right in what I have so far said, pictures of god; that is, they express some aspect of transcendent consciousness and agency. Language-games other than religious belief in their turn may similarly be said to be constituted by pictures which are pictures of their constitutive concept. These constitutive pictures, or rather the language which states them, cannot be regarded as ordinary assertion within the language-game concerned. Nor, I shall argue below, is there any other language-game in which propositions which embody these pictures can be placed and then tested for truth or falsity.[27] I think Wittgenstein had this, or something of all this, in mind with regard to religion when he said : 'What we call believing in a Judgment Day or not believing in a Judgment Day — The expression of belief may play an absolutely minor role'.[28] It is not that the believer says that he believes that such-and-such is the case, and the unbeliever says that he does not believe it, within some common universe of discourse where it can be resolved whose belief is true and whose, false. The real 'expression of belief', in fact, is the whole way of explaining and experiencing which makes up the one state of mind as against the other. These fundamental pictures which make up religious belief in its various forms are the kind of thing which other writers have variously described as 'bliks' (R. M. Hare), 'onlooks' (D. D. Evans), 'end-statements' (P. van Buren).[29] In so describing them, they were making the point that some statements of belief embody the standard of sense and nonsense in religion. If I am right, such bliks, onlooks or end-statements are all about god in one way or another.

Much of what I have been saying in this section may strike the reader as obvious. Does anyone deny that religious explanations and experiences are constituted by the concept of god?, he may ask. To which my reply is : implicitly they may well do so. For it is often thought that asking for explanations, or seeking experiences, *leads* one *to* god. What I have been saying is that *logically* god is, so to speak, in the explanation and the experience from the start. You cannot (logically) ask a question which is not conceptually 'loaded'. You cannot (logically) have an experience which is not conceptually 'made'. St Paul on the road to Damascus was surprised by a strange light and a strange sound. 'Who art thou, Lord?' he asked (*Acts* 9:5). Suppose he had asked instead 'What has gone wrong with my eyes and ears?'. He would have got a different kind of answer and had a different kind of experience. His question was 'loaded' with the concept of god and the point which I have been making throughout this section is that this predetermined what the experience was for him and what it taught him.

Conclusion

I have, then, marked off religion as a logically distinct language-game constituted by the concept of god, its tacit presupposition. I have said that religious explanations and experiences can only occur within this language-game or form of life. In conclusion let me note a criticism which is often made of the view which I have taken and say why I think that there is nothing in this criticism.

It is sometimes said that the sort of view which I take of religious belief is, in one way or another, too narrow. One critic of my views has suggested that they betray a 'ghetto mentality'.[30] Another critic wrote 'The god or God who needs to be protected from other dimensions of life will not inspire total commitment'.[31] Such criticisms seem to me to show a remarkable lack of comprehension. There is no ground at all for supposing that my view of religious belief consigns the latter to an intellectual slum or robs it of its moral and spiritual dynamism. It is my whole intention to show that the logic of religious discourse is similar in its fundamental structure to that of any main kind of discourse – morality, science, or whatever. I have not consigned religious language to an intellectual ghetto. On the contrary I have been at pains to show that it is, so to speak, a neighbourhood the map of which is not dissimilar to that of any other major provenance of the human mind. Different from other language-games or forms of life it undoubtedly is, but not necessarily more disreputable by contrast. If 'total commitment' means taking religious questions and answers seriously, allowing them to occupy the forefront of one's mind, to regulate all in one's life – I see no reason at all why my account of the logical structure of religious belief should inhibit all that.

Let me rebut further conceivable criticism by emphasising that two things are undoubtedly possible given my account of the logical structure of religious belief.

One is wide-ranging exploration leading to new explanations and experiences. I have emphasised above the complexity of the concept of god. Let me now emphasise its 'open-texture'. Philosophers have called attention to the 'open-texture' of empirical concepts. They point out that what is meant by a material object term, e.g. 'table' can never be given *final and complete* definition in sense-contents. This 'open-texture' is evident in two ways : (i) one can never complete the empirical description of a material object; it is always logically possible to extend the description by adding some further details; (ii) one can never be sure that some new and unforeseen experience will not cause one to modify or retract the empirical description hitherto given to a material object. Now, god is not, of course, a material object, but there are two features of the concept of god which seem to be recognized in most, if not all, systems of religious belief. One is that the concept of god is like an empirical concept in that its content is in part, if not entirely, a function of human experience; the word 'god' stands for someone or something which men encounter in their experience of life or the world about them. The other is that the transcendence of god is taken to imply that more may always be said in describing god than has been said. The concept of god is thus open-textured in that : (i) it is never possible to complete the description of god; and (ii) one can never be sure that some new and unforeseen experience will not cause one to modify or retract the description of that which one calls god. It follows that to be exploratory, or at least open-minded, in one's religious beliefs is not only a religious or moral virtue (if it is either of these), but a logical requirement of employing the concept of god correctly. Religion can (logically) be a universe of discourse as full of the possibility of new developments as science or morality. So far from having 'to be protected from other dimensions of life' and thus failing to 'inspire total commitment', (whatever my critic meant by this) religious belief is as open to new discoveries or new dimensions as any universe of discourse could be.

The other possibility which my view leaves open is that of discussing any subject-matter whatever within the religious language-game. Religious discourse would collapse if god were reduced to anything else, just as for instance moral discourse would, if some other concept were substituted for that of moral obligation. That much is analytically true in both cases. But it does not follow that nothing but god can be talked about in religious discourse. All that does follow is that nothing can be talked about in religious discourse *except* in terms of god. Does the religious believer *qua* religious believer wish to talk in any other terms? He may, of course, want to say something about morality or science or politics or whatever. But as a religious believer he will want to say it in religious terms, i.e. in terms of god. This is the point I want to emphasise : being a religious believer means putting to the *whole* of nature and human nature questions in terms of god. That does not make religious discourse a ghetto. It makes it, if you like, a university of the spirit to which all comers are welcome.

The relationship between religious belief and other language-games is dynamic. The believer can ask questions in terms of god about the subject matter with which, say, the scientist or the historian deals. What was god's purpose in creating nature as it is? What was his will in history as it happened? And so on. As the scientist or the historian discovers more, so the religious believer's thought of god may be enlarged. The creator is the creator of this ever more amazing universe; the lord of history, the lord of that ever more fascinating process. And so on. My view of religious belief does not cut it off from other universes of discourse. It simply avoids the muddles which arise from confusing one thing with another.

There are, however, as I indicated in my Introduction, three questions which press upon us, given my account of the logical structure of religious belief. They are as follows :

(i) Does god exist? There is a language-game logically constituted by the concept of god, but is that language-game *about anything which objectively exists*? This I call the problem of objectivity.

(ii) Is god out of date? Wittgenstein said that language-games sometimes 'become obsolete and get forgotten'. Is religious belief one such? This is what I call the *challenge of secularization*.

(iii) Is it rational to think and speak in terms of god? The religious language-game is played but is it rational to play it? This is what I call the *question of rationality*.

2 The Problem of Objectivity: (i) Conceptual Analysis

If an account of religious belief such as I have offered in the first chapter is accepted, then the question arises : is religious belief about anything which exists objectively? This is what I mean by the problem of objectivity.

I have spoken of religious belief as a language-game or form of life constituted by the concept of god. To this, reply may be made as follows. True, this game is played; this form of life occurs. People think and speak in terms of god. But is god more than a word? Is god real in the sense that whatever is meant by 'god' exists independently of the discourse which the concept of god constitutes? In the next three chapters I shall discuss respectively three ways of dealing with this problem of objectivity which have arisen within theism. They have to do of course specifically with the existence of that in terms of god in which theists believe, i.e. with the existence of a Supreme Being who is in some sense personal and is called *God* (with a capital 'G'). According to the first of these ways, God can be known to exist from *conceptual analysis* alone : in the very thought of God it is logically implied that he exists. According to the second, God's existence can be proved from *empirical evidence* alone : there is proof in the physical world around us or in the experience of our own lives that he exists. According to the third way of dealing with the problem of objectivity, the question 'Does God exist?' is – at least as it has been traditionally understood – a *pseudo-question* which cannot (logically) be asked and so should not trouble anyone. The two former ways of dealing with the problem have each a long history in the philosophy of theism but the third is of more recent date.

In this chapter I shall discuss the opinion which some philosophers have held that what I call the problem of objectivity can be solved – at least so far as theism is concerned – simply by a logical analysis of the concept of God. They think that God's existence can be demonstrated by the so-called ontological argument or proof. The most famous exponent of this argument was Anselm (1033-1109), sometime Archbishop of Canterbury; but with certain modifications it has been reiterated by a number of later philosophers, notably Descartes and Leibniz. In our own day interest in the ontological argument has been revived by the attempts of Norman Malcolm, Charles Hartshorne and others to rehabilitate it.

Anselm's Ontological 'Proof'

Anselm tells us that he wanted to find a single argument which would demonstrate the existence of God. For a time it eluded him but then one day, he says, 'the proof of which I had despaired offered itself'.[1] This 'proof' ran as follows. Religious believers mean by 'God' 'that than which nothing greater can be conceived'.[2] What they believe is that such a being exists. Unbelievers deny this belief. In so doing they must necessarily mean by 'God' the same as believers, otherwise their denial would be no denial. But, Anselm argued, if unbelievers do mean the same as believers by 'God', then their denial is logically impossible because to say 'That than which nothing greater can be conceived does not exist' is to contradict oneself.

In making out his case that this is so, Anselm seems to have used two lines of argument. He himself did not differentiate them very sharply from one another but some modern philosophers think that it is very important to do so because there is far more to be said for the latter of these lines of argument than for the former. Briefly, the two lines of argument were as follows.

(i) The former turns on the contention that *existence-in-reality* makes a being greater (or more perfect) than *existence-in-the-understanding* alone. Suppose a being has perfections, or kinds of greatness, a, b, c, but exists only as a fiction (i.e. *only* in the understanding); then a greater than it can be conceived, namely a being who has a, b, c, existence-in-the-understanding *and* the additional kind of greatness, existence-in-reality. Said Anselm :

... Even the fool (sc. the 'fool' of Psalm 14 : 1, who says in his heart that there is no God) is convinced that something exists in the understanding, at least, than which nothing greater can be conceived. For when he hears of this (sc. of God) he understands it. And whatever is understood, exists in the understanding. And assuredly, that than which nothing greater can be conceived, cannot exist in the understanding alone. For, suppose it exists in the understanding alone : then it can be conceived to exist in reality; which is greater.[3]

(ii) Anselm's second line of argument turns on the contention that *necessary existence* makes a being greater (or more perfect) than merely *contingent existence.* The contrast here is between a being which has the characteristic of existence-which-*cannot*-be-conceived-not-to-be (i.e. necessary existence), and one which has that of existence-which-*can*-be-conceived-not-to-be, i.e. (contingent existence). Said Anselm :

For, it is possible to conceive of a being which cannot be conceived not to exist; and this is greater than one which can be conceived not to exist.[4]

We have here, then, two claims concerning the implications of the word 'greater' in the definition of 'God' as 'that than which nothing greater can be conceived' : namely (i) that God is a being who *really exists* as opposed to one who is only the subject of thought or imagination; and (ii) that God is a being who *necessarily exists,* as opposed to one whose existence can be conceived to have a beginning or an end, to occur in one finite place rather than another, to be dependent on something other than itself, or, in any other way, to be merely contingent existence.

The traditional objection to Anselm's 'proof', whether the latter is supported by the one line of argument or the other, is to the effect that it is based on a confusion between two quite distinct contentions. These are : (i) the contention that *a certain word,* '*God*', *can apply only to that which exists* (whether 'in-reality' or 'necessarily', according to which of Anselm's two lines of argument is being pursued); and (ii) the contention that (whether 'in-reality' or 'necessarily') *there exists that to which a certain word,* '*God*', *does apply.* I will now try to show the grounds on which this traditional objection rests; and I will consider whether it applies in the case of both Anselm's lines of argument equally. Some philosophers have recently argued that, although this classic objection applies to Anselm's first line of argument, it does not apply to his second.

Anselm's First Line of Argument

Anselm's first line of argument attempts to prove that God, by definition, exists *in-reality*.

This line of argument appeals to the distinction between existence-in-reality and existence-in-the-understanding. That distinction is real enough. It constitutes, for instance, the difference between horses and unicorns. Unicorns exist in the understanding alone; we can imagine them but they do not exist outside our minds. Horses, like unicorns, exist in our minds because we can conceive of them; but they also exist in a reality outside our minds. Anselm would have said, if he had used this example, that horses are more perfect or greater than unicorns because they have *two* perfections – namely existence-in-the-understanding and existence-in-reality, whereas unicorns have only one perfection, namely the former.

Critics of Anselm's first line of argument have tried to show that existence-in-reality is not a perfection or element of greatness; and that it is therefore invalid to deduce God's existence-in-reality from the premise that God is that than which nothing greater can be conceived. Gaunilon, a contemporary of Anselm, for example, tried to show that existence-in-reality is not a perfection by the following *reductio ad absurdum* :

> . . . It is said that somewhere in the ocean is an island, which, because of the difficulty, or rather the impossibility, of discovering what does not exist, is called the lost island. And they say that this island has an inestimable wealth of all manner of riches and delicacies in greater abundance than is told of the Islands of the Blest; and that having no owner or inhabitant, it is more excellent than all other countries, which are inhabited by mankind, in the abundance with which it is stored.
>
> Now, if someone should tell me that there is such an island, I should easily understand his words, in which there is no difficutly, but suppose that he went on to say, as if by a logical inference : 'You can no longer doubt that this island which is more excellent than all lands exists somewhere, since you have no doubt that it is in your understanding. And since it is more excellent not to be in the understanding alone, but to exist both in the understanding and in reality, for this reason it must exist.

For if it does not exist, any land which really exists will be more excellent than it; and so the island already understood by you to be more excellent will not be more excellent.'

And he adds this caustic comment :

... If a man should try to prove to me by such reasoning that this island truly exists, and that its existence should no longer be doubted, either I should believe that he was jesting, or I know not which I ought to regard as the greater fool : myself, supposing that I should allow this proof; or him, if he should suppose that he had established with any certainty the existence of this island. For he ought to show first that the hypothetical existence of this island exists as a real and indubitable fact, and in no wise as any unreal object, or one whose existence is uncertain in my understanding.[5]

In reply to this criticism Anselm pointed out that it is one thing to say that something is greater than all other *existing* things and another to say that nothing greater than it can be conceived.[6] Existence is *only one* amongst many possible perfections. So the lost island of Gaunilon's example could indisputably have *more* perfections than all other *existing* places and yet lack existence. But if this lost island were said to be a place than which no greater (i.e. more perfect) place could be *conceived* (and not merely one which is more perfect than all other existing places), then this would imply that the island referred to possessed *all* conceivable perfections and these would necessarily include existence.

Does this reply dispose effectively of Gaunilon's criticism? It is true that Gaunilon spoke of his lost island as 'more excellent than all other countries, which are inhabited by mankind', i.e. than all other existing countries rather than all other conceivable ones. That was careless of him and Anselm was entitled to take him up on the point. But suppose that Gaunilon *had* spoken of his lost island as more excellent than any other conceivable place, would Anselm have had any reply to that?

His reply would presumably have been that islands as such cannot, in the very nature of the case, possess all conceivable perfections but God can. A perfect island could not be, for example, omniscient or morally perfect as God is. Therefore, even if Gaunilon had stated his point as carefully as may be, he could not have reduced to absurdity an argument about that than which nothing greater can be conceived by applying it to an island. Such is the reply which Anselm appears to be driving home in the following sarcastic passage :

> ... Now I promise confidently that if any man should devise anything existing in reality or in concept alone (except that than which a greater cannot be conceived) to which he can adapt the sequence of my reasoning, I will discover that thing, and will give him his lost island, not to be lost again.[7]

The difficulty about Anselm's reply at this point – supposing that I have interpreted it correctly – is that God himself cannot possess all conceivable perfections any more than an island can. Islands cannot be omniscient or morally good, it is true. But if God is an invisible being, then it is equally true that God cannot be of the most beautiful or the most pleasing shape. Islands cannot have all the perfections of God; but neither can God have all the perfections of islands. Anselm's sarcastic dismissal of Gaunilon's *reductio* seems, to say the least, to have been somewhat hasty.

Even if Gaunilon's *reductio* were unsuccessful, however, his main criticism of Anselm – that the latter confused 'hypothetical existence' with 'real and indubitable fact' – would seem to be well founded. So long as a distinction is drawn, as it was drawn by Anselm, between existence-in-reality and existence-in-the-understanding, then it is legitimate to insist, as Gaunilon did, that this distinction should be clearly recognized and taken seriously. If there is a difference between concepts and objects, words and things, i.e. what exists-in-the-understanding-alone and what exists-in-reality, then it is not enough to show that existence-in-reality is part of the *concept* of God. All that would follow from this is that nothing can be *called* God unless it really exists. It would not follow that there must be *something existing* in reality which is God. What I called the traditional objection to Anselm's 'proof' seems to be fatal so far as his first line of argument is concerned. The defining characteristics of the word 'God' are one thing. Whether or not God exists as more than a word is another.

Anselm's Second Line of Argument and Recent Philosophy
Anselm's second line of argument attempts to prove that necessary existence is a perfection attributable to God by definition. Anselm

evidently thought that a being which *cannot* be conceived not to exist is greater or more perfect than one which *can* be conceived not to exist. God is that than which nothing greater can be conceived. So God must be a being which cannot be conceived not to exist, i.e. a necessary being. There is however a problem about what 'necessary existence' should be taken to mean here.

The expression, 'a being which cannot be conceived not to exist' may mean either : (a) a *logically* necessary being or (b) a *factually* necessary being. A logically necessary being is one whose existence it is impossible to deny without self-contradiction. A factually necessary being is one whose existence is not dependent upon any being other than itself. In which sense was Anselm using the expression? He is taken to have meant that God is a logically necessary being by many scholars; for instance, Professors J. N. Findlay and Norman Malcolm as we shall see below take him to have meant this. But others, such as Professor John Hick, contend that Anselm had factual, rather than logical, necessity in mind when he spoke of God as a being which cannot be conceived not to exist.[8] John Hick points out that in his reply to Gaunilon, Anselm states explicitly what he means by 'a being which cannot be conceived not to exist' :

> . . . All those objects, and those alone, can be conceived not to exist, which have a beginning or end or composition of parts : also . . . whatever at any place or at any time does not exist as a whole.
>
> That being alone, on the other hand, cannot be conceived not to exist, in which any conception discovers neither beginning nor end nor composition of parts, and which any conception finds always and everywhere as a whole.[9]

This seems clearly to mean factually necessary being. And it ties in with the distinction which Anselm drew in his *Monologium* between what he calls existence *a se* and existence *ab alio* :

> . . . The supreme Substance . . . does not exist through any efficient agent, and does not derive existence from any matter, and was not aided by being brought into existence by any external causes. Nevertheless, it by no means exists through nothing, or derives existence from nothing; since, through itself and from itself, it is whatever it is.[10]

Aseity (existence *a se*) is what I have hitherto spoken of as factually necessary being. It is not existence which cannot be denied without self-contradiction. But it is existence which cannot be conceived not to be in the sense that it is eternal (i.e. has no beginning or end and is not subject to the decay or decomposition of its parts as other beings are) and self-sufficient (i.e. owes its existence to no being beyond itself). For what my opinion is worth, I think those scholars who take Anselm to have conceived of God as a necessary being in this (factual) sense are correct.

More important for our purposes than such points of scholarship, however, are two questions which may be asked of necessary existence in either the logical or the factual sense. They are : (i) *Can* such existence be conceived as a perfection possessed by God?; and (ii) *Must* it be so conceived?

With regard to *logically* necessary being, Findlay has argued from the paradoxical premises : (a) that this *cannot* be attributed to God, but (b) that it *must* be if he is to be an object worthy of religious worship, to the conclusion that God is a logical impossibility and therefore does not exist.

The 'cannot' in premise (a) is a logical 'cannot'. Findlay took this premise from Hume and Kant. Hume called attention to the fact that, whereas *no* logically necessary proposition can be denied without self-contradiction, *all* existential propositions can; and he contended that it is therefore logically impossible for *any* existential proposition to be logically necessary. In his own words :

> ... Nothing is demonstrable unless the contrary implies a contradiction. Whatever we conceive as existent, we can also conceive as non-existent. There is no being, therefore, whose non-existence implies a contradiction. Consequently there is no being whose existence is demonstrable. I propose this argument as entirely decisive, and am willing to rest the whole controversy upon it.[11]

Kant made the same point with reference to analytic propositions or, as he called them, identical judgments. When 'an identical judgment' is denied (e.g. 'It is not the case that the triangle ABC has three sides') the subject (the triangle ABC) is retained, whilst the predicate which is implicit in the subject by definition ('has three sides') is rejected and thus a contradiction arises; but when an existential proposition is denied (e.g. 'It is not the case that the triangle ABC exists') the subject itself with all its predicates is rejected and hence no contradiction can arise. Illustrating his point with specific reference to God, Kant wrote :

> ... 'God is omnipotent' is a necessary judgment. The omnipotence cannot be rejected if we posit a Deity, that is, an infinite being; for the two concepts are identical. But if we say, 'There is no God', neither the omnipotence nor any other of its predicates is given; they are one and all rejected together with the subject, and there is therefore not the least contradiction in such a judgment.[12]

If Hume and Kant were right, then logically necessary existence cannot be attributed to God, or indeed to anything else, because the expression 'logically necessary existence' is self-contradictory.

The 'must' in Findlay's premise (b) above is also, presumably, a logical 'must'. Findlay's point appears to be as follows. God is by definition an object of religious worship. It is self-contradictory to say that a being is a worthy object of religious worship and to deny that it is, to quote Findlay (see below), 'one whose existence and whose possession of certain excellencies we cannot possibly conceive away'. But if it is a being whose existence we cannot possibly conceive away, then it must possess logically necessary existence. Here is the argument in Findlay's own words :

> The religious frame of mind seems, in fact, to be in a quandary; it seems invincibly determined both to eat its cake and have it. It desires the Divine Existence both to have the inescapable character which can, on Kantian or modern views, only be found where truth reflects a connection of characteristics or an arbitrary convention, and also, the character of 'making a real difference' which is only possible where truth doesn't have this merely hypothetical or linguistic basis. We may accordingly deny that these approaches allow us to remain agnostically poised in regard to God : they force us to come down on the atheistic side. For if God is to satisfy religious claims and needs, He must be a being in every way inescapable, One whose existence and whose possession of certain excellences we cannot possibly conceive away. And the views in question really make it self-evidently absurd (if they don't make it ungrammatical) to speak of such a Being and attribute existence to him. It was

indeed an ill day for Anselm when he hit upon his famous proof.
For on that day he not only laid bare something which is of the
essence of an adequate religious object, but also something
which entails its necessary non-existence.[13]

Both of Findlay's paradoxical premises, which were set out above
and which underlie his argument, can be challenged. As for
premise (a), that God cannot exist necessarily, Charles Hartshorne
has attempted – successfully I think within the terms of the argument – to turn the tables on Findlay. He points out that in the
closing words of the above quotation Findlay speaks of 'necessary
non-existence'. But, says Hartshorne, if it makes sense to speak of
necessary non-existence, then it must (logically) make sense to
speak of necessary existence. So Findlay's argument can be turned
on its head. If – as that argument implies – 'necessary non-
existence' is meaningful, then 'necessary existence' must be so too.
And if 'necessary existence' is meaningful, then – again according
to Findlay's argument – God can, and must, be said to exist necessarily. Within the terms of his own argument Findlay is here
refuted, as I think he would now himself acknowledge.[14] It is, however, important to see precisely what Findlay's mistake was. I do
not think that Hartshorne clearly grasped this. Findlay was wrong
to suppose, as evidently he did, that if it does *not* make sense to
say that God necessarily *does* exist, then it *does* make sense to say
that God necessarily does *not* exist. But, not so. If 'God necessarily
does exist' is nonsense, then, provided 'necessarily' and 'does exist'
are being used in the same senses, 'God necessarily does not exist'
is nonsense also. If ontological proof is logically impossible, so is
ontological disproof. I think that Hartshorne supposed that in
pointing out Findlay's mistake he had rehabilitated the ontological
argument, but, of course, he had not.

Findlay's other premise (b), that God in order to be a worthy
object of religious worship must be a logically necessary being, is
also open to damaging criticism. Surely he is wrong about this.
The God whom theists worship – the God of the Bible for example
– is not normally conceived as a logically necessary being, i.e. a
being whose existence cannot be denied without self-contradiction.
Denials of God's existence in the Bible are variously described as
false, foolish or wicked but never as self-contradictory. We saw
above reason to think that when Anselm himself spoke of God as

'a being which cannot be conceived not to exist', he was probably thinking of factually, rather than logically, necessary being.

I return now to the question : what precisely is meant by logically necessary existence or non-existence? Findlay thought that he had discovered an ontological disproof of God's existence, an argument which proved the exact opposite of what Anselm thought that his 'proof' had demonstrated. Hartshorne, in refuting this argument of Findlay's, evidently thought that he had in some sense rehabilitated Anselm's ontological proof. He went on to drive this point home by saying that, in the case of necessary existence, no distinction can (logically) be drawn between 'possible' and 'actual' and that the ontological argument is hypothetical to this effect : 'If, "God" stands for something conceivable, it stands for something actual'. This hypothetical, he asserts, must not be taken to mean : 'If the necessary being happens to exist, that is, if as mere contingent fact it exists, then it exists not as contingent fact but as necessary truth'. Instead of 'this nonsense', he says, we must take the hypothetical to mean : 'If the phrase "necessary being" has meaning, then what it means exists necessarily, and if it exists necessarily, then *a fortiori,* it exists'.[15]

However, both Findlay and Hartshorne were deceived in thinking that they had propounded an ontological argument. Talk of necessary existence or non-existence in the sense in which these expressions are used by Findlay and Hartshorne respectively – i.e. *logically* necessary existence or non-existence – tells us nothing about objective, i.e. extra-conceptual, extra-linguistic, reality. When we say that something, in the sense referred to, necessarily either exists or does not exist, we are talking only about logical implications in some conceptual or linguistic scheme. To say, for instance, 'X is a triangle and therefore the three sides of X necessarily exist' is to say something about the meaning of the words (or concepts) 'triangle', 'three' and 'side'. To say 'X is a triangle and therefore a fourth side to X necessarily does not exist' is likewise to say something about those words and the additional word 'fourth'. Logically necessary existence or non-existence has to do with what can, or cannot, be said or conceived. For example, the fact that there are no square circles is a fact about language and that is why we do not need to search the world in order to discover it. But all this fact amounts to is that the expression 'square circle' makes no sense. You cannot (logically) say 'A square circle exists'. But, by the same token, you cannot say 'A square circle does not exist' – unless of course this is just your way of saying that the expression 'square circle' makes no sense. If it means nothing to say 'A square circle exists' because the subject of the sentence is meaningless, then it also means nothing to say 'A square circle does not exist' for the same reason.

Findlay and Hartshorne seem to have ignored all this. I think that when Findlay spoke of the 'necessary non-existence' of God he meant more than that the expression 'God' makes no sense: witness his preference for saying that God's existence is 'impossible' rather than simply 'senseless', which we noted above. Again, Hartshorne certainly intended his claim that God necessarily exists to mean more than that the word 'God' could conceivably be defined to mean 'a logically necessary being' : witness his remark, quoted above, 'if it (the necessary being) exists necessarily, then *a fortiori,* it exists'. What Findlay and Hartshorne respectively thought that they had found was grounds for believing in the non-existence (Findlay) or the existence (Hartshorne) of God, i.e. the being to whom the word 'God' refers. But their disagreement, if it was about anything, was simply about what can, or cannot, be said. I think Hartshorne got the better of Findlay by discovering the latter's inconsistency. But, of course, the whole thing is simply about the words 'God', 'necessary', 'existence' and 'non-existence'. It does not answer the question 'Does God exist?'. When Hartshorne said : 'if it exists necessarily, then *a fortiori* it exists' he was sliding over the point which Findlay, in the first of what I called his paradoxical premises, had grasped : that logical implications are one thing, ontological realities another. The traditional objection to the ontological argument is simply that it blurs this distinction. Findlay's ontological 'disproof' and Hartshorne's 'proof' both fall foul of that objection.

So far I have applied the two questions posed above – (i) *Can* necessary existence be conceived as a perfection possessed by God? and (ii) *Must* it be so conceived? – only to logically necessary being. What of *factually* necessary being? The latter, it will be remembered, is being independent of others and having others dependent on it. Can we – must we – conceive of this as a perfection possessed by God?

Undoubtedly we *can*. It is entirely in accordance with the

ordinary meaning of the word 'perfection' to conceive of factually necessary being as a perfection or an element in greatness. Incidentally, it stands contrasted in this respect with logically necessary being. I do not know what is meant by calling the latter a perfection. There is nothing in the ordinary use of 'perfection' or 'greatness' to justify the idea that logical necessity makes anything greater or more perfect. But the kind of independence which a factually necessary being has is another matter. Dependence on others is a limiting factor and, in many contexts at least, being greater or more perfect means being less dependent. Are not countries, for example, deemed greater as they are more able to sustain, or defend, themselves independently of other countries? Is not a great man – whether we regard him as such for his wealth, intelligence or character – one who can exist with a greater degree of self-sufficiency than lesser men? So there is nothing strained in the thought of God's perfections including factually necessary being.

Against this, Professor N. Malcolm thinks that factually necessary being cannot constitute the independence necessary in a perfect God.[16] He says that if anything lacks logically necessary being (i.e. if its existence can be denied without self-contradiction) then it must (logically) depend on other things for coming into and continuing in existence. God, he contends, cannot be so conceived and remain the God of theistic thought and devotion. But this is mistaken. Professor A. Plantinga has recently pointed out that it is, for instance, perfectly conceivable that there are certain elementary physical particles which have always existed. In that case they would not depend upon anything else for coming into or continuing in existence. But it would not follow that 'Such particles do not exist' is self-contradictory. True, it is not part of the concept of an elementary physical particle that it should have necessary being as it may be part of the concept of God that he should have such being, but that does not affect the point. It is perfectly conceivable that God should have factually necessary being (i.e. have always existed as an independent being) without the statement 'God does not exist' being self-contradictory.[17] We *can*, therefore, conceive of God as factually necessary being.

Must we conceive of God as factually necessary being? I think the answer again is yes. The characteristic which Findlay and Malcolm both mistake for logically necessary being, namely the characteristic in God which makes him the object of such typically

religious attitudes as absolute trust, is in fact his being independent
of all other things and able to sustain all other things as dependent
on him. This characteristic is a necessary condition of that limitless, sustaining love for which believers worship him. We have not
conceived of the God of theistic thought and devotion unless we
have conceived of him as factually necessary being. So to conceive
of him is not to define 'God' stipulatively but reportively. Here
again there is a contrast with logically necessary being. I said that
God could be defined as the latter but that it was against the
ordinary use of the word 'God' so to define him. By contrast, it is
entirely in accordance with the way in which believers (and unbelievers alike) normally think and speak of God to define him as
a factually necessary being. If we purport to use the word 'God'
as it is normally used then we must so define it. So my answer to
the questions posed above, with regard to factually necessary
being, is that we *can* conceive of this as a perfection possessed by
God and that we *must*.

Once again, however, we have not arrived at any sort of ontological proof of God's existence. We have simply been thinking
about the defining characteristics of God. Whether or not he is
what he is taken to be – whether or not he exists at all – is another
question. And it remains. What I called the traditional objection to
Anselm's ontological 'proof' seems to be just as fatal to his second
line of argument as to his first.[18]

Conclusion
My conclusion, then, is that the traditional objection to the ontological proof is effective against both Anselm's lines of argument.
The essence of that objection is that the logical distinction between
words and things, between on the one hand logical implication
within a conceptual or linguistic scheme and on the other hand
ontological reality, cannot be eliminated. Not even in the case of
God. In stating this conclusion, it is perhaps important to make it
abundantly clear just what I *am* insisting upon here and what I
am *not*.

The point upon which I *am* insisting is as follows. The very
meaning of the question 'Is God an ontological reality?', or 'Does
God exist objectively?', implies that it cannot be answered by any
analysis of the meaning of the word 'God'. For *within the meaning
of that question* a distinction is drawn between what is being *said*

and what, if anything, it is being said *about*. All analysis of the meaning of what is being said is necessarily on one side of that divide. When the linguistic tale is fully told – when everything which can be explained about the meaning of the word 'God' has been explained – the question 'Is God an ontological reality?' or 'Does God exist objectively?', remains unanswered. For the point of that question is to discover whether the word 'God' corresponds to anything beyond itself. All ontological questions are, in this sense, endlessly elusive to answers derived from the conceptual analysis of that with regard to which they are asked. Implicit within them there is always a distinction between what is being *said* and what it purports to be said *about*. If there were no such distinction, there could (logically) be no ontological questions about God or anything else.

What I am emphatically *not* insisting upon, however, is that there must be some way of discovering *beyond language altogether* what is ontologically real, or what objectively exists. I am not concerned to deny that 'the limits of my language mean the limits of my world'.[19] The expressions 'ontologically real' or 'objectively existing' are themselves pieces of language and as such only have meaning within their appropriate language-game. What it makes sense to say about ontological reality or objective existence is not decided by any discovery which goes beyond language. It may be the case – in Chapter 4 I shall argue that it is the case – that these expressions call in the last analysis for a *choice* on the part of those who press their use to the limit. The speaker may have to decide what he means by them: it may be their logical character that he has to do so. But if it is, then it is because of what 'ontological reality' and 'objective existence' *mean*. And their meaning is something they only have *within* language.

3 The Problem of Objectivity: (ii) The Appeal to Empirical Evidence

Numerous attempts have been made to solve what I have called the problem of objectivity from what is deemed to be empirical evidence that God really exists. In this chapter I shall refer to four such attempts, generally known respectively as the cosmological argument, the argument from design, the argument from religious experience, and the moral argument.

The Cosmological Argument

Thomas Aquinas, the predominant philosopher and theologian of the Middle Ages, propounded the cosmological argument in the first three of his famous *Five Ways*. The Third of these Five Ways is generally taken to contain the definitive form of the argument. I will quote it as it appears in Aquinas's *Summa Theologica* and then turn to explanation and criticism.

> . . . Some things we encounter have the possibility of being and not being, since we find them being generated and corrupted, and accordingly with the possibility of being and not being. Now it is impossible for all that there is to be like that; because what has the possibility of not being, at sometime is not. If therefore everything has the possibility of not being, at one time there was nothing. But if this were the case, there would be nothing even now, because what is not does not begin to be except through something which is; so if nothing was in being, it was impossible for anything to begin to be, and so there would still be nothing, which is obviously false. Not everything therefore has the possibility (of being and not being), but there must be something which is necessary. Now everything which is

necessary either has the cause of its necessity outside itself, or it does not. Now it is not possible to go on for ever in a series of necessary beings which have a cause of their necessity, just as was shown in the case of efficient causes. So it is necessary to assume something which is necessary of itself, and has no cause of its necessity outside itself, but is rather the cause of necessity in other things, and this all men call God.[1]

For the purpose of explanation and criticism I intend to break this passage up into four parts and to discuss them in turn.

(1) *Some things we encounter have the possibility of being and of not being, since we find them being generated and corrupted, and accordingly with the possibility of being and not being.*

Aquinas started here from what is empirically observable, namely the impermanence of things in this changeful world. Though he did not refer to Anselm by name, he expressly rejected the ontological argument in favour of a more empirical approach. God, he said, is not known by us to exist through our seeing that the proposition 'God exists' is true by definition of 'God', but through what we can observe of his 'effects' in the world. Aquinas did hold however that, *if* we knew enough about the essence of God, we would be able to show that his essence includes his existence; but not knowing enough to do that, we must find some other way of proving God's existence. Hence his appeal to what is empirically observable in the world about us. He wrote :

> ... I declare then this proposition, *God exists,* though of itself self-evident – since subject and predicate are identical, for God in his existence, as will be shown hereafter – is nevertheless not self-evident to us, because we do not know what the essence of God is; it requires to be demonstrated by proofs more evident to us though less evident in themselves, namely his effects.[2]

Aquinas's statement here of his reason for turning to God's 'effects' is open to a damning objection. He could not possibly have known what is of itself self-evident though not self-evident to him; for this would have meant that he knew what he would know if he knew what he did not know, which is absurd. But I leave it at that. All I want to bring out at the moment is the fact that Aquinas did appeal to empirical evidence as his starting-point. His line of argument was as follows. We see certain things happening in the world around us. Any rational man who reflects on why they happen as they do will find himself irresistibly led to the conclusion that it is because of God's existence and activity. Aquinas's appeal was to intuition working on what is empirically observable : to what we can intuit as self-evident in consequence of what we see in the world about us. In due course I will say something about this intuition to which he appealed; and I will also show why the God whose 'effects' we observe needed in Aquinas's opinion – despite his rejection of Anselm's 'proof' – to be a God in whom essence and existence are one, i.e. a necessary being.

The particular empirically observable aspect of the world to which Aquinas called attention in his Third Way was the fact that 'some things . . . have the possibility of being and not being'. What precisely did he mean by this? It was not simply the logical possibility of certain things not existing to which he was referring. It is logically possible, for instance, that the sun and the moon do not exist but Aquinas did not think that either of these bodies had, at least with regard to the future, 'the possibility of not being'. A passage in his *Contra Gentiles* shows us what Aquinas did mean by this latter expression. *Possibilitas ad non esse* is there taken to be synonymous with *potentia ad non esse.*[3] Things are said to have this *potentia,* this 'power of not being (or existing)' if 'the matter in them is in potency to another form'. This means, to quote Dr Kenny's recently published study of the Third Way, 'if the stuff they consist of is such that they can turn into something else'.[4] Some things certainly do have this *potentia* or *possibilitas.* It is beyond dispute that we find things, as this Third Way has it, 'being generated and corrupted'. Both processes may be either natural (e.g. the birth and death of animals) or artificial (e.g. the erection and demolition of buildings). Both processes involve the turning into something else of the 'stuff' of which the things concerned consist. Given then, as his point of departure the empirically observable impermanence of some things, Aquinas developed his argument as follows.

(2) *Now it is impossible for all that there is to be like that; because what has the possibility of not being, at some time is not. If therefore everything has the possibility of not being, at one time there was nothing.*

The argument is that every real possibility would be realised in infinite time; and so, if everything had a power, or possibility of not existing, then at some time in the past there would have been nothing at all.

Is this step in Aquinas's argument valid? It seems not. The following is undoubtedly valid.

Each thing has a possibility of not being
There is infinite past time
At one time *each* thing was not

But the following argument is invalid :

Each thing has a possibility of not being
There is infinite past time
At one time *everything* was not (i.e. there was nothing)

Aquinas's argument is of the latter form. It is invalid because the times at which some things were not could (logically) have been different times from those at which other things were not; and so there might conceivably have been no time at which everything was not.[5]

Aquinas, as we shall see in a moment, wished to show that there could (logically) *not* have been a time when there was nothing at all. Before we come to his attempt to do so, notice that he did not beg the question by assuming either (a) the truth of the Christian doctrine of creation or (b) the logical impossibility of an infinite regress into the past of causally-connected temporal events. As for the doctrine of creation, he did, of course, believe in that as a Christian and the influence of this belief is evident in some of his opinions, e.g. in his view that the sun and moon, though they lack the power or possibility of not being as to the future, have not, as Aristotle supposed, existed eternally because God created them. Aquinas, however, was looking for an argument which would prove creation not presuppose it. As for the logical impossibility of an infinite regress of temporal events, he certainly did not presuppose that impossibility : on the contrary, he must have thought that it was logically possible to speak of such an infinite temporal regress since his argument turns upon the supposing of it.

(3) *But if this were the case (if at one time there was nothing) there would be nothing even now, because what is not does not begin to be except through something which is; so if nothing*

was in being, it was impossible for anything to begin to be, and
so there would still be nothing, which is obviously false.

At this point the Third Way rests upon the First. Coming into
existence is regarded by Aquinas as an instance of motion. In the
First Way he argued, following Aristotle, that nothing can be
conceived to move unless it is conceived as moved by something
else. His reasoning ran as follows.

Whatever is in motion is in a state of potentiality with regard
to that towards which it is moved. It is set in motion by something
else. To set a thing in motion is to cause it to pass, in some particular respect, from potency – i.e. from being in this respect deter-
minable – to actuality – i.e. to being in this respect determinate.
A piece of wood, for example, is potentially hot, before it is placed
in the fire. When it is amongst the flames, the actual heat of the
fire causes the wood in its turn to become actually hot. Motion in
this, as in every case, is caused by something which is actual; a
thing cannot be brought from potentiality to actuality except by
something which is itself in actuality. But it is impossible for a
thing to be, at one and the same time, in any given respect, X,
both potentially X and actually X. This would be contradictory,
since what is potential is by definition not actual. It is, therefore,
impossible for a thing to be, at the same time and in the same
respect, moved and its own mover. This is why everything that is
in motion must be moved by something else. The mover may, of
course, itself have been moved : the actual heat in the fire from
which the wood took flame was potential heat until the actual heat
of, say, a torch, moved it towards actuality. This mover, the actual
heat of the torch, was itself at some point moved from potency to
actuality : when the torch, say, was lit from some other fire. Must
we, then, conceive of this inference to act from potency as
regressing *ad infinitum*? No, said Aquinas, because if it did so
there would be no first mover and so no motion at all. We therefore reach by this line of argument a first mover which is not
moved by anything else, and this is what all men take God to be.

It seems reasonable enough to say, as Aquinas did in this First
Way, that to move is to pass from potency to actuality. But why
must this movement be affected by something else? It is undoubtedly a truth of grammar that precisely the same entity cannot at one and the same time be both the subject and the object

of the *transitive* verb 'to move'. One part of a whole may move
another part; but it would not make sense to say that the same part
had moved the same part. But what of the *intransitive* verb 'to
move'? In Latin, as Kenny[6] points out, to express the intransitive
sense of 'move', one simply writes the passive of the transitive verb.
So *movetur* translates both 'is moving' (intransitive) and 'is being
moved' (passive). The latter (is being moved) grammatically
implies some entity other than the subject of the verb which is
doing the moving : but the former (is moving) does not. Kenny
suggests that Aquinas was seriously misled at a crucial point in
his argument by this feature of the language in which he wrote.
What Aquinas said was : *omne quod movetur ab alio moveri*
(whatever is in motion must be moved by something else). But
why? Why should not some things at any rate simply be in motion
without being moved by other things? This is not inconceivable,
as Aquinas supposed. Newton's First Law conceives of it.

If some things could be in motion without having been moved
by any other thing; and if beginning to be is an instance of motion;
then some things could have begun to be without being brought
into being by something else. Therefore, it does not follow that if
at one time there was nothing, there would be nothing now, as
Aquinas supposed. This step in his argument is fallacious.

As the next step in his Third Way, Aquinas attempted to define
the 'something', not having a possibility of not being, which he
mistakenly thought is required to explain the existence of those
things which we observe to have a possibility of not being. This
something is necessary being. Aquinas defined the nature of its
necessity thus :

(4) *Not everything therefore has the possibility (of being and
not being), but there must be something which is necessary. Now
everything which is necessary either has the cause of its necessity outside itself, or it does not. Now it is not possible to go on
forever in a series of necessary beings which have a cause of their
necessity, just as was shown in the case of efficient causes. So it
is necessary to assume something which is necessary of itself, and
has no cause of its necessity outside itelf, but is rather the cause
of necessity in other things, and this all men call God.*

Here Aquinas meant by 'necessary being' what we called, when
discussing Anselm, *factually*, as distinct from logically, necessary

being. Commentators mostly take Aquinas to have thought of God in his earlier writings as a necessary being in the sense that the denial of God's existence is self-contradictory; but it seems to be agreed among them that, in his later writings, particularly in *Summa Theologica,* he had moved under the influence of Averroes to the view that God is a necessary being in the sense of an eternal and imperishable being who has all other beings dependent upon him whilst he himself is dependent upon none.[7]

Aquinas in the above quotation speaks of two kinds of (factually) necessary being. A necessary being may have the cause of its necessity 'outside' itself or its necessity may be 'of itself'. The sun, the moon and human souls are, according to Aquinas, necessary beings of the former kind. They are necessary in the sense that, though they have a power of not existing with respect to the past, they do not have also a power of not existing in respect of the future, as buildings or human bodies for example do. If they cease to exist, it will not be because they are corruptible but because God has destroyed them. Such beings once did not exist and so they required a cause to bring them into being. They could not have been their own cause : according to Aquinas in his Second Way nothing can be the efficient cause of its own existence since it would then have to have existed prior to itself, which is impossible. So these necessary beings which are caused require as the cause of their existence that 'something which is necessary of itself, and has no cause of its necessity outside itself', namely what all men call God.

The classic objection to this line of argument is of course as follows. Why does there have to be a first cause? We have already noted that Aquinas evidently did not think an infinite regress of causally connected events to be logically impossible. If it makes sense to conceive of such a regress, why is a first cause necessary in order to explain the existence of things? There does not seem to be any convincing answer to this. A great deal has been made by some defenders of Aquinas to the effect that he was arguing in the first Three Ways not for a first *temporal* cause but a first *ontological* cause. Fr F. C. Copleston, for example, has written :

We have to imagine, not a lineal or horizontal series, so to speak, but a vertical hierarchy, in which a lower member depends here and now on the present causal activity of the member above it.

It is the latter type of series, if prolonged to infinity, which Aquinas rejects. And he rejects it on the ground that unless there is a 'first' member, a mover which is not itself moved or a cause which does not itself depend on the causal activity of a higher cause, it is not possible to explain the 'motion' or the causal activity of the lowest member.[8]

I cannot see how this makes Aquinas's argument more acceptable. Whether the cause is ontological or temporal, it remains a cause. Why a series of ontological dependants should not be prolonged to infinity is no more evident than why a series of temporal causes should not. Why there has to be a first term to the 'vertical hierarchy' is no more apparent than why there has to be one to the 'horizontal series'. Copleston seems to think that it is self-evident that there has to be a ground of all being even though it is not self-evident that there has to be a first mover of all process within the world. But he is mistaken.

Aquinas, in the first Three Ways, analyses the concepts of motion, cause and contingent being, respectively. In each case, he ends up with something which completely lacks the logical character of that which he is supposed to be analysing. There is no motion, he says, without a mover; and, since potency cannot move itself, the mover is always an actuality; therefore the logically first term here is pure actuality, i.e. an *unmoved* mover. There are no effects without causes; and, since no effect can be its own cause, there must always be something else which causes the effect; therefore the logically first term here is pure cause, i.e. an *uncaused* cause. There is no contingent being without might-not-have-been-ness; but might-not-have-been-ness cannot account for its own being; therefore the logically first term here is being without any might-not-have-been-ness in it, i.e. pure, or *non-contingent,* being. So motion is reduced to the unmoved, cause to the uncaused, contingency to necessity. How did Aquinas purport to effect this reduction? He did so by regressing to infinity with the questions (respectively) 'What moved this?', 'What caused this?' and 'What gave this being?'. He argued that if one persists with these questions then at infinity one must (logically) end with unmoved motion, uncaused cause and non-contingent being.

His argument suffers from a fatal ambiguity so far as the idea of an infinite series of connected events is concerned. It applies that idea to (respectively) motion, cause and contingency. On the one hand, it says in effect that this lands us in absurdity; and on the other hand, that it does not. According to Aquinas's argument, it must be *logically impossible* to apply the idea of an infinite series of connected events to (respectively) motion, cause and contingency : because the only justification that there can be for rejecting the ideas of motion, cause or contingency, infinitely extended, as Aquinas rejects them, is the fact (if it were a fact) that it would not make sense so to extend them. But on the other hand, according to Aquinas's argument, it must be *logically possible* to extend motion, cause and contingency (respectively) to infinity : because he says that it is only when they have been so extended that we arrive at the ideas of unmoved motion, uncaused cause and non-contingent being.

What, in reality, Aquinas was doing in his first Three Ways was this. He was in each case pushing a question beyond the point at which it can logically be answered, and insisting that even so it is still a significant question to ask. 'What moved X?', 'What caused X?', 'What gave X being?' : it makes sense to ask these questions *within* the world, where the world is X *and* something else – call it Y – which is *more* than X. The answer can then be drawn from Y. But if these questions are put of X + Y, i.e. of the world *as a whole,* where is the answer to come from? The logical difference between these questions when asked, in the one case, of *things in the world,* and in the other, of *the world as a whole* is this : it is a necessary condition of the questions being answerable in the case of the world as a whole that there should be *something else besides the world as a whole,* from which the answer can be drawn, whereas this is not a necessary condition of their being answerable in the case of things in the world. Because these questions can be answered when asked about things in the world, it does not follow that they must (logically) be answerable when asked of the world as a whole. Aquinas's mistake was to assume that it does follow.

It is of course true that we may feel *psychologically* compelled to ask what caused the world as a whole. Metaphysicians certainly do. This is not, perhaps, surprising. The principle of causation has an *a priori* character. If a scientist comes on an event of which he cannot discover the cause, he does not simply say, 'Here is an uncaused event!' and leave it at that. He looks for the cause more diligently. That every event has a cause is the guiding principle which he brings to his work. It is *a priori* in that sense. Now, it is not *prima facie* unplausible to suppose that the metaphysician is simply applying the same principle as the scientist. Copleston for instance says that he is : 'The physicist presupposes, at least tacitly, that there is some sense in investigating nature and looking for the causes of events . . . The metaphysician assumes that there is sense in looking for the reason or cause of phenomena . . . I consider that the metaphysician is as justified in his assumption as the physicist'.[9] But there is an important difference between the scientist and the metaphysician in how they apply the principle of causation. The scientist may work on the principle that, if only he seeks long and hard enough, he will find the cause of any given effect; but the application of this principle is, with him, always subject to the test of empirical observation. He does not assume that, apart from the confirmation of empirical observation, the causal principle informs us about reality. But this is precisely what the metaphysician does assume. When 'What caused this?' is asked of the empirically observable world *as a whole,* any answer is necessarily *beyond* the test of empirical observation. The question then can (and this is a logical 'can') only be asked on the assumption that the principle itself – i.e. that every event must have a cause – informs us about reality, that it tells us that there must be a cause of the world as a whole.

However, let us now suppose for a moment that all these criticisms of Aquinas's cosmological argument fail and that he has successfully proved that there is necessary being which has 'no cause of its necessity outside itself'. The question will then arise : why does this have to be God, as he thought? Why could it not simply be the universe as a whole? There is nothing self-contradictory in the idea of the universe existing eternally. We may note in passing that this is so, even if the universe consists entirely of things which have each a possibility of not being. It is true that if A changes into B, as distinct from merely succeeds B, then there must (logically) be some element common to A and B; and if B changes into C, some element common to B and C. But as Kenny has shown[10] this does not mean that there must be some element common to all three. What is common to A and B may have ceased to exist before there begins to be whatever is common to B and C. It does not follow from :

In every change there must be a common element between the terms of change.

that :

There must be some element common to the terms of every change.

The universe, therefore, could conceivably consist of parts, each of which turns into something else in infinite time; yet nevertheless be itself a necesary being which has 'no cause of its necessity outside itself'.

Aquinas evidently thought that such a necessary being can only be God on the ground that it does not make sense to ask what caused God as it does, what caused the universe. But if that was his ground, it is, to say the least, debatable. The question 'What caused God?' is not obviously more nonsensical than the question 'What caused the universe?' Why should we cease to look for a cause of what exists simply because we have arrived at the thought of God as existing?

Two kinds of answer to this question have in fact been offered by, or on behalf of, Aquinas.

One is: *because it can be shown* that, in the case of God, essence and existence are one. This is what Anselm's ontological argument purported to show. We have already noted that Aquinas did not think that argument valid. But we have also noted that he thought that the proposition 'God is his existence', though 'not self-evident to us' is 'of itself self-evident'.

I said above that Aquinas's claim to know that what is not self-evident to him is of itself self-evident does not make sense. Nor does it; but we ought perhaps in fairness to look a little more closely at what Aquinas evidently wished to say about the relationship between essence and existence in God. He recognized that in the case of everything except God essence (what the defining characteristics of anything are) is one thing; and existence (whether there exists in reality anything which fulfils these defining characteristics) is another. Within the notions of both essence and existence he draws a further distinction.

Understanding the *essence* of anything may mean simply (i) knowing what the word for it means (being able to give an accurate ostensive definition or an adequate verbal definition of e.g. 'man'); or it may mean understanding the nature of the thing in question (e.g. being able to give a comprehensive scientific account of human nature in physiological, psychological, sociological, etc. terms).

Speaking of the *existence* of anything may involve : (i) saying that it belongs within one of Aristotle's ten categories and thereby conceiving it to exist in reality; or (ii) saying something where 'is' functions simply as a *verbalis copula.*

As an example of the latter, Aquinas offered the following : 'it is said that blindness *is* in the second sense, in so far as the proposition "something is blind" is true; but it *is* not in the first sense, for it has no *esse* in reality but is rather the privation of an *esse*'.[11]

As to the former, he distinguished three kinds of predicate which may be attributed to a substantive as subject : (i) where 'to be' is followed by a predicate within the first of Aristotle's categories, i.e. substance, e.g. 'Socrates was a man'; (ii) where 'to be' is followed by a predicate within any of the other nine Aristotelian categories, e.g. 'Socrates was white'; (iii) where 'to be' stands alone, e.g. 'Socrates was'. This third case, the *esse simpliciter,* is, said Aquinas, reducible to the first, the *esse substantiale.* The *esse simpliciter* is constituted by that which makes any individual what it is (or was or will be) substantially as distinct from accidentally. 'Socrates was a man' expresses what is meant by 'Socrates was' (*esse simpliciter*) as 'Socrates was white' does not. *Esse* – whether *substantiale* or *accidentale* – is the actuality of some Idea or Form (in the Platonic sense). The difference is that some Forms constitute the *essence* of a thing as others do not.

So much for essence and existence in general. Now we turn to the special case of God.

How then, did Aquinas interpret God's *essence*? He claimed that we can know what the word 'God' means (the Five Ways are sometimes interpreted as no more than attempts on his part to make this meaning explicit); but that we do not fully understand the nature of God (even if the Five Ways are more than was supposed in the last parenthesis, Aquinas would have said that they do not represent an understanding in depth of the divine nature). This sounds reasonable enough. It makes sense to say that there is – or rather that there *may be* – more to God than we know. We cannot *know* that this is so because that would amount to knowing something which we do not know, which is absurd. While we may in some sense, know that there is something which we do not know – e.g. we may know that we have not yet mastered the whole of a foreign language or some other difficult subject of study – we cannot know that something which no man yet knows is there to be known. We can believe that it is. We can have good reason to believe this; e.g. the great increase of scientific knowledge hitherto is surely good ground for believing that man has more to learn about the universe. But we cannot (logically) *know* that he has; we cannot know for instance, that the universe will eventually be discovered to be older than at present it is thought to be. Similarly, then, we may with good reason believe that the essence of God is more than at present we understand it to be.

Passing from essence to existence, how did Aquinas interpret God's *existence*? He held in some of his writings that although God's essence and existence are not self-evidently one for us, it can be shown by *discursive* reasoning that they are one. This claim seems to rest on an argument about what God *must* be. In a word, an argument to the effect that God must be *being*. Kenny refers to a passage from Aquinas's *De Potentia* as the clearest statement of this argument and translates it thus :

> Wherever causes whose proper effects are diverse produce also a common effect, the additional common effect must be produced in virtue of some superior cause of which it is the proper effect. For example, pepper and ginger, besides producing their own proper effects have it in common that they produce heat; they do this in virtue of the causality of fire, of which heat is the proper effect. Now all created causes have their own proper effects, but they also have *a single common effect which is being* (*esse*). Heat causes things *to be* hot, and builders cause there *to be* houses; both alike, therefore, *cause being. There must, therefore, be some superior cause whose proper effect is being:* and this, we are left to conclude, is what men call God.[12]

The argument, here, appears to amount to this. There is in the world what there is. Anything which is part of what there is has being. So everything there is has the 'common additional effect', being. This being which everything in the world has must be an effect *of something*. What it is the effect of must have being in order to cause being as its effect. So God must have being. And therefore the essence of God must include existence.

If this was Aquinas's argument, then it was a very bad one. For one thing it begs the question in a twofold way. The question, from which this present discussion of ours proceeds, remember, was : why should we not ask what caused God if we ask what caused other things? In calling the being of everything else an 'effect' Aquinas begged the question as to whether or not we must ask what caused things other than God. If everything else is spoken of as an 'effect' then it must have a cause. Again, Aquinas begged the question 'Why, if everything else, because the verb "to be" can be applied to it, must have a cause of its being other than itself, must *not* God, to whom "to be" can also be applied, also have a cause of his being other than himself?' If he did not actually ignore this question, Aquinas evidently thought that we know by intuition that God must not. But we shall see in a moment that this is not really a defence against the charge of having begged the question.

There is perhaps an even more fundamental objection to Aquinas's argument. We saw above that, in his view, what *esse simpliciter* means is expressed by *esse substantiale*, and that the latter is the actuality of some Platonic Form or Forms. In speaking both of a 'common additional effect', i.e. the being of all things, and of its cause, i.e. the being of God, Aquinas treats being as though it could be conceived as a form comparable to manhood, etc. He treats *esse*, whether *simpliciter* or *substantiale*, as needing for its intelligibility some further predicate. 'Socrates is' (*esse simpliciter*) means 'Socrates is the actuality of manhood' (*esse substantiale*). Now, the difficulty is to make sense of the view that 'being' can be used in just the same way as 'manhood' is used here. 'Socrates is', when its meaning is made clear, needs something added to 'is', e.g. a reference to manhood. But what would be added if 'being' is substituted here for 'manhood' or any other such substantival expression? What have you added to 'Socrates is . . .' when you have said 'Socrates is the actuality of being or "isness" '? You have certainly not completed the sentence as you have in the case of other substantival predicates.

This criticism applies to 'God is being' just as forcefully. 'God is the actuality of being or isness' fails to complete 'God is . . .' as it is completed by, for instance, 'God is the actuality of creator-hood (or fatherhood, or whatever)'. When you have said that exis-tence, i.e. being or isness, is of the essence of God, therefore, you have said something of a logically different kind from saying that creatorhood, etc, are of the essence of God. Aquinas seems to have been deceived into thinking that because it makes sense to say that these latter are of the essence of God, it *must* also make sense to say that existence is of his essence. But the question whether or not it does remains, at least, open. Aquinas appears to beg it.

The other conceivable answer to the basic question under discussion, namely, 'Why should we cease to look for a cause of what exists simply because we have arrived at the thought of God as existing? is: *because we intuit* that God must exist. Copleston seems to think that this is the correct answer. He speaks of a 'metaphysical' point of view, distinct from the 'scientific'. From the latter scientific point of view he says, we may be impelled to go on asking for causes. But if we reflect metaphysically we can come to see that the question 'What caused this to exist?' does not arise about God, for it becomes clear to us that everything depends upon God. Copleston recognizes that 'nobody can compel me to adopt this (metaphysical) point of view'.[13] But it is not enough simply to concede that much. The issue is not whether *compulsion* can or cannot be effected. The question which arises about Copleston's argument is : what *reason* is there to adopt his 'metaphysical' point of view? Copleston gives none.

He speaks of 'adopting' this metaphysical point of view and 'maintaining it' until it 'becomes clear' that God is uncaused necessary being. But what then has happened? What does 'become clear' amount to here? All that has happened is that the metaphysical point of view has been adopted because it has been adopted. One adopts it and then it 'becomes clear'. For the view to become clear seems to mean no more here than that those who adopt the view become *sure* of it. Now it may be psychologically accurate to say that the way to become sure of anything is to think and speak as if one were convinced of it until one finds that one is convinced. This may not always work but sometimes it seems to do so. However, even if the psychological trick worked every time the logical question would remain : what *reason* is there to feel sure? The fact that one feels sure of something never answers the question : ought one to feel sure of it? Yet that is the question which those who say that it is clear that 'What caused God?' does not make sense purport to be answering when they claim that we can be sure of this by metaphysical intuition.

In .the end, then, we must conclude that the cosmological argument fails. A reason for believing that God really exists has not been provided by Aquinas's appeal to empirical evidence. I pass, therefore, to the next kind of argument which constitutes such an appeal.

The Argument from Design
The argument from – or perhaps it would be more accurate to say to – design purports to ground religious belief in objective empirical fact by showing that the order everywhere observable in the natural world can only be explained as the work of a Supreme Designer.

This argument has a long history. Anaxagoras (born c.500 B.C.), the Greek philosopher, was perhaps the first to propound it in any form. His account of creation ran : 'All things were together, infinitely numerous, infinitely little; then came mind (Greek *nous*) and set them in order.' Mind, he said, created a vortex at one point in the mixture; this disturbed the particles and they came together like with like, earth with earth, water with water, etc., until the world as we know it was created. Anaxagoras, in an age when philosophers in general applied the word 'god' (Greek *theos*) very indiscriminately, used it only of cosmic mind and, on this ground, he has been called 'the founder of theism'.[14] In the Christian era, the argument from design found classical formulation as the Fifth Way of Aquinas :

> We observe that some things which lack awareness, namely natural bodies, act for the sake of an end. This is clear because they always or commonly act in the same manner to achieve what is best, which shows that they reach their goal not by chance but because they tend towards it. Now things which lack awareness do not tend towards a goal unless directed by something with awareness and intelligence like an arrow by an archer. Therefore there is some intelligent being by whom everything in nature is directed towards a goal and this we call 'God'.[15]

After the Renaissance and the Enlightenment, Christian apologists, however hard pressed they might be to defend some tenets of their faith, were convinced that here, in the argument from design, they had a knock-down case for the existence of God.

Richard Price (born 1723), the moral philosopher, dissenting minister and political radical, wrote :

> It is impossible to survey the world without being assured, that the contrivance in it has proceeded from some contriver, the design in it from some *designing* cause, and the artistry from some artist. To say the contrary, or to assert, that it was produced by the accidental falling together of its component parts, must appear to every man whose understanding is not perverted, a folly as gross as it would be to assert the same of any other work of art that could be presented to him; of a commodious house, of a fine picture, or an exquisite machine.[16]

This sort of argument is still used by Christian apologists, though in a more sophisticated form than those which have so far been mentioned. Professor C. A. Coulson, for example, in his McNair Lectures, published as *Science and Christian Belief,* has much to say concerning 'the act of reflection' which 'leads us stage by stage through Natural Theology to Christian belief'.[17] The stages are as follows : (i) Science is seen to be not simply a matter of conceptual invention : the scientist is dealing with a reality that is *given*; every discovery appears to him as a revelation of this reality and not just a product of his own imagination. (ii) Science is seen to be a unity : this is true at all levels – within one science; as between one science and another; and in regard to the relation between man and nature. (iii) It is seen that this unity 'has a quality about it which can only be described as *spiritual*'; science is the 'carrier of spiritual meaning'. (iv) This spiritual quality of the unity which we experience and to which science contributes, must be expressed in terms 'which are at least personal'. By this fourfold 'act of reflection', according to Coulson, we apprehend the giveness, the oneness, the spiritual and the personal quality of the natural world respectively; and thus it is, he says, quoting Jeans, that we come to see that 'the universe shows evidence of a designing and controlling power that has something in common with our own individual minds'. Were Coulson merely describing here the stages through which some believers have in fact passed, he might well be right. But he writes as one who is not simply offering a psychological description of some people's religious experience, but constructing a logical bridge across the gap between the concepts of science and religion. He is, of course, fully aware of the difficulty of the task. He warns

against confusing concepts, which he says is 'as disastrous as mix-
ing drinks';[18] and he concedes, at the end of his account of the
stages of 'reflection', that 'the argument may not be logically convincing'.[19] His point however is not simply that, if the Christian
faith is accepted, science must be interpreted theologically in terms
such as those which he uses for his stages of reflection. With that
we might have no quarrel. For all his hesitation about its logical
cogency, his point is this : if any rational man looks carefully at
the natural world, he will see that it must (logically) have had one,
spiritual, personal Creator. Sophisticated and qualified as his
statement of the argument from design is, it is in its essentials the
same argument as that of Anaxagoras, Aquinas or Richard Price.

To this line of argument there are serious objections. They have
probably never been better stated than they were by David Hume
(1711-1776) in his *Dialogues Concerning Natural Religion.*

Hume pointed out what one is logically entitled to say concerning a cause in the light of its effect. In forming an inference from
effects to their causes, a man 'must form that inference from what
he knows, not from what he is ignorant of.'[20] If our argument is
from what we observe in nature, then we must attribute to God
only that degree of power, intelligence and benevolence which
would be necessary to create the natural world as we know it. We
are not entitled to claim that, although the world appears in some
degree to be the work of a malevolent creator, this is not really the
case and only appears to be so because we do not see the whole of
God's handiwork or know the full extent of his design. Hume's
point here has been taken by most Christian apologists who have
become familiar with it. Richard Price, Hume's contemporary,
was careful to say that, though the design evident in nature made
it folly to deny a designer, it is more difficult to show that this
designer is good.[21]

Hume, however, had a more radical objection to raise. The
argument from design is an argument from analogy. Where we
have observed, in a number of cases, a connection between effects
of species A (e.g. houses) and causes of species B (e.g. the work of
architects), then by argument from analogy, if we come on a new
case of species A, we can infer that it must have had a cause of
species B. All the houses we have observed hitherto had architects;
we see something new which is indisputably a house; and we infer
by analogy that this must also have had an architect. Put in the

plainest terms, the argument from design is to the effect that there is a resemblance between things like houses and the universe, and, since we have observed houses to have architects, we are entitled to infer by analogy that the universe also had one.

An argument from analogy never amounts to a logical demonstration. It is always conceivable, for instance, that although all the houses we have seen or heard about had architects, the one which we are now observing did not. The most we can say is that it probably did. The non-demonstrative character of the argument from analogy is not, of course, denied by those who use this form of argument in their attempt to prove the existence of a divine designer. Their claim is simply that the order in the universe is such that it is as probable that it had a designer as it is that any house we may come upon had an architect.

The probability of such an argument from analogy increases to the extent to which two conditions are fulfilled. Bear in mind that the argument which we are considering is to the effect that, since all effects of species A which we have hitherto observed were connected with causes of species B, a new phenomenon of species A must have had a cause of species B. Now, the probability that the new species A phenomenon was so caused increases : (i) the *more* cases of effects of species A connected with causes of species B which we have observed. (ii) the *closer* the resemblance between the new instance of species A and the previous instances of species A which we have encountered.

To illustrate (i) : we have observed very many cases of houses having architects; but if we only knew of two or three houses which had architects it would be that much less probable than it is that any new house we come upon had an architect.

To illustrate (ii) : when we see a house we are usually in no doubt at all that it is a house; but if we came upon some object and were uncertain whether or not it was a house, it would be, to the extent of that uncertainty, less probable that it had an architect.

How does the argument from design stand with regard to the two conditions which I have just mentioned?

With reference to the former condition, Hume had this to say : 'When two *species* of objects have always been observed to be conjoined together, I can *infer*, by custom, the existence of the one wherever I *see* the existence of the other : and this I call an argument from experience. But how this argument can have place, where the objects, as in the present case, are single, individual, without parallel, or specific resemblance, may be difficult to explain.'[22] Resemblance, that is, to other objects of the same species. If, he is saying, we had had experience of many universes conjoined with (caused by) many creators, then we could infer by analogy that this universe probably had one. But that condition cannot be fulfilled because the universe is an effect without parallel in our experience.

Prof. T. McPherson has argued that there is a way of escaping Hume's objection here.[23] The argument from design is not necessarily from the universe as a whole. Particular parts of it, which exhibit order, may be compared to manufactured objects and the inference drawn that, since the latter have designers, the former also must. This seems to leave us with many designers of the universe but to avoid that conclusion, it could perhaps be argued that, since the ordered parts of nature appear to 'work in with' one another, it must have had a Supreme Designer. We have experience of many objects (houses would be a case in point) where different ordered parts 'work in with' one another (e.g. the brickwork, the carpentry, the plumbing, the electrical circuits, etc. in a house) and in all such cases there is a supreme designer (the architect).

Much that religious believers ascribe to God could not, of course, be inferred concerning McPherson's Supreme Designer of the ordered parts of nature. For instance, it could not be inferred that he had created *ex nihilo* or that he created the laws of nature. Manufactured objects, such as houses, are not made out of nothing and their manufacture consists in exploiting the laws of nature, a process radically different from creating them. But, along the lines which McPherson suggested, it is perhaps possible to some degree to reduce the force of Hume's objection that the argument from analogy is invalid because the universe is 'an effect . . . entirely singular'.

As to the latter of the above conditions, Hume contended that, even if it were allowable to draw an analogy between the universe and other objects, those which it was found most closely to resemble would not be objects which have been designed, such as machines, houses, or works of art. Living organisms exhibit order as well as manufactured objects. In our experience, living organisms arise, not as the products of a designing intelligence, but of vegetation and generation. Generation produces human beings who both reproduce themselves through further generation and also exercise designing intelligence. Generation produces, one might therefore say, the order *both* of living organisms and of manufactured objects. In the universe we are confronted by both kinds of order. The cause of the universe, therefore, more closely resembles generation, which in our experience gives rise to *both* of these kinds of order, than intelligence, which in our experience *only* gives rise to the order or design of manufactured objects. As Hume put it : 'Judging by our limited and imperfect experience, generation has some privileges above reason; for we see every day the latter arise from the former, never the former from the latter'. Recalling the Brahmin legend that the world was spun by a giant spider, he concludes : 'Why an orderly system may not be spun from the belly as well as from the brain, it will be difficult . . . to give a satisfactory reason'.[24]

I do not suppose that theists will be unduly dismayed by Hume's argument that the universe resembles a living organism more closely than an artefact. The generation which, in our experience, gives rise to both the order produced by further generation and the order produced by intelligence is birth from personal beings. Human parents have children who, in due course, exhibit (a) the order produced by generation through having children themselves, and (b) the order produced by intelligence through the things which they make or do. This being so, a Christian apologist might well argue that what is needed to explain both the order of genera-tion and the order of intelligence or design, which the universe exhibits, is by analogy, God the Father rather than merely God the Architect.

However, it will scarcely do to leave the matter there. Human beings, so far as the empirical evidence goes, are themselves the product of an evolutionary process extending back to lower forms of life and, presumably, to inanimate matter. How human life has evolved from lower forms of life is something of a mystery still; and how life evolved from inanimate matter, if it did, an even greater mystery. But all the empirical evidence which we have to go on is a process with considerable gaps, whereby ever more com-plicated forms of life appeared on this planet until eventually human beings appeared. So if we are going to run personal life back to its origins, as known to us, and argue that God the creator must be conceived after that analogy, then the order of generation and intelligence in the universe will take us back, not to God the Architect, much less God the Father, but to God the amoeba, God the vegetable, even God the exploding Sun.

A more radical difficulty with regard to the argument from design than those so far considered concerns the whole concept of order in nature, on which that argument rests. Suppose a species of fruit tree, which had hitherto always yielded apples, were suddenly one year, to yield pears, and, on existing theories, scientists could not account for this. They would not conclude that nature is chaotic. They would try to revise their theories in such a way as to account for both the apples and the pears. It is a methodological rule with scientists that natural laws can have no exceptions and that, when theories have to be changed in order to meet something new in experience, they should be so revised as to explain, not only the new state of affairs, but the old one as well.[25] In other words, nothing is allowed to count as empirical evidence of *dis*order in nature. The appeal to order in nature, therefore, cannot be lost; and in so far as the argument from design is based on that appeal, it cannot be invalidated. We shall see, in a moment, that this disqualifies that argument from comparison with scientific explanation.

The proponent of the argument from design might conceivably reply that his point has been missed : that he is not appealing to the methodological rule whereby natural laws have no exceptions but to the empirical fact that nature has chimed in so closely with the predictions of scientists. It is conceivable that this should not have been so. The following might have happened. Scientists, having observed events X1, X2, X3, propounded a theory, or set of theories, T1, and from T1 predicted event X4. But, in fact, X5 occurred. So scientists revised their theories in such a way, T2, as to account for X1, X2, X3, and X5 and, from T2, predicted event X6. But in fact X7 occurred so they revised their theory again, T3, and from T3 predicted X8. But X9 occurred. And so on . . . Scientists could conceivably have stuck to their methodological rule that natural laws have no exceptions but their predictions in practice have always been falsified. (Or, at any rate, these predictions could have been falsified in an embarrassingly large proportion of cases : there would have had to be some regularity in nature or there would have been nothing which could be thought of as a thing, or an event, and so no possibility of science at all.) But this is not what has happened. The history of scientific prediction has not been predominantly one of defeat but of victory. As scientific theories have become increasingly universal and precise, they have proved increasingly reliable. Is not this remarkable : that nature should have confirmed science, that the unified framework which scientists have constructed should, so far as all our experiences can tell, *fit* nature so much more closely than, for example, the discrete, chaotic system of animism? The natural theologian could go on to argue that this remarkable fact requires explanation. When things 'chime in' with one another in our experience, it is commonly because an architect, designer, or composer has arranged that they should. By analogy, the fact that nature 'chimes in' with science leads to the conclusion that this state of affairs – the order in nature – has been arranged by a Divine Designer or Composer.

Suppose that conclusion is allowed. It may then be asked : is the belief that nature is the creation of one intelligent Designer of stable character, therefore comparable to a scientific hypothesis? Natural theologians think that it is. With the argument from design in mind they compare religious belief to scientific hypothesis.

The crucial question in deciding whether or not they are entitled to do so is this : can religious belief be given the same kind of objective grounding as scientific knowledge? Note first the stages which lead to scientific knowledge. (i) Certain empirical facts, the initial conditions, require explanation. (ii) A theory is propounded or invoked to explain them. (iii) Empirically observable predictions are deduced from this theory together with the initial conditions. (iv) Appropriate observations are made to see whether or not these predictions are fulfilled. If they are, the theory is corroborated; if not, the theory is falsified. This is the 'hypothetic-deductive' account of scientific method as propounded by K. R. Popper. It seems to me to be the correct account. Take as an instance of scientific knowledge Newton's theory of gravitation. It is well known that it received classic confirmation in the following way. It had been noticed that the orbit of the planet Uranus did not exactly coincide with scientists' calculations as to what it ought to be. Newton's theory of gravitation laid it down that planetary motion is determined by gravitational force according to a certain formula.

Scientists took it that the deviation of Uranus must be a case in point. It must be due to the attraction of some object hitherto unobserved. At least two of them, Leverrier in France and Adams in England, worked out what the track of such an object would have to be for it to exert the necessary gravitational pull. Leverrier sent his calculations to Berlin, where the largest telescope in the world was then situated and this was trained, at the appropriate time, on a certain part of the heavens which Leverrier indicated. The planet which we now call Neptune swam into view. In this example we see the following elements : (i) initial conditions (the deviation of Uranus) which require explanation; (ii) a theory (the law of gravitation) invoked to explain them; (iii) from this theory together with the initial conditions certain predictions (the existence of Neptune) deduced; (iv) these predictions put to the test of empirical observation. The view which we are considering is that the argument from design establishes the existence of God in a similar way.

This view might be set up as follows. (i) Certain empirical facts – the order in nature – call for explanation. (ii) The theory of a Cosmic Designer who is to some extent consistent in his ordering of nature is invoked to explain them. (iii) From (i) and (ii) – the initial conditions and the theory – certain empirically observable predictions are deduced to the effect that nature will continue to manifest consistent order in for example day following night, etc. (iv) Appropriate observations are made to see if these predictions are fulfilled.

Can this comparison between the discovery of a natural fact like the existence of Neptune and the discovery of the existence of God be sustained? It cannot for at least two reasons.

(i) If the evidence for a Cosmic Designer is the extent to which nature chimes in with scientists' predictions – and we suggested a moment ago that this is how the argument from design might be put – it is appropriate to ask to what precise extent nature would have to fail to chime in to falsify the hypothesis of a Cosmic Designer? This is appropriate because the *sine qua non* of a scientific theory is that it should be falsifiable by empirical evidence. If it is not possible to say what would falsify a theory, that theory does not qualify as a candidate for admission to the corpus of scientific knowledge. So if belief in a Cosmic Designer is to be compared to a scientific hypothesis, natural theologians must be prepared to say precisely what would falsify it. Can they do so? In asking that question I am not merely suggesting that they might share the general reluctance of religious believers to admit anything as falsifying their beliefs. I am wondering how a natural theologian would differentiate between cases where a scientist's prediction failed to be fulfilled because the scientist's knowledge was defective from cases where it failed to be fulfilled because nature was disorderly. The problem here is the problem of identifying the evidence of disorder.

Given the argument from design, evidence of disorder in nature would falsify the hypothesis of a Cosmic Designer. But how could one tell what was evidence of disorder in nature and what was simply evidence of ignorance in scientists? If the answer is that one could not, then the argument from design – in the particular form that we are here considering it – is unfalsifiable and so not comparable to a scientific hypothesis.

(ii) Even if the argument from design could be cast in a form which is empirically falsifiable, does it meet the demands of scientific simplicity? Is it the simplest possible explanation of the facts? If not, it falls under Occam's razor – entities must not be multiplied without necessity – and that is a fate which no theory can survive and remain scientific. It seems that the argument from design is not the simplest explanation of the order in nature. If nature, in our experience, chimes in with science then we are entitled to work with the theory that nature is a unified system. But that is all. Our evidence is drawn from nature and our conclusion concerns nature. Our theory will then enable us to make predictions about the course of nature but nothing more. That is the whole business of science : working with theories which have to do with nature, it forecasts natural events : being able to do this efficiently is what is meant by scientific explanation. But this is not the whole business of religion. The latter brings God in to explain the unity of nature. This complicates the issue unnecessarily from a scientific point of view. As Laplace, who was a devout Christian as well as a scientist, said, the scientist *qua* scientist has no need of the hypothesis, God. The argument from design, then, is not comparable to a (good) scientific hypothesis because it is unnecessarily complicated.

I have been widening the gap between religious belief and scientific explanation in these last remarks but a point of similarity between them has emerged in what I have been saying. I said that a scientist *qua* scientist is committed to the methodological rule that natural laws have no exceptions. This means that, if any event occurs which falsifies his present theory, he modifies the latter in order to explain the falsifying event. But in no case does he forsake his belief that nature admits of scientific explanation. Even if he cannot think of the explanation in a given case, he affirms that there must be one and continues to seek it. Now, similarly, a religious believer *qua* religious believer is committed to a methodological rule something like this: there are no exceptions to the government or providence of God. Events may occur which conflict with his present doctrine concerning that government or providence. He may, for instance, believe that God will never allow his native land to be defeated in battle and then find that it is defeated. In such a case, he will try to think of some explanation, which covers the present defeat as well as any past victories which his native land has enjoyed. For instance, he may come to think that God's purpose for his native land, though in the past served by victories, can now only be fulfilled by a people who have known defeat. It was in some such vein that their prophets explained the defeats of the early Israelites. In no case will the religious believer surrender his belief that events admit of religious explanation. Believers and scientists alike, if they cannot think of a convincing explanation, will affirm that there must be one, even though it does not yet occur to them. This similarity between religious belief and science, however, only highlights the point which I was making just now; that belief in God is *not* comparable to the acceptance of a scientific hypothesis. The methodological rules of science are *not* scientific hypotheses. They are logical starting points for the scientific way of interpreting experience. Belief in God is similarly not an empirically testable hypothesis. It is a commitment from which the distinctively theistic method of interpreting experience proceeds.

The argument from design fails, at least for the purpose under consideration in this chapter. Its appeal to order in nature will not serve as evidence of that in nature which justifies belief in God's objective existence. If an affirmative answer to the question 'Does God really exist?' can be substantiated from empirical evidence it is not by this argument.

Religious Experience

We have noted in the last section that scientific theories are tested by empirical observation, i.e. *in experience*. They are corroborated when men find observable predictions deduced from them to be commonly and recurrently verified; and discredited when they find such predictions falsified. The objectivity of scientific knowledge derives from this appeal to common and recurrent experience. To recall an example used above, any normally sighted person who looked through the Berlin telescope, when it was focused in the appropriate way, could not have failed to see Neptune. The question which we must now consider is: can religious beliefs similarly be put *to the test of experience*? The claim that they can has a longer history even than the argument from design. the confident prediction of the Hebrew lawgiver could be paralleled a thousand times from religious literature, ancient and modern :

> If . . . thou shalt seek the Lord thy God, thou shalt find him, if
> thou seek him with all thy heart and with all thy soul. When
> thou art in tribulation, and all these things are come upon thee
> . . . if thou turn to the Lord thy God . . . he will not forsake
> thee . . .   (*Deuteronomy* 4 : 29-31.)

Here is a belief in God and, deduced from it, a forecast concerning human experience. It is tempting to liken this kind of forecast to the predictions which scientists make in order to test their theories. I have already pointed out some objections to doing so with particular reference to the argument from design. Here I want to consider religious experience in a wider context. We are seeking empirical evidence for God's existence. Does anything called religious experience provide it?

It cannot be disputed that religious experience occurs, if by 'religious experience' is meant either : (i) ordinary experience which has occurred in accordance with predictions which religious believers, on the grounds of their beliefs, have made; or, (ii) experience having a peculiar feeling-tone, a 'numinous' quality to use Otto's word. The fulfilment of St Paul's prediction during the storm at sea, 'There shall be no loss of any man's life among you, but of the ship . . . for I believe God that it shall be even as it was told me'. (*Acts* 27 : 22-25) illustrates the former meaning. **Wordsworth's** remarks in his *Lines above Tintern Abbey* about 'a presence which disturbs me with the joy of elevated thoughts' is an illustration of the latter meaning. The question which has to be answered is : does religious experience, in either sense, provide logically adequate grounds for asserting that God exists objectively?

If, of course, God is defined as to any degree transcendent and if 'transcendent' here means 'lying beyond human experience' then necessarily the answer is no. For in such case, no premises solely concerning human experience could (logically) prove his existence. It is logically impossible to experience that which by definition lies beyond experience. If, however, by 'transcendent' is meant 'having the greatest degree of goodnesss, power, or whatever, – even of mystery – of which we can conceive', then human experience could conceivably justify our calling God, in this sense, transcendent.

Even without the benefit of the word 'transcendent', however, there is a logical gap which can be opened up between accounts of religious experience and the belief that God exists objectively. It is the same gap as that which can be opened up between any statement reporting what some given subject has experienced and any statement asserting the existence of an object other than that subject. To illustrate the nature of this logical gap let us consider briefly the relationship between statements concerning sense experience and statements concerning physical objects. Take this example :

A : 'There is a table in the next room.'
B : 'How do you know?'
A : 'Because I have seen it.'

A's claim to knowledge concerns a physical object, namely a table. The reason given for making it, however, concerns only sense experience, namely A's experience of seeing. Now, no statement (or statements) about sense-experience will serve as the necessary or sufficient condition for a statement about physical objects. If the statement (or statements) about sense-experience were a *necessary* condition, then one could say, 'If this physical object exists, or has such-and-such properties, then these sense-experiences occur'. Or alternatively, 'If these sense-experiences do *not* occur then the physical object does *not* exist or have these properties.' But it does not necessarily follow from the fact that the requisite sense-experiences do not occur, that the physical object in question does not exist, or have the properties it has been said to have. It makes sense to say that there may always be a table in the next room even though, through some circumstances beyond our knowledge, neither I nor anyone else can see it. Again, if the statement (or statements) about sense-experience were a *sufficient* condition of an assertion about a physical object, one could say, 'If these experiences occur, then this object exists or has these properties.' Or, alternatively, 'If this object does *not* exist, or have these properties, then these experiences do *not* occur.' But it is logically impossible to give any description of sense experiences from which it would necessarily follow that a certain physical object exists or has certain properties. The distinction between reality and hallucination can (logically) always be drawn and the possibility of the latter conceived. It is always conceivable that, although the physical object does not exist, we should suffer the hallucination that it does.[26]

Two points emerge here. (i) An assertion about a physical object can never be logically reduced to an assertion, or assertions, about sense experience. (ii) It is always logically possible to introduce a hypothesis (namely, that we are being deceived by sense experience) to save the physical object statement from conclusive confirmation or refutation by the empirical evidence. The statements in which scientists express their conclusions, however sophisticated they may have become, are all physical object statements. They are, therefore, all subject to these two logical limitations.

Now, in order to protect the comparison between religious belief and scientific knowledge, some apologists for religion have argued that, if this is so in the case of scientific statements, then the facts : (i) that it is never logically possible to reduce a statement about God to a statement or statements about human experience; and (ii) that it is always logically possible to save a religious statement from conclusive falsification by introducing some saving hypothesis, do *not* render theological assertions unscientific. True, the statement for example 'God has given me peace through prayer' cannot be reduced to 'I have found peace through prayer'. True again, the belief for instance that God cares for his people can be saved from falsification by such occurrences as their defeat in battle if we introduce such saving hypotheses as that through defeat he is fulfilling some good purpose for them. But here we simply have parallels in the case of religion to the facts that no physical object statement can be reduced to, or conclusively falsified by, any statement about sense experience.

Is this comparison between religious statements and scientific ones legitimate? Notice first that, although no sense experience statements are logically equivalent to physical object statements, scientists and plain men of common sense do in practice accept the former as evidence of the latter. 'There is a table in the next room' for instance is treated as a hypothesis which can be confirmed or discredited by sense experience such as 'If anyone goes into the next room he will have X experiences', where X can be specified, e.g. 'He will see brownness, shininess, roundness', 'He will feel hardness', etc. We say that the table exists, if these sense experiences are common and recurrent. Now can this be taken over and applied to religion? One apologist for religion wrote not long ago :

> An apparently existential statement such as 'There is a God' . . . would have to imply that certain experiences are generally and permanently available at least to certain people under certain conditions, just as 'grass is green' implies that certain people (those who are not blind or colour-blind) under certain conditions (in normal light, and without the use of rose-tinted spectacles) would have common experiences for which we use the word 'green' . . . All we need is a certain number of people with a common and recurrent experience and some way of distinguishing genuine from illusory experience.[27]

These conditions appear, at first sight, to be satisfied. There are a number of religious people who claim that they have certain experiences commonly and recurrently, under certain conditions, e.g. peace in sorrow when they pray, or guidance in difficulty when they ask for it. They differentiate genuine from illusory experience after their own fashion, e.g. they say such things as 'I thought God wanted me to stay there but I had to move and I see now that I was mistaken.' But the question remains : are the scientific conditions *really* fulfilled in the case of religion?

A prediction such as 'If anyone goes into the next room, he will have X experiences' may, in some cases, be unfulfilled. For instance, the person concerned may be blind. The prediction must be stated more carefully to allow for this kind of falsification : 'If anyone goes into the next room, and if that person is not blind, he will have X experiences'. The crucial point to take is that the auxiliary hypothesis, '. . . and if that person is not blind', can be put to empirical tests which are *independent* of e.g. his seeing or not seeing the table. An oculist could apply many such tests. But compare the saving hypothesis here with the sort of saving hypothesis which is frequently introduced when predictions concerning religious experience are unfulfilled.

The verses from *Deuteronomy* quoted earlier in this section will illustrate the point. That quotation predicted that if one seeks God, God will not forsake one. Well, suppose someone does seek God (i.e. worships, studies Scripture, obeys the Commandments, or whatever else 'seek' is defined to mean here) yet is forsaken by God (i.e. he is not delivered from tribulation, feels abandoned, or whatever else 'forsaken' means). There is certainly in the text a saving hypothesis to cover just this contingency : 'if thou seek Him with all thy heart and with all thy soul.' But the important question is : can this saving hypothesis be put to an empirical test which is *independent* of what we mean by being or not being forsaken? Do we know the measure of effort in heart and soul which is required to avoid being forsaken, so that we can test whether it is present or absent, as we can test whether a man is blind or not, independently of whether he sees this or that particular table? If not, then the position we are in is this. We have a prediction which purports to put belief in God to an empirical test. ('If thou shalt seek the Lord . . . he shall not forsake thee'.) This is not fulfilled and so the belief is empirically falsified. But we have a saving hypothesis ('If thou seek Him with all thy heart and with all thy soul') which enables us always to avoid admitting empirical falsification. We can always argue that the prediction is unfulfilled, not because the belief on which it is based was mistaken, but because the subject did not try hard enough to find God. It is however a fatal objection to such a move if the contention that he did not try hard enough is confirmed only by the fact that the original prediction ('he shall not forsake thee') was falsified *and by nothing else*. A fatal objection, that is, to any comparison between the belief in question and scientific knowledge. The kind of saving hypothesis which is never allowable in science is the kind which is not corroborated by anything except the non-fulfilment of the predictions deduced from the theory which it is invoked to save. Science can be defined by its exclusion of just this kind of move.

Another requirement of scientific enquiry is that the predictions with which the scientist tests his theory are, or ought to be, always *precise* enough to be tested *experimentally*. That is, the exact conditions under which the test needs to be made can be specified and exactly what will happen, if the theory is confirmed, can be forecast. In religion the demand for this kind of experimental precision seems frequently to be evaded. There is an attempt to have it both ways : to claim that one is arguing from experience like a scientist, but to be vague about precisely what experience one is arguing from. Professor Paul Tillich, for instance wrote :

> The verifying test belongs to the nature of truth; in this positivism is right. Every cognitive assumption (hypothesis) must be tested. The safest test is the repeatable experiment . . . But it is not permissible to make the experimental method of verification the exclusive pattern of all verification. Verification can occur within the life-process itself. Verification of this type (experiential in contra-distinction to experimental) has the advantage that it need not halt and disrupt the totality of a life-process in order to distil calculable elements out of it (which experimental verification must do).[28]

If the point here were simply that the predictions which test a religious theory have to do, not with moments of experience, but prolonged phases of it, that might be allowed. But, if the comparison with science is to be preserved, there must be no loss of precision. The natural theologian must say exactly what difference 'seeking God' for instance makes. However difficult to devise, he must allow experimental tests : for instance, he must collate evidence which will give him two significantly large groups of people, A and B, similar in intelligence, temperament, upbringing, etc. where A seeks God and B does not; and he must show that the predicted difference characterises members of A as against those of B. Tillich's point seems to be not that this would be hard to do, but that it does not need to be done :

> Verifying experiences of a non-experimental character are truer to life, though less exact and definite . . . The test, of course, is neither repeatable, precise, nor final at any particular moment. The life process itself makes the test. Therefore, the test is indefinite and preliminary; there is an element of risk connected with it.[29]

This is precisely the sort of risk which a scientist *qua* scientist does not take. Tillich said that there are 'two cognitive attitudes, the controlling and the receiving',[30] corresponding to experimental and experiential verification respectively. But he seems to consider them both definable as cognitive by the same criterion, that is, they are both verifiable in experience. If this is his point, then what his argument amounts to is that religion is science, but of an imprecise kind. To which the only reply is that an activity which is so imprecise that its tests are not 'calculable', 'exact', 'definite', or 'repeatable', is not like science at all.

An apologist on behalf of religion could conceivably accept all that I have said about the need for science to be empirically falsifiable and precise and still persist in his contention that belief in God can be compared to accepting a scientific hypothesis. He would of course have to concede that what passes for religion must be brought into line so that : (i) the existence of God is empirically falsifiable; and (ii) the experiences which test it can be specified precisely. But he may be willing to do so. This would be a courageous move on his part. The apologist to whom I referred a few moments ago (see p. 70) seemed prepared to make this move. He seemed to think that if a rational case is to be made out for religion, certain precise empirical predictions must be deduced from the theory that God exists or has certain qualities, and if these predictions are not commonly and recurrently fulfilled, that theory must be renounced. This move would certainly bring religion into line with science, but would it be at the cost of reducing religion to something other than itself? *Not* putting God to this test seems to be definitive of at least some forms of religion. 'Though he slay me yet will I trust in Him'. (*Job* 13 : 15). Refusal to surrender belief, whatever the empirical evidence, has been taken by many to be a *sine qua non* in religion. If it is, then this makes religion very different from science.

We noted above that physical object statements cannot (logically) be reduced to statements about sense experience. Then, is the table *really* there or is there only a family of sense-data which for convenience we call by the name 'table'? This is a question with which the scientist as such does not concern himself at all. If the point were put to him I suppose he could accept with equanimity that there may conceivably be no thing-in-itself 'out there' which is the table; that all science may be only about human

experience and the patterns which it assumes. This view need not
appear to him to render his conclusions invalid or his discipline
pointless. But could a religious believer accept with similar equanimity that 'God' may be just a convenient way of referring to a
family of human experiences? I am not saying simply that this
would involve a redefinition of 'God' as it would involve a redefinition of 'table' if we came to think of it as the name for a family
of sense-data and nothing more. What I am saying is that it seems
to matter more to a religious man that God really exists than it
does to a scientist as such that the physical world really exists.

The attempt to establish the existence of God in the way that
scientific hypotheses are corroborated by empirical evidence does
not succeed. The problem of objectivity is not to be solved by an
appeal to religious experience.

The Moral Argument
I turn now to an argument – put forward in various forms – to
the effect that from the fact that men form moral judgments it can
be inferred that God exists.

In one form this line of argument is simply a variant of the
argument from design. We observe in the world a certain phenomenon, namely man, a being who forms moral judgments. The
cause of which this phenomenon is the effect must be, or have
been, sufficient to produce the effect. What is moral cannot (logically) have been caused by what is non-moral. Therefore, a moral
being, namely God, must be, or have been, the creator of men. All
the arguments deployed above against other variants of the argument from design apply against this one and we need not therefore
spend any more time on it.

Another form which the moral argument for God's existence
takes is that represented by Kant and in this form it requires more
detailed consideration. I do not find it easy to interpret Kant but
what follows is, I think, a correct account of the definitive form
of his argument as it appears in *The Critique of Practical Reason*.
An essential element in the *summum bonum,* i.e. the highest good
conceivable for man, is, according to Kant, 'happiness propor-
tioned to . . . morality'. This is a state of affairs in which the
virtuous are happy and the vicious unhappy in direct proportion
to their virtue or vice respectively. Happiness Kant defined as the
condition of a rational being for whom everything goes according

to his desires; and unhappiness as the opposite condition. Now, whilst men can, and should, will the realization of this state of affairs as part of the *summum bonum*, they cannot by the exercise of their will ensure that it will be realized. A good man, as such, wills the realization of the *summum bonum* but this act of willing does not operate as a cause in the physical world; it cannot of itself effect the realization of the *summum bonum*. Says Kant:

> Nevertheless, in the practical problem of pure reason, i.e. the necessary pursuit of the *summum bonum*, such a connection (sc. between morality and proportionate happiness) is postulated as necessary : we ought to endeavour to promote the *summum bonum*, which therefore must be possible. Accordingly, the existence of a cause of all nature, distinct from nature itself, and containing the principle of this connection, namely of the exact harmony of happiness with morality, is also postulated. Now this supreme cause must contain the principle of the harmony of nature, not merely with a law of the will of rational beings, but with the concept of this *law*, in so far as they make it the *supreme determining principle of the will*, and consequently not merely with the form of morals but with their morality as their motive, that is, with their moral character. Therefore, the *summum bonum* is possible only on the supposition of a supreme Being having a causality corresponding to moral character . . . Now it was seen to be a duty for us to promote the *summum bonum*; consequently it is not merely allowable, but it is a necessity connected with duty as a requisite, that we should presuppose the possibility of this *summum bonum*; and as this is possible only on condition of the existence of God, it inseparably connects the supposition of this with duty; that is, it is morally necessary to assume the existence of God.[31]

The fundamental premise of this argument seems to be that 'ought' implies 'can'. That is, it does not make sense to say that anyone ought to do X unless he can do X. There is much to be said for this premise and I have no wish to quarrel with it here. But if we accept it, does the rest of Kant's argument stand up to criticism? He seems to be making two main points : (i) that because we ought to endeavour to promote the *summum bonum*, the *summum bonum* must (logically) be possible in the sense of realizable; (ii) that because the *summum bonum* must be realizable God must (logically) exist in order to make it so. Let us look more closely at each of these lines of argument. Both, I think, are mistaken.

As for the first, it is doubtless true that if we could not 'endeavour to promote' the *summum bonum* it would make no sense to say that we ought to do so. If we really ought to endeavour to promote the *summum bonum* – and Kant believed that we have an intuition of this – then it must really be the case that *we can* do so. But notice carefully what *is* the case. Not, that the *summum bonum* is realizable. Only that *we can try to realize it.* Even if we knew that it was physically impossible because of some element in the natural world for anyone ever to realize the *summum bonum,* it would still make sense to say that we ought to try to do so. Moral values might conceivably be realized only by attempting the impossible and hence it be our duty to do just that. Therefore, Kant's first line of argument is mistaken : from the fact that we ought to endeavour to promote the *summum bonum* it does not follow that the *summum bonum* must be realizable.

Kant's second line of argument, if I understand it correctly, is also misconceived. What it amounts to is this. No man could, simply by willing it to be so, make the *summum bonum* realizable. But God could. Since in the world as it is the *summum bonum must* be realizable (see the first line of argument), it follows that the world *must* (logically) have been created by a being who had (a) the will that the *summum bonum* should be realizable and (b) the power to create a world in which it would be realizable. Such a being is what we mean by God. Therefore God must exist. Here I think there is some confusion between a necessary and a sufficient condition of the *summum bonum* being realizable. If there exists a being who (a) wills that the *summum bonum* shall be realizable and (b) has the power to make it so, then certainly the existence of this being is a *sufficient* condition of the *summum bonum*'s being realizable. But Kant, as I understand him, is not saying this. He is saying that if the *summum bonum* is realizable, then it is a *necessary* condition of that state of affairs that there exists a being who (a) wills that the *summum bonum* shall be realizable and (b) has the power to make it so. If this is what Kant is saying, he is mistaken. If it is true that the *summum bonum* is realizable, then necessarily it is also true that there does not exist anything which prevents it being realizable; and that there exists something which makes its realization possible. But this condition could quite conceivably be fulfilled if God does not exist. There would, of course, be a mystery then as to why this condition was fulfilled. But it is one thing to say that we do not know why something is the case and quite another to say that it is inconceivable that it should be the case. Kant, as I understand him, is saying that we cannot conceive of a world in which the *summum bonum* is realizable without also believing that God exists. But he has not given us good ground for this contention.

It may be objected that Kant was talking about what men must believe if they are to 'endeavour to promote' the *summum bonum* with confidence. God's existence is 'postulated' in the sense that, unless we believed that the *summum bonum was* realizable, we should not try very hard to promote it; and the best guarantee that it is realizable being the existence of God, that belief is demanded where men do try very hard to promote it.[32]

But I doubt if this is even true as a contribution to the psychology of morals. Unless one is going to engage in sophistry to the effect that every man who tries to promote the *summum bonum* in so doing affirms his belief in God because trying to promote the *summum bonum* is what belief in God *means*, then it seems quite certain that many atheists and agnostics can, and do, 'endeavour to promote' the *summum bonum* very vigorously indeed even though they do not believe in God. Be that as it may, I do not think that Kant intended his moral argument for God as a contribution to the psychology of morals. He intended, I think, to deduce from something, which he took men to know, certain conclusions as to what in consequence must be true. Men, Kant held, know by moral intuition that it is their duty to endeavour to promote the *summum bonum*. It seemed to Kant in consequence true as a matter of logical necessity that: (a) the *summum bonum* is realizable; and (b) God exists as the necessary condition of its being so. I have given reasons why I think these conclusions do not follow.

Some modern authors argue from moral experience to God's existence. They start from the putative fact that we intuit moral properties in actions or states of affairs as (a) *sui generis* and (b) objective. By such moral intuition, they claim, we know that an objective order of moral values exists and they deduce from the existence of this moral order the existence of God.

How is the objective order of moral values related to the existence of God? Some hold that it is identical with the latter; others,
dependent upon the latter. Professor W. G. Maclagan represents
the former view.[33] He holds that 'the objective order of values is
God' and that to say this is to 'suggest a meaning for the term
"God".' Prof. H. P. Owen, on the other hand, takes the view that
absolute values must not be identified with God but 'inhere in the
personality of God'.[34] I do not intend to concern myself with the
particular issue which divides these two schools of thought but to
examine critically the premises from which, as I have already
indicated, both proceed, i.e. that we intuit moral properties which
are *sui generis* and objective. First I will say something about the
sui generis character of moral properties. Then I will consider the
claim that they are *objective*.

Moral terms are indeed *sui generis* in the sense that they cannot
be defined, without change or loss of meaning, in non-moral terms.
Many classical moral philosophers pointed this out in one way or
another,[35] but it will suffice if we take the point as it was made by
a modern philosopher, G. E. Moore, in his *Principia Ethica*
(London 1903). Moore concentrated his attention on the word
'good' and argued that, when used in a strictly moral sense, it
stands for what he called a 'simple', 'indefinable' or 'unanalysable'
notion. He wrote:

> It may be true that all things which are good are *also* something
> else, just as it is true that all things which are yellow produce a
> certain kind of vibration in the light. And it is a fact, that Ethics
> aims at discovering what are those other properties belonging
> to all things which are good. But far too many philosophers
> have thought that when they named those other properties they
> were actually defining good; that these properties, in fact, were
> simply not 'other', but absolutely and entirely the same with
> goodness. This view I propose to call the 'naturalistic fallacy'
> and of it I shall . . . endeavour to dispose.[36]

His method of disposing of it was as follows. When 'good' is
defined, a question and a statement, both of which most people
would consider significant, become insignificant.

Suppose 'to be good' is defined as 'to give happiness'. The contention then is that for 'to be good' in any context we can substitute some form of 'to give happiness' without any change or loss

of meaning; for instance, 'Albert Schweitzer was a good man' can be re-written 'Albert Schweitzer was a man who gave happiness'. But now suppose someone asks 'But is what gives happiness good?' Is this question *self-answering*? Does it, that is to say, amount to no more than 'Does what gives happiness give happiness?' to which the answer 'Yes' is analytically true?

Again, suppose that someone wishes to express the view that it is good to do what gives happiness and says 'What gives happiness is good'. Is he uttering nothing more than the *tautology* 'What gives happiness gives happiness'? If 'good' really did *mean* 'gives happiness', then the question to which I referred a moment ago *would be* self-answering and the expression of opinion to which I have just referred *would be* a mere tautology.

But it seemed clear to Moore that *whatever definition* (call this D) is given to 'good' the question 'Is what is D good?' is *not* self-answering; and the statement 'What is D is good' is *not* a mere tautology. His main target of criticism was those moral philosophers who have wanted to do two things; (a) to utter a significant generalization and (b) to claim that it is true by definition. To say, for example, 'Whatever gives happiness is good because that is what "good" means', the implication being that anyone who says 'Whatever gives happiness is not good' is not simply morally in error but does not understand the language which he is using. Against those who attempt to support their moral judgments with this sort of knock-down argument, Moore aimed to show that moralists and moral philosophers cannot have it both ways. 'Whatever gives happiness is good' cannot (logically) be both a significant ethical generalization and not a mere tautology and at the same time true by definition. This, he insisted, is not simply because 'gives happiness' or whatever is the *wrong* definition of 'good'; but because 'good' is indefinable.

Others writers, such as W. D. Ross or H. A. Prichard, extended Moore's case for the *sui generis* character of moral discourse by showing that the points which he made about 'good' can *mutatis mutandis* be made equally cogently about 'right' or 'ought' (along with their opposites and cognates).[37] If 'right' for instance, is defined as 'conformable to the principle of utility', then, 'What conforms to the principle of utility is right' becomes tautologous and 'Is what conforms to the principle of utility right?' becomes self-answering. If, 'ought' is so defined that 'X ought to be done' means for instance 'X is a case of obeying God rather than men', then 'Ought we to obey God rather than men?' becomes a self-answering question. Some religious moralists may be well content so to regard it. But would they be content – which follows by the same token – to regard 'We ought to obey God rather than men' as a vacuous tautology meaning no more than 'For us to obey God rather than men is for us to obey God rather than men'?

It seems to me that moral language is beyond dispute *sui generis* in the sense that it is not logically possible to replace it in any context by non-moral language without some loss or change of meaning. But this is simply a point about language. Does anything follow from it concerning extra-linguistic reality? With that question before us we turn to the claim that moral values are objective.

I must begin the discussion of this claim by distinguishing two theories (already noted in Chapter 1) as to the meaning which language in general, and moral language in particular, has. According to one of these, the meaning of language is, and only is, that to which it *refers*. The meaning of 'table' for instance is the thing which we call a table, the meaning of 'good' is the property of acts or states of affairs to which we give that name. Unless an element of language, like the word, 'good', has a referent it does not, according to this theory, have a meaning. The alternative theory is to the effect that we discover what any piece of language means by asking not 'To what does this refer?' but 'What *job* does this do?' Does it describe, exhort, praise, blame, terrorise, encourage, etc? Does it do so in some particular way or in accordance with certain distinctive rules? According to this theory, the uses to which language can be put are exceedingly varied and so are the meanings which elements or combinations of elements within it may have.

Now, if (a) moral language is *sui generis* and (b) its meaning is its *referent*, then, given that moral language is meaningful, there must be some distinctive reality – that is, objective moral value – corresponding to it. But from the premises that (a) moral words like 'good' and 'right' are *sui generis* and (b) their meaning is their *use*, it does not necessarily follow that an objective moral order exists. Words like 'good' or 'right' need not refer to anything objectively existing. They may simply be devices for registering certain distinctive moral attitudes which the speaker has towards certain actions or states of affairs. For reasons which I have offered elsewhere[38] and shall not rehearse here, I think that the latter of the two theories of meaning about which I have been speaking is the correct one. The meaning of moral language is the job or jobs which it does.

In considering *what* job or jobs it does it is important to differentiate between description and evaluation. This distinction can be briefly illustrated thus. Suppose a man has something to sell. Asked what he has to sell, he replies 'It is a house'. This description of it may be true or false : what he has to sell may, or may not, be a house. Asked 'How much is it?', he replies 'It is £20,000'. This price which he puts upon it cannot be either true or false : there is nothing objective to him to which his price does or does not correspond as there is something to which his description 'a house' does or does not correspond. Others may think £20,000 an unfair price and they may well have reasons for doing so, e.g. the house is badly affected by subsidence, the lease is about to run out, it has no garage, etc., etc. These reasons will certainly be true or false. But the reasons for putting a price on a house are logically quite distinct from the price itself. Whether we think the price of a house unfair or not depends, not simply upon whether it is affected by subsidence etc. or not, but upon that together with our evaluation of the effects of subsidence etc. We have, so to say, to put a price on our reasons as well as on the house. The point is never reached where evaluation – the price put upon the house – can (logically) be reduced to mere description, i.e. to things said about the house which are capable of being true or false. He may indeed be a very odd fellow who thinks that the effects of subsidence, or the imminent expiry of the lease, make a house *more* valuable. But it is always conceivable that this odd fellow should turn up.

As for moral value-terms, they may function either descriptively or evaluatively. Suppose Black has seduced a girl and she is going to have a baby. White asks me 'Will he do the right thing by her?' In the society to which he and I belong it is generally accepted that the right thing for a man to do in those circumstances is to marry the girl if he is free to do so. So White does not need to add '. . . I mean will he marry her?' I know that that is what he means. His 'do the right thing by her' functions as a description of Black's action in just the way that 'marry her' would. So when I reply to White's question with 'He will' or 'He won't' what I say is capable of being true or false : it is verified if Black marries her, falsified if he does not. But now suppose that White says to me 'Is it the right thing for Black to marry her?' My reply to that is not a prediction but a value judgment. It will be neither true nor false : for I shall not be describing Black's action but, in a moral sense so to speak, putting a price on it. I shall be ascribing to it positive or negative moral value.

Of these two uses of moral language, the descriptive and the evaluative, the latter is primary. As Professor R. M. Hare has shown[39] two considerations lead to this conclusion. (i) The descriptive meaning may vary from context to context : in any given set of circumstances 'the right thing' would describe a very different course of action in some societies from what it would describe in our own. But, used evaluatively, 'right' has the *same* range of meaning in all contexts : it commends, expresses approval, guides choices, advises, persuades, grades, etc.[40] (ii) We use 'right' evaluatively to challenge, or change, its descriptive meaning, as White's question gave me an opportunity of doing, had I wished, in the above illustration. Had I said 'No. It's not the right thing for Black to marry her' – and gone on to offer some convincing reasons for this – then I might have changed White's mind about the matter and – who knows? – my re-valuation might have functioned as part of a movement within our society whereby the descriptive meaning of 'the right thing' ceased to be 'marrying her'.

It is appropriate to add a brief word here about the difference between what Wittgenstein called 'the surface grammar' and the 'depth grammar' of an utterance. The sentences 'It is a house' and 'It is £20,000' have the same grammatical form in the sense that their syntax is the same. But as we have seen there is a logical difference between them : one is a description and the other an evaluation. Their 'depth grammar' differs. Similarly 'It is red' and 'It is right' are syntactically similar but the latter is – if the view which I have taken above is correct – primarily not a description but a moral evaluation. Wittgenstein, we noted in Chapter I, spoke of philosophy as 'battle against the bewitchment of our intelligence by means of language'[41] and some philosophers would say that those who regard moral terms as primarily descriptive – e.g. the classical intuitionists or even contemporary descriptivists –

have been bewitched by the grammatical similarity between moral judgments such as 'It is right' and naturalistic descriptions such as 'It is red' into supposing that moral words like 'right' and 'good' fundamentally refer to objective moral properties which inhere in actions or states of affairs. However, I have discussed moral intuitionism and descriptivism elsewhere and shall not do so at any length here.[42]

One word about contemporary moral descriptivism is perhaps in order. If moral philosophers such as Mr G. J. Warnock and Mrs P. Foot are right,[43] then fundamentally to say that something is morally right or good is to say something like that it meets human wants, needs or interests — with of course a good deal of sophisticated qualification. Whether or not a given action does satisfy such wants etc. is a factual question, and if the view which we are now considering is true, then 'right', 'good' and other moral terms signify these objective properties (meeting human wants, etc.) which the actions or states of affairs so described possess. But of course there is all the difference in the world between saying this and saying that they refer to objective *moral* values. If modern descriptivists are right, then all that this amounts to is that, with regard to certain natural properties (e.g. being the satisfaction of such-and-such wants) the so-called 'naturalistic fallacy' (see Moore above) is not a fallacy after all. Moral terms are not *sui generis*: they can be replaced by these non-moral terms. But from this it certainly does not follow that there are objective moral values in the sense required by the form of the moral argument for God which we are here considering.

I conclude, then, that the claim that there are objective moral values fails. But suppose for a moment that it does not. Suppose that classical intuitionists were right and that moral terms refer to objective, non-natural, moral properties of actions or states of affairs. This in itself would not constitute a moral argument for God's existence. It would not necessarily follow that God exists unless God is identified with moral value. Maclagan, we noted above (p. 78), does so identify him. But this is a stipulative definition of 'God'. Certainly 'God' as generally understood means one who is good, amongst other things. But 'God is good', as commonly understood, most certainly does not reduce to the analytic triviality 'Good is good'.

Quite apart from the issues which I have just been discussing, there are two other lines of argument used by Owen and Maclagan respectively, in support of the view that there is an objective order of moral values, which both seem to me to be misconceived. I will conclude what I have to say about objectivity by offering a few comments on each of these arguments.

(i) Owen says that 'subjectivism' – by which he means the emotivist or prescriptivist account of moral language – 'contradicts experience'. He attempts to show that this is so as follows:

> Let us suppose that I have a friend whom I admire. He is honest and kind in all his dealings with me. He is (as I should put it) always 'good to' me. Can I suppose that 'good' in this context merely refers to my 'pro-attitude'? On the contrary, the more I know of him the more I feel his goodness as an objective fact that confronts me and compels my admiration. Admittedly this appeal to experience does not constitute an argument; but such an appeal is ultimately inevitable.[44]

On the inevitability of this appeal to experience, it is true of course that in so far as knowledge rests upon empirical observation the observer has to trust his senses. He has – after taking all possible safeguards – to believe that he really is seeing, hearing, etc. what it seems to him that he is. But it is a far cry from accepting this to accepting – as Owen evidently wishes us to accept – that because a friend seems to him to be very good that friend's goodness is 'an objective fact'. The grounds of that goodness (i.e. the honesty, kindness to which Owen refers) will be objective facts. But there is a logical distinction between grounds of goodness and goodness itself and it is the latter of which Owen is speaking. It is this latter which he thinks cannot be 'merely. . . (a) pro-attitude'. He is saying, not that his friend must be honest or kind as a matter of 'objective fact', but good. Why? Owen's assurance that this is so seems to be the only reason given for why it is so. Whether this is (a) assurance that his friend is good or (b) assurance that the goodness is objective is not altogether clear to me. But either way, it makes no saving difference. If it is assurance (a) – that his friend is good – then we must point out that the fact that a pro-attitude is firm, fixed, undoubted, does not make it more than a pro-attitude. And if Owen's assurance is (b) – that his friend's goodness is objective – then we must reply that the fact that anything is firmly believed to be the case does not make it the case. Goodness cannot (logically) be an objective property of Owen's friend *simply* because Owen believes that it is.

(ii) Maclagan argues that unless there are objective moral values it is logically impossible to 'rectify' as against merely 'alter', to 'correct' as distinct from simply 'change', anyone's moral judgments. He writes :

> I do not see how without this assumption of an objective 'order of values' we can suppose that the fundamental valuations of different persons (conflict between which is at least conceivable) could be said to be capable of rectification, as distinct from mere alteration, true though it is that correction properly so-called might still be possible *within* a valuational system, in the form of a replacement of incoherence by consistency. And, neither do I see, without a belief in corrigibility as contrasted with mere changeability, how any of us could, as we do, take seriously the task, which is sometimes an anxious and exacting one, of attaining (as we very naturally express it) a *right* judgment of where our duty lies.[45]

Maclagan evidently thinks that something more than correction 'within a valuational system' is necessary in order to make sense of the expression 'attaining a *right* judgment'. But why?

Talk of 'rectifying' or 'correcting' moral judgments brings out the fact that discussion and argument are appropriate in moral discourse; and it is of course very important to recognise this. Where a moral judgment has been expressed the speaker is expected to have a reason for what he says, to have an answer to the question 'Why?', as he is not expected to where a mere expression of taste or liking has been voiced.

> 'Strawberries are delicious.'
> 'Why?'
> 'What do you mean "Why?"?'

The last remark here is not at all odd. But compare that dialogue with this :

> 'Drug taking is morally wrong.'
> 'Why?'
> 'What do you mean "Why?"?'

The last remark here is very odd. Anyone who rejects the demand
for reasons to support his moral judgments will not be taken
seriously; he is not, if you like, playing the game. If someone says
that something or other is 'a moral issue', he means amongst other
things that it is a matter about which people hold strong opinions
and concerning which it is appropriate that there should be discussion and argument with reasons given and then either challenged or accepted. By contrast, if it is said that something is 'a
matter of taste' this normally means that it is a matter about
which people have strong predilections *but* about which there is
no point in arguing. Emotivists and prescriptivists have never said
that moral issues are matters of taste in that sense. A great deal
in the writings of C. L. Stevenson,[46] the exponent of emotivism,
and of R. M. Hare, the protagonist of prescriptivism, is about the
role played by reasons in moral judgment. Quite apart from
whether or not these points of view are right – as against, say,
classical intuitionism or modern descriptivism – a perfectly plausible account of 'rectification, as distinct from mere alteration' *can*
be given *within* them.

A 'right judgment', both points of view allow, is one supported
by good reason. 'Good reason' here must mean at least two things :
(i) Reasons for moral judgements, being reasons, must be adhered
to consistently. If anyone holds, for instance, that drug taking is
morally wrong because it is against the Law, but that tax evasion
is not wrong, his judgment can be challenged. The 'moral
language-game' is such that (a) he is expected to have some reason
for the judgment that drug-taking is wrong and (b) he is expected
to regard anything else which also instances that reason *ceteris
paribus* to be wrong as well. (ii) Reasons given for moral judgments are in the last analysis always themselves grounded in moral
judgments. It is a fact, to use this example again, that drug-taking
is against the Law. But it is not simply the truth of the non-moral
statement 'Drug-taking is against the Law' which makes this a
good reason for judging drug-taking to be morally wrong. The
further premise is required, 'Whatever is against the Law is morally wrong'. The reason given for a moral judgment is always, when
correctly analysed, a combination of : (a) a general moral principle
and (b) a statement of fact. From these two premises the moral
judgment itself follows as the logical conclusion.

In argument someone who has delivered a moral judgment

may be challenged in either of two ways corresponding to (a) or (b). Does he consistently hold to the moral principle implicit in the reason which he gives for his judgment? (e.g. Does he think whatever is against the Law to be wrong?) And : Is the reason which he has given true to fact? (e.g. Is what he says is against the Law really against it?) As the argument proceeds a speaker can be asked why he subscribes to (a), i.e. the general moral principle implicit in the reason which he has given for his moral judgment (e.g. why does he think that whatever is against the Law is wrong?) His answer to this will itself be a reason which consists of (a) a statement of fact and (b) an implicit general moral principle. For instance it might be : 'Because only if the Law is kept, will the greatest happiness of the greatest number be realized'.

Now, the point which emerges from all this is as follows. Rectification or correction in moral discourse necessarily always occurs 'within a valuational system' (to recall Maclagan's words). When we rectify or correct another person's judgment we *either*: (i) Get him to see that what he takes to be an instance of his general moral principle is really not so. (If, for instance, it were the case that drug-taking is *not* against the Law, we could correct a man who said 'Drug-taking is wrong because it is against the Law' by showing him that it is not against the Law and therefore to his way of thinking not wrong.) *or* (ii) Get him to reject the general moral principle implicit in his reason by showing him that it is one to which he does not consistently subscribe and so does not really hold as a reason but only as a prejudice. (If, for instance, we could show the supposed speaker above that law-breaking does not reduce the general happiness, we could get him (in so far as he was rational) to abandon his general moral principle, 'Whatever is against the Law is wrong', and so his particular judgment, 'Drug-taking is wrong', in so far as it was grounded in that principle.) Both these moves to a right judgment, notice, occur 'within a valuational system'. The former occurs within a system constituted by the general moral principle 'Whatever is against the Law is wrong'. The latter occurs within one constituted by the general moral principle 'Whatever does not reduce the general happiness is not wrong'. It is impossible to conceive of any other way in which the move to a right judgment could occur. The moved and the mover, the speaker who comes to a right judgment and the speaker who brings him to it, must, in the last analysis, stand *on common moral ground.* All this can mean is that they stand *within one valuational system.* If two speakers can find no common moral ground, then no moral reasoning – and so no rectification or correction, no coming to a right judgment – can occur between them. Maclagan speaks as if 'correction . . . *within* a valuational system' were some sort of second best kind of rectification. I am saying that correction is *only* possible within such a system and that Stevenson and Hare have in common at least this much, that they give a plausible account of such rectification.

In pursuit of his argument for objective moral values, Maclagan seems to think that there is necessarily *more* to 'rectification', 'correction', and 'a right judgment' than writers such as Stevenson and Hare suppose. The right judgment must not only be *thought* to be right, but must *be* right. This is a distinction which can certainly be drawn but it does not follow as Maclagan seems to think that there must be ultimate and objective moral ground – the real values which exist independently of what any man judges to be good or evil, right or wrong – which we can and must discover if we are to speak of 'a right judgment'. The concept of rectification – of thinking something right but coming to see that it is not right – can be accounted for in terms of rejected and accepted pro-attitudes. In the light of pro-attitudes to which I now adhere I may reject pro-attitudes to which I once adhered, and I may perfectly intelligibly speak of this rejection as the rejection of what I once (mistakenly) thought right. The logical possibility of the distinction between the statements 'X is right' and 'X is thought right' does not render an account of moral judgment in terms of pro-attitudes unintelligible.

In none of the forms which we have considered is the moral argument successful.

Conclusion

In this chapter we have carefully considered four kinds of appeal to empirical evidence in the attempt to arrive at an affirmative answer to the question 'Does God really exist?' but have found reason to reject them all. From considering attempts to answer that question we shall now turn our attention to the question itself.

4 The Problem of Objectivity: (iii) The Rejection of the Question

The question with which we have been preoccupied throughout the last two chapters is: does God really, i.e. objectively, exist? In chapter 2 we were concerned with attempts to demonstrate God's existence as a matter of logical necessity, to show that it has the kind of objectivity which truths of logic have. In chapter 3 we considered various appeals to empirical evidence by which attempts have been made to show that God exists in the same way as matters of physical or historical fact do. Along both these lines of argument – that of conceptual analysis and that of appeal to empirical evidence – we have been seeking grounds for affirming the proposition, 'It is the case *that* God exists'. But we have failed to find any such grounds.

What follows from the fact that we have failed to find such grounds? To some it seems to follow that religious belief must be rejected; that the question, 'Does God really exist?' must be answered in the negative. But there is an alternative view. What if it is *this question* itself, 'Does God really exist?', which has to be rejected? What if the belief that God exists in the way that logical truths or physical and historical facts exist is a travesty of religious belief? What if, to quote a recent writer (see Malcolm below), 'a "belief that God exists" . . . would be of no interest, not even to God'.[1] In other words, we must consider the possibility that religion is something logically different from the belief *that* God exists in any of the ways in which the thinkers who we have considered in the last two chapters have tried to prove that he exists. I turn then to the contention that the correct way to solve the problem of objectivity is to reject the question 'Is it the case *that* God exists?'

I will discuss in this chapter three ways of dealing with that question. The two former are ways in which other writers have rejected it and of these I shall be critical. The third way is that in which I wish to deal with it.

Belief In and Belief That

Note carefully that the question rejected is 'Is it really (or objectively) the case *that* God exists?' Some philosophers have rejected this question on the ground that it misconceives the nature of religious belief by supposing the latter to be belief *that* God exists rather than belief *in* God. Belief-*in,* they insist, must not be confused with belief-*that.*

A recent analysis of 'belief in' or 'believe in' by Mr J. J. MacIntosh in *Mind*[2] shows that these expressions have two main uses. (i) On the one hand they are performatives[3] with strong commendatory overtones. They normally express or report approval of the object believed in; and they commit the speaker to certain actions with regard to that object, e.g. to support where support may be needed. If in this sense a headmaster, for example, said that he 'believed in' one of his pupils, Jones, we should normally take him to mean that he thought well of Jones and would do what he could to ensure Jones' success. (ii) On the other hand, 'belief in' or 'believe in' may, to quote MacIntosh, 'make and take away an existence claim'.[4] In this sense 'I believe in X' means that the speaker believes that X exists but it implies that the speaker recognizes that there is room for some doubt as to whether X really does exist or not. So, one might say, 'I believe in the abominable snowman' but one would not say 'I believe in snow'.

Belief-in God admits of both interpretations. (i) It may express trust in God, and (ii) it may indicate that the existence of God is a matter doubted by some, though not by the speaker. The former interpretation is the one which is of interest to us at the moment.

In his Gifford Lectures entitled *Belief* (London, 1969), H. H. Price carefully differentiates belief *in* God from belief *that* God exists. The former, he points out, involves trust and of trust he writes :

Trusting is not a merely cognitive attitude . . . There is something more than assenting or being disposed to assent to a proposition, no matter what concept the proposition contains . . . trusting is an affective attitude.[5]

This is undoubtedly true. It is equally beyond doubt that religious belief amounts to *more* than the belief that God exists. When a believer says for example, 'God is our Father' what he purports to do is not merely to state a putative fact but to express an affective attitude. To use J. L. Austin's terminology the illocutionary force of his remark is commissive. That is, in saying 'God is our Father' the believer characteristically commits himself to God.[6] This will be apparent if we consider how odd it would be for a believer to say 'God is our Father but I don't trust him'. If any believer said that we should assume that either he was not sincere or he did not know the meaning of the English words which he was using.

Religious belief is clearly *more* than the belief *that* God exists, but is it entirely *independent* of such belief? Does 'belief-in' *imply* 'belief-that'? Price, with reference to human beings says that it certainly does. He writes: 'I cannot trust my doctor unless I at least believe that there is a person to whom the description "being my doctor" applies'.[7] He concedes that when we trust people, we are likely to know them by acquaintance and not merely by description, but he does not consider this to impugn the contention that one cannot (logically) believe in anyone, i.e. trust them, and at the same time not believe that they exist.

In the case of God, however, some philosophers give the impression that belief-in can subsist without any implied commitment to belief-that. Or, if that is putting it too strongly, they seem to think that religious belief is so essentially a matter of trusting in God that any doubts as to whether it is really the case that God exists are irrelevant to it. I takes as a case in point Norman Malcolm's way of rejecting the question, 'Is it the case that God exists?' He writes:

> Now one is inclined to say that if a person believes in God surely he believes that God exists. It is far from clear what this is supposed to mean. Of course, if 'believing that God exists' is understood to mean the same as 'believing in God' (and this is not an entirely unnatural use of language) then there is no problem. But the inclination we are discussing is to hold that you could believe *that* God exists without believing *in* God. As I understand it, we are supposed to think that one could believe that

God exists but at the same time have no affective attitude towards God. The belief that he exists would come first and the affective attitude might, or might not come later. The belief that he exists would not logically imply any affective attitude toward him, but an affective attitude toward him would logically imply the belief that he exists.

If we are assuming a Jewish or Christian conception of God I do not see how one can make the above separation. If one conceived of God as the almighty creator of the world and judge of mankind how could one believe that he exists, but not be touched *at all* by awe or dismay or fear? I am discussing logic, not psychology. Would a belief that he exists, if it were completely non-affective, really be a belief that he exists? Would it be anything at all? What is the 'form of life' into which it would enter? What difference would it make whether anyone did or did not have this belief? So many philosophers who discuss these matters assume that the first and great question is to decide whether God exists: there will be time enough later to determine how one should regard him. I think, on the contrary, that a 'belief that God exists', if it was logically independent of any and all ways of regarding him, would be of no interest, not even to God.[8]

Notice that Malcolm's point is, as he says, not psychological : he is not merely pointing out that believers always happen to have an affective attitude towards God as well as a belief that he exists. It is the logic of religious belief about which Malcolm wishes to say something. But what?

Malcolm's main point is clear enough : it does not make sense to speak *simpliciter* of 'belief that God exists'. It is of such belief that he asks : 'Would it be anything at all?' But I am not certain what precisely Malcolm is saying with regard to such belief. Two possibilities suggest themselves.

(i) Is he arguing that belief-that *simpliciter* where God is concerned does not make sense *and therefore* it makes no sense to say that belief-in implies belief-that? In line with this interpretation is his remark that it is 'far from clear' what it means to say 'that if a person believes in God surely he believes that God exists?' (ii) Or is he, on the other hand, simply contending that belief in God is a necessary condition of belief that God exists *and therefore* it would make no sense to affirm belief-that and deny belief-in? In line with this interpretation is his puzzlement as to how 'we are supposed to think that one could believe that God exists but at the same time have no affective attitude toward God'. Malcolm appears to be rejecting the question 'Is it the case that God exists?' on one or other of these grounds though I cannot be sure which. Whichever of the two it is, however, it will not support such rejection.

(i) If Malcolm is arguing that belief-that is unintelligible where God is concerned, he certainly does not prove his point. It may well be true that the belief that God exists has no religious value, which is presumably what he means by saying that it is 'of no interest, not even to God'. But this belief is not without intellectual interest. Malcolm asks : 'What is the "form of life" into which it would enter? What difference would it make whether anyone did or did not have this belief?' Well, it has entered into the 'form of life' constituted by Christian apologetics and advocacy as we have seen throughout the last two chapters and the difference, say, between someone who thinks that the ontological proof is valid and someone who thinks that it is not is a real enough difference which must be described as the difference between thinking it proved *that God exists* and thinking it unproved. Moreover, even if a penetrating analysis of religious language shows as I claimed above, that speech acts expressing religious belief, e.g. 'God is our Father', normally have an illocutionary force which is commissive, this fact about religious language is only to be explained, as I explained it, by showing that religious beliefs do *more* than simply state putative facts about God's existence or attributes. And this explanation implies the intelligibility of statements to the effect that God exists, or has certain attributes, because, if such statements were not intelligible, no one could understand what was meant by saying that affirming religious belief is doing *more* than make them. There appear, then, to be no good grounds at all for saying that belief-that, where God is concerned, is unintelligible. So if Malcolm's argument in the above passage is to the effect that it makes no sense to say that belief-in implies belief-that where God is concerned because the latter is unintelligible, it is unsound.

(ii) If, on the other hand, Malcolm is contending that belief in

God is a necessary condition of belief that God exists *and there-fore* it would make no sense to affirm belief-that and deny belief-in, where God is concerned, then two questions arise : (a) Is that argument sound?; (b) If so, does it give Malcolm good ground for rejecting the question, 'Is it the case that God exists?' The argu-ment that belief in God is a *necessary* condition of belief that God exists, when the latter constitutes anything recognizable as religious belief, seems to me to be perfectly sound. This is what I meant by saying that religious beliefs characteristically have a commissive illocutionary force. But as Professor K. Neilsen has pointed out in criticising Malcolm, this 'does nothing to show that one could believe in God and not presuppose that God exists'.[9] It is beyond doubt true to say that belief in God is a necessary condition of religious belief and that therefore it is pointless to affirm belief that God exists while denying belief in God. But when we have shown that religious belief necessarily implies an affective attitude towards, or a belief in, God we have not answered or eliminated, the question 'But is it the case that God exists?' It makes perfectly good sense, when told as by Malcolm above, that one cannot 'believe that he (God) exists' and 'not be touched *at all* by awe or dismay or fear', to reply 'Yes, I quite see that but does the object of these attitudes really exist?' Malcolm, if he thinks that he has answered or eliminated that question, is confusing a necessary condition of religious belief with a *sufficient* condition of it. He is supposing that belief-in is enough to constitute religious belief given the explicit exclusion of belief-that. This is plainly mistaken. It is true that religious belief is not simply the belief that God exists but it is equally true that it is not thus exclusively belief in God.

Our conclusion must be that it is not logically possible to reject the question 'Is it the case that God really exists?' simply by draw-ing a sharp distinction between belief-in and belief-that.

God and Love

Another way of rejecting the question 'Is it the case that God really exists?', which some philosophers take, is as follows. They attempt to reduce the concept of the existence of God to the con-cept of the existence of something else whose existence is not problematic.

Professor D. Z. Phillips, for instance, seems to think that the question of God's real existence is settled by the fact that what he calls eternal love is possible. By 'eternal love' he means love which, to quote his own definition, 'is not dependent on how things go, . . . cannot change and . . . cannot suffer defeat'.[10] Phillips writes : '. . . seeing that there is a God . . . is synonymous with seeing the possibility of eternal love'.[11]

Now, two points can be granted with regard to God and eternal love. (i) The possibility of eternal love does appear to be a *necessary condition* of God's existence. If such love were not possible then it would not make sense to say, as Christians and others do say, that God is a God of love essentially. (ii) Furthermore, it may be that where such love is manifest one has the *best clue* one could have to the existence or activity of God. If anything shows that Christ comes from God, Christians would say, it is his eternal love. But Phillips has gone far beyond these two points.

His remark quoted above : '*Seeing that there is a God* is *synonymous* with seeing the possibility of eternal love' (italics mine) could, I think, be interpreted in either of the following ways : (i) (Somewhat loosely) that the possibility of eternal love is a *sufficient* condition of God's existence; or (ii) (more strictly) that the existence of eternal love is not just a condition of, but *identical* with, the existence of God. Both these interpretations are unacceptable. Consider them in turn.

There is no reason to think that the possibility of eternal love, as Phillips defines the latter, is a sufficient condition of God's existence. Love which 'is not dependent on how things go, . . . cannot change and . . . cannot suffer defeat' could conceivably be evinced by one human being towards another even if God did not exist. There is nothing self-contradictory in advocating such love whilst denying the existence of God. Bertrand Russell who was certainly agnostic about God's existence, for instance, could write :

There are certain things that our age needs, and certain things it should avoid. It needs compassion, and the wish that mankind should be happy : it needs the desire for knowledge and the determination to eschew pleasant myths : it needs, above all, courageous hope and the impulse to creativeness . . . The root of the matter is a very simple and old-fashioned thing, a thing so simple that I am almost ashamed to mention it for fear of the derisive smile with which wise cynics will greet my words. The thing I mean – please forgive me for mentioning it – is love, Christian love, or compassion. If you feel this you have a motive for existence, a guide in action, a reason for courage, an imperative necessity for intellectual honesty.[12]

He is advocating what Phillips calls 'eternal love'. But it would be absurd to maintain that when Russell recognized, as he did in this passage, the possibility of love which is 'eternal' in Phillips' sense he was, though unaware of it, affirming by implication that there is a God.

Phillips, as I said above, can be alternatively interpreted as identifying the possibility of eternal love with the existence of God. But then we must reply that it is one thing to say that such love is our best clue to the existence or activity of God, and quite another to say, as Phillips does, that 'seeing the possibility of eternal love' is 'synonymous' with 'seeing that there is a God'. This latter can only be true strictly speaking if the existence of God and the possibility of eternal love are the same thing. But, as the words 'God' and 'love' are normally used, the expressions just used in which these words occur are certainly not identical. If you try to identify them, as Phillips does, you do not prove that God exists because the possibility of eternal love exists. All you do is to evacuate propositions such as 'God is love' of any but a trivial meaning. If anyone wishes to propose that we should all stop talking about God and start talking about love, then let him by all means propose it. But he will not be entitled to pretend that all he has proposed is a correct understanding of religious language. What he has proposed is the elimination of religious language.

In his attempt to show that seeing that there is a God is synonymous with seeing the possibility of eternal love, Phillips invokes the authority of Kierkegaard. He quotes the latter at some length to the effect that when a man ceases to love his neighbour it is not only the neighbour who is deprived of love but the man himself. Then Phillips comments :

In this way Kierkegaard illustrates the truth that for the believer love itself is the real object of the relationship between himself and another person. This love is the spirit of God, and to possess it is to walk with God. Once this is realized, one can see how love and understanding are equated in Christianity. To know God is to love Him.[13]

His point appears to be that the existence of 'love itself' in a loving relationship between two persons is in some way the existence of God. To love the love which subsists within such a relationship is to 'love', to 'understand', and to 'know', God. But I find it hard to make any sense of the remark 'love itself is the real object of the relationship' where one person loves another. If this means anything, presumably it means that the person concerned is the sort of person who not only enters into loving relationships with others but places the highest possible value upon such relationships. But it only confuses the matter to speak of this evaluation as loving the object of the relationship. A relationship is between two persons and the object of the relationship for each of them is the other person. Anyone who loved his neighbour for the sake of the love rather than for the neighbour's own sake, would, to put it mildly, be in danger of impoverishing, if not destroying, the love-relationship itself. It seems to me even more meaningless to say that loving the love, i.e. valuing the relationship, is loving God. When a believer says 'God is love' he does not mean 'Love is love'. He means that love is the most important element in the divine nature as we know it. Nothing, therefore, could be more important than the recognition of the connection between God and love but it is a connection, not an identity.

The Question Elusive to an Affirmative Answer

My own way of dealing with the question 'Is it the case that God really exists?' is to point out that the expression 'really exists' is systematically elusive to final definition. I do not claim, as Malcolm and Phillips appear to do, that this question, as it has traditionally been understood, is meaningless. On the contrary, it seems to me to make perfectly good sense. What I do claim, is that the logic of the word 'real' and its cognates is such that it does not make sense for anyone to claim that he has discovered what in a final or absolute sense really does exist.[14]

First, let me point out what seems to me to be wrong with an attempt such as that of Phillips, to reject the question as meaningless. Phillips rejects the question 'Does God really exist?' as traditionally understood, on the ground that it misconceives the existence of God by regarding the latter as a matter of fact comparable to matters of physical or historical fact. The difference between believers and unbelievers is not, he avers, 'over a matter of fact', at least as we use 'fact' in speaking of physical or historical facts. The latter are facts because they can be located in space or time. But God, by definition, cannot be so located, says Phillips. That is why :

> When the positivist claims that there is no God because God cannot be located, the believer does not object on the grounds that the investigation has not been thorough enough, but on the grounds that the investigation fails to understand the grammar of what is being investigated, namely, the reality of God.

The question of the reality of God is not a question of whether or not he exists as a matter of spatio-temporal fact. Rather, says Phillips, '. . . the question of the reality of God is a question of the possibility of sense and nonsense, truth and falsity, in religion'.[15]

But surely this will not do. Sense and nonsense, in religion can certainly subsist whether God really exists or not, and in a sense, so can truth and falsity. The fact that some propositions make sense within theism and others do not does not settle the question whether or not God really exists – it is possible to talk sense or nonsense about Santa Claus but who supposes that this proves that he really exists? Given any system of belief, there will be some propositions which can legitimately be labelled true as against others which must be called false : e.g. within Christian theism it is true that God regards all men with good will and false that he regards any with malice; but all this is so quite apart from the question whether Christian theism is true in the sense of corresponding to objective reality or not.

Phillips goes on to say :

> Discovering that there is a God is not like establishing that something is the case within a universe of discourse with which we are already familiar. On the contrary it is to discover that there *is* a universe of discourse we had been unaware of.[16]

I am ready to admit the force in the first part of this quotation, namely, 'discovering that there is a God is not like establishing that something is the case within a universe of discourse with which we are already familiar.' But I feel less happy about what follows :

'on the contrary, it is to discover that there *is* a universe of discourse we had been unaware of.' To discover the religious universe of discourse is to learn how to play the religious language-game; but this is not, in any normal sense of the words, to discover that there is a God because it would make perfectly good sense to say that religious believers, i.e. those who play that game, are deluded. What is it for a believer to be deluded? Simply for the universe of discourse which constitutes his belief to be a figment of his imagination *and nothing more*; for him to suppose himself to have discovered something when in reality there was nothing to discover. What people wish to know when they ask if God really exists is whether or not believers are thus deluded. Phillips's argument has done nothing to show that this question is meaningless.

The question 'Does God really exist?' could conceivably be answered *in the negative* with finality. If all propositions concerning God are necessarily self-contradictory because God is a self-contradictory concept, then all such propositions must be false. It is logically impossible for a self-contradictory proposition to be other than false; and what is logically impossible is not contingently possible. If God is an inherently self-contradictory concept, then 'God exists' must logically be false. In such case, the question 'Does God really exist?' *can* be answered with a final, absolute, *no*.

Some authors, for example Professor K. Nielsen, claim that this is, in fact, the case. He first concedes a point, to which I shall return, namely that 'real', with its synonyms and cognates such as 'really,' is 'context-dependent'. He writes:

The question 'What is real?' has no determinate sense. What is real and what is unreal is a very context-dependent notion. What in a specific context counts as 'real' or 'reality' as in 'a real trout', 'a real champion', 'an unreal distinction', 'the realities of the economic situation', 'a sense of reality', 'the reality of death', or 'the reality of God', can only be determined with reference to the particular matter we are talking about. We have no antecedent understanding of reality such that we could determine whether language agreed with reality. . . .[17]

But nevertheless Nielsen claims that it is in accordance with the ordinary meaning of 'real' to say that in so far as talk of anything is incoherent there is a good reason for denying that it is about something which really exists. What does he mean by talk being 'incoherent'? Or, as he has it, 'put together in a strange way'? Examples of such talk which he gives are talk of God as a *person* though he cannot be identified as a spatio-temporal individual; or of God as *acting* even though he has no body; or as being *both three and one*; or as *encountered* by us in prayer even though he is *transcendent*. Such talk according to Nielsen strains the ordinary use of language to the point of unintelligibility and violates such basic rules of logic as non-contradiction. Therefore, he argues, even though 'real' is 'context-dependent' such talk cannot be about what is real.

> 'Reality' may be systematically ambiguous, but what con-
> stitutes evidence, or tests for the truth or reliability of special
> claims, is not completely idiosyncratic to the context or activity
> we are talking about. Activities are not that insulated. As I have
> already remarked, once there was an on-going form of life in
> which fairies and witches were taken to be real entities, but
> gradually, as we reflected on the criteria we actually use for
> determining whether various entities, including persons, are or
> are not part of the spatio-temporal world of experience, we
> came to give up believing in fairies and witches. That a
> language-game was played, that a form of life existed, did not
> preclude our asking about the coherence of the concepts
> involved and about the reality of what they conceptualized.[18]

I shall argue in Chapter 6 that talk of God within theism does not have to be incoherent in the sense in which Nielsen uses this latter description. But if it were necessarily incoherent in his sense, i.e. self-contradictory, then he would probably be right to say, as he does, that God cannot really exist. I say 'probably' because there is perhaps a problem here as to what people mean when they say – as some do say – things like 'Ultimate reality can only be des- cribed in self-contradictory terms.' Is that remark nonsensical? If it is not, then Nielsen's analysis of 'real' is incomplete. I am inclined to think that the remark just quoted *is* nonsensical. The 'can' in it is a logical 'can' and it seems clear enough that the whole notion of logical possibility and impossibility collapses if there is something which can (logically) be described in self-contradictory terms. However, even if I am mistaken in this opinion, that only increases the *openness* of the concept of reality for which I shall argue in a moment.

If talk of God can be delivered from self-contradiction, as I shall maintain in Chapter 6 that it can, it does *not* follow, of course, that the answer to the question 'Does God really exist?' is *yes* (as it follows that the answer is *no*, if it cannot be so delivered). All that follows is that the answer *may* be *yes*.

The problem is : given that the answer may be yes, how are we supposed ever to be able to discover, in a final, absolute way, that it is?

It is no use treating the question 'Does God really exist?' as a question *within* religious discourse. True, there is a sense in which this question might be discussed within religious discourse. If religious discourse is taken to be constituted by the concept of god (as I argue in Chapter 1); and if theism is taken to be the view that 'God is god', then the question can be discussed : Are there good religious reasons for taking what exists as god to be God? This is a religious question and will involve a comparison of theism with other forms of religious belief. But this is not what the question 'Does God really exist?' normally means. For 'God' here we could write 'god' also. What the questioner wishes to know is something like this : Are there grounds for believing that God (or god) exists *outside* religious discourse? In what follows, I shall take the question in this sense. Note that, as I take it, it is a question about the existence of the constitutive concept of religious belief, i.e. god or transcendent consciousness and agency, as much as about the God whom theists, as such, take to be what exists as transcendendent consciousness and agency.

Where, then, do we go with this question 'Does God (or god) really exist?' Anything which exists, exists *as* something. The things physical scientists talk about, for example, exist as physical objects, the things moralists talk about as moral obligations, and so on. Scientists try to discover what really exists *as* physical object and what does not; moralists, what really exists *as* moral obligation and what does not; and so on. It is no use taking the question 'Does God (or god) really exist?' to either of them because god is by definition neither physical object nor moral obligation. What applies here to the cases of physical science or morality will apply *mutatis mutandis* to any other non-religious universe of discourse. So it would seem that we are in the following dilemma with the

question 'Does God (or god) really exist?' as traditionally understood. It cannot be answered *within* the religious universe of discourse because there the existence of god – and so of God for purposes of this argument – is presupposed. But neither can it be
answered in any non-religious universe of discourse because god
(or God) is by definition not the kind of thing which can be shown
to exist or not exist within any such.

It is conceivable that there should be a universe of discourse in
which questions about the real existence of the several constitutive
concepts of universes of discourse such as physical science,
morality, religious belief, etc. could be answered affirmatively.
These universes of discourse are not completely isolated from one
another. We have already seen that the writ of the law of non-
contradiction, so to speak, runs in all of them. Moreover, certain
concepts are common to more than one of them, e.g. those of
action or consciousness to religion, morality and psychology. It
may seem conceivable, therefore, that there should be an 'over-all
universe of discourse', or a 'common conceptual scheme'[19], within
which questions such as 'Do physical objects really exist', 'Does
god really exist?' could find an affirmative answer. If there were
such a universe or scheme, it would be a metaphysical or ontological one, constituted by a certain ultimate, irreducible concept
(or concepts). This ultimate irreducible concept (or concepts)
would then determine the criteria of what is real in a final and
absolute sense. For any X, the question 'Does X really exist?'
would mean 'Does X exist as an instance of this ultimate irreducible concept (or concepts)?'

But whatever we suppose such ultimate irreducible concept or
concepts to be – call this C – the question 'Does what is C really
exist?' still makes sense. Suppose we take our common conceptual
scheme to be constituted in the last analysis by the concepts of a
person and a physical object, so that these serve as our criteria of
what is real. It makes sense, does it not, to say 'But do persons
really exist?' 'Do physical objects really exist?' As I suggested
above, even if the ultimate irreducible constituents of our overall
universe of discourse are logical rules such as the law of non-
contradiction, we come up against the objection that it might still
make sense to ask 'Is what really exists self-contradictory?' The
point which I am endeavouring to bring out is that there is the
same kind of *openness* to the concept, *real*, as G. E. Moore claimed

that there is to the concept, *good*. It may help to make what I am saying about 'real' clearer, if we briefly recall what Moore and others have said about 'good' (cf. Chapter 3 above).

In *Principia Ethica* Moore said that 'good' is indefinable. If anyone says of any X, 'X is good' he can properly be asked what it is about X which makes it good. But his answer can (logically) never consist in an appeal to a definition of 'good'. Suppose his answer were 'X will produce the greatest happiness of the greatest number.' According to Moore, the statement 'What produces the greatest happiness of the greatest number is good' is not an insignificant tautology nor is the question 'Is what produces the greatest happiness of the greatest number good?' a self-answering question – as they would be if 'good' *meant* 'produces the greatest happiness of the greatest number.' *Whatever* other reason were given for saying that X is good the same would hold *mutatis mutandis,* said Moore. This is what he meant by saying that the word 'good', as ordinarily used, is indefinable. Some later moral philosophers have claimed that a speaker can, on this view, choose his own criteria of goodness. These criteria may be very unusual, even bizarrely different from those to which most users of the word 'good' subscribe; but in using 'good' in accordance with his own criteria, however odd the latter, a speaker would not be talking nonsense. There is an openness to the word 'good' such that its normal use always allows for the provision of new defining characteristics. (I am not concerned here to defend Moore's account of the meaning of 'good' against all criticism. Some modern philosophers would challenge the contention that 'good' is indefinable; and Moore himself would not have agreed that it follows from the indefinability of 'good' that a speaker can choose his own criteria of goodness. Whatever may be the case with 'good', all I am maintaining is that 'real' is indefinable in somewhat the same way as Moore and others – whether rightly or wrongly – have said that 'good' is.)

Anyone who says that something is real can legitimately be called upon to say what he takes the criteria for the use of 'real' and its cognates to be. But when he has given them, the question can (logically) always be asked, 'Is what is in accordance with these criteria real?' No such question is manifestly self-answering according to the ordinary use of the word 'real'. It follows, I would claim, that anyone who uses the word 'real' can (logically) decide in

accordance with what criteria he is using it. He is not tied down
to one set of defining characteristics, in accordance with which he
must describe anything as real. If he questions the reality of, say,
physical objects or persons (or whatever criteria of 'real' one proposed), he will probably be regarded as engaging in a highly
sophisticated kind of discourse. Positivist philosophers may say
that he is talking nonsense. But ordinary users of the English word
'real' need not say that.

Reality, in a final or absolute sense, is not something which we
can discover. In the last analysis what we take to be 'real' is a
matter of choice. We have to make our own ultimate ontological
decision; we have to make up our own minds what criteria we will
use for the application of the word 'real'.

It may be, of course, that there are certain criteria for its use
which *rational* men definitively adopt. That is to say, it may be
part of the meaning of 'rational' – in some contexts anyhow – that
men so described adopt certain criteria for the use of the word
'real'. If by these criteria God is unreal, or does not really exist,
then those who speak of him as real or really existing cannot be
rational in the sense supposed. Their talk of God will, from the
rational point of view, be nonsense. But it will be nonsense, not
fundamentally because of what 'real' means but because of what
'rational' means. I think, incidentally, that if we take 'rational'
in its usual sense, then some of the things which religious believers
have said about God are rational and some are not, but I certainly
do not think that all talk of God is irrational. My reasons for this
view will, I hope, become clearer in Chapter 6 when I turn specifically to the question of rationality.

For the present, however, I hope that I have said enough to
justify this twofold position : (i) that the question 'Does God really
exist?' is meaningful; and (ii) that no one can claim to have discovered finally or absolutely what really does exist. To bring out
these two points seems to me the correct way to deal with the
problem of objectivity. All kinds of questions remain for the
religious believer; I have instanced one, 'Is he, as such, rational?'
But there is one question which need not worry him, namely, 'How
can I prove that God really does exist?' That question is systematically elusive to the kind of answer traditionally demanded. In
this regard, be it noted, religious belief as such is in no worse case
than any other universe of discourse. 'Do physical objects really

exist?' 'Does moral obligation really exist?' – such questions are just as elusive to a final affirmative answer as 'Does God really exist?' But this does not lead scientists to give up talking of physical objects or moralists, of obligation. Nor should the systematic elusiveness of an affirmative answer to 'Does God really exist?' prevent anyone from sharing in religious belief.

5 The Challenge of Secularization

Wittgenstein remarked that language-games sometimes 'become obsolete and get forgotten'.[1] They may do so for different reasons. I will take two such reasons. (i) It may be apparent that a certain language-game is internally incoherent : that the moves made within it contradict one another or are in some other way irrational. If so, then reasonable men as such will find the language-game concerned an abortive and unprofitable exercise and they will turn their attention to something else. To the extent of their rationality the offending language-game will become obsolete and get forgotten. (ii) On the other hand, a language-game may be such that, given its presuppositions and procedures, it is not self-contradictory or otherwise incoherent, but its presuppositions and procedures may have become so far removed from those generally accepted or approved in a given society that it has fallen into desuetude within that society. An example would be animism in our own society. Provided that one adhered consistently to the presupposition that certain things have, each within it a spirit which makes it move, then I suppose one could (logically) explain all the movements of such things in terms of the movements of the spirits within them. Animism is obsolete and has got forgotten not because it contradicts itself but because its presuppositions and procedures are now far removed from those according to which we normally think and speak.

The question to which I turn is this : is religious belief *as a whole* in danger of becoming obsolete and getting forgotten for either of the reasons which have just been outlined? (i) Is it irrational? I shall discuss that question in my next chapter. (ii) Is it out of date? I shall discuss that question in this chapter.

What I call the challenge of secularization. is the contention that the fate which has undoubtedly befallen animism has in reality befallen the religious language-game as a whole : that its presuppositions and procedures are now so far removed from those to which modern man as such is committed that the language-game which they constitute is, for our contemporaries, meaningless.

In this chapter I shall attempt three things : (i) to show the precise nature of the challenge of secularization; (ii) to assess the response to it of some representative modern religious thinkers; and (iii) to offer a response of my own to what I call the various levels of the challenge.

(i) THE NATURE OF THE CHALLENGE

It is necessary first to distinguish clearly between *practical* and *intellectual* secularization. By *practical* secularization I mean the decay of religious *practices,* whether public or private. By *intellectual* secularization I mean the absence of religious *belief.* Practical and intellectual secularization – decline of practice and of belief–are *not* necessarily connected either empirically or logically. As to empirical fact, it is arguable for instance that American society has become increasingly secular in its beliefs and values whilst at the same time a large and growing percentage of the population has been going to church. As to logical implication it is possible to differentiate the concepts of practice and belief as we are using them here quite clearly from one another. It would not be in the least self-contradictory to say of some individual that he engaged regularly in the practice of private or public prayers even though he had no religious beliefs. Someone might say that he could not really be praying if he did not believe but that is a matter of what is involved in the concept of prayer; it is not to say that the concepts of practice and belief merge into each other.

I must now try to explain a little more clearly what I mean by intellectual secularization. In bringing to light this notion of intellectual secularization so that we may see the challenge which it constitutes for religious belief, I think that we have to uncover three levels of it.

The Decline of Belief
The first level is a very obvious one. Intellectual secularization means, at its simplest, that a great many people in the modern

world do not believe in God. In 1968 the Independent Television Authority commissioned a survey of popular attitudes to religion as a guide for those responsible for its religious programmes.[2] The survey was conducted by the trained field staff of Opinion Research Centre and took place in the first week of February, 1968. One feature of the survey was the construction of a 'religiosity scale' (called such non-pejoratively) designed to serve as a 'measure of how important religion (was) to each individual in his or her daily life'. The scale was constituted by nine questions or variables. These were put to a random sample of 1,071 adults. The table below shows what percentage of the sample gave 'religious' replies in the case of each variable. The distribution of 'religiosity' in Great Britain was then calculated by taking into account each individual's answers to all nine questions and showing what percentage of the sample gave totals of nine, eight, seven, . . . nought 'religious' answers respectively.

The percentage giving 'religious' answers to each variable in turn was as follows :

		%
1.	They are 'very religious' or 'fairly religious'.	58
2.	They are 'certain' that to lead a good life it is necessary to have some religious belief.	42
3.	They are 'certain' that without belief in God life is meaningless.	41
4.	They are 'certain' that religion helps to maintain the standards and morals of society.	55
5.	They are 'certain' that there is a God.	56
6.	They believe that 'God does watch each person'.	59
7.	They are 'very likely' to think of God when they are worried.	43
8.	They are 'very likely' or 'fairly likely' to think of God when they are happy.	51
9.	Their daily lives are affected 'a great deal' or 'quite a lot' by their religious beliefs.	46

'Religiosity' gradings were accorded as follows :

None of 1 'religious' replies:	– –
2, 3, or 4, 'religious' replies:	–
5, 6, or 7, 'religious' replies:	+
8 or 9 'religious' replies:	+ +

The distribution of these various grades of 'religiosity' throughout the sample was as follows :

	Total	Men	Women
+ +, +	49%	39.%	58%
- -, -	51%	61%	42%

+ +, + rose through the decades of age from 36 per cent at 16–24 years of age to 61 per cent at 65 + ; and – –, – fell from 63 per cent at 16–24 to 39 per cent at 65 +.

These figures simply bring out the degree to which, at a rather unsophisticated level, modern men participate in the religious language-game. There would appear to be a good deal more religious belief than practice in our society. The percentage for 'religious' answers and + + and + 'religiosity' gradings are far in excess of the percentage of people in this country who attend church regularly.

Nevertheless, even judged by the elementary standards of the 'religiosity' scale, there are rather more people in our society to whom religion is unimportant in daily life than to whom it is important. Moreover, this secular majority would appear to be rapidly increasing, if we take into account facts such as this : the Gallup Poll, conducted for ABC Television in 1964, found only 6 per cent of the population in Britain denying membership of any church, whereas the 1968 survey conducted by Opinion Research Centre found 22 per cent doing so.

All of this may be regrettable from the point of view of religious belief but, in itself, it does not immediately discredit that point of view. Fewer people believe in God. But when did the intellectual respectability of religion depend upon how many people believe it? We shall see in the next sub-section that this is not quite as simple a rhetorical question as it may appear. There may be a sense in which not only the intellectual respectability but the very intelligibility of an opinion depends upon how many people subscribe to it; and we shall turn in a moment to the view that this is so where religion is concerned. But at present I am making the simple, though perhaps superficial, point that religious belief could conceivably be a perfectly respectable intellectual stance even though few people as a matter of fact adopted it.

The Prevalence of a Secular World-View
Philosophical considerations arise when we proceed to what I
choose to think of as the *second* level in the analysis of the notion
of secularization. To speak of 'secularization' may not simply be
to refer to the empirical fact that many people do not nowadays
believe in God. It may be to refer to norms of intelligibility, standards of sense and nonsense, which prevail in our society and which
are logically alien to religious belief. Secularization, many would
claim, is a feature of our society in the sense that the world-view to
which we all now subscribe leaves no place for traditional religious
belief. The religious language-game, they would say, has become
obsolete and is getting forgotten, not simply in the sense that a
decreasing number of people are 'playing 'it, but in the deeper
sense that anyone who does 'play' it is thereby participating in a
'form of life' of which it becomes increasingly difficult for modern
men to make sense.

What is to be said in reply? It can be granted at once that
religious belief is not a logically self-contained universe of discourse. There are standards of intelligibility which apply to religious and non-religious discourse alike and so we cannot, as it
were, entirely compartmentalize religious language and hold that
what it does or does not make sense to say in religious terms has
nothing whatever to do with what it may or may not make sense
to say in other terms. Language-games do not subsist in complete
logical isolation from one another. Recall what was said in Chapter
I about someone being trained to believe in God as Father. I
pointed out that he would have to learn how the use of the expression 'father' when applied to God is (a) like and (b) unlike its
use when applied to a human father. If 'father' as applied to God
had no semantic connection whatever with 'father' as otherwise
applied, then there would be no point in using that word rather
than any other for whatever it was that we wished to say about
God. The intelligibility of the fatherhood of God, that is to say, is
related to – indeed is parasitic upon – the intelligibility of fatherhood in a more general sense. Again, consider the universal
application of the law of non-contradiction. In any universe of
discourse contradictions are self-stultifying. To say that X is Y and
not Y is, for all practical purposes, equivalent to saying nothing
about X at all. If I simultaneously affirm and deny any statement

or any judgment, then unless I am using some figure of speech, it is as if I had said nothing. If I say, 'God is our father and not our father', I have told you nothing about God – unless of course I am using this form of words to mean 'God is in some respects like a human father (e.g. he cares for his children) but not in others (e.g. he is not any man's male progenitor)', which is not a contradiction. But even if it were the intention to say that, it would still be important to remember that the concept of fatherhood must not be so qualified when applied to God that its meaning is eroded to the point at which to speak of God as our father becomes in effect to utter the contradiction that he is, and is not, our father.

There are then such logical relationships between religious and non-religious discourse. They show that there are standards of intelligibility which overlap universes of discourse. The intelligibility of what is said within a language-game is not – normally at any rate – defined entirely *within* that language-game. It is therefore conceivable that the use of terms in religion should become so different from their use elsewhere as to be unintelligible to modern man. Nothing which I have said so far shows that this has in fact happened. All I am saying is that the contention that it has cannot be dismissed with the knock-down argument that the intelligibility of religious belief is determined within the religious language-game and nowhere else. Some writers I think have recently come very close to saying, if they have not actually said, that the challenge of secularization can be countered in that way. But the considerations which I have been presenting show that it cannot: religious belief is not a logically self-contained universe of discourse.

Let us then look more closely at this second level of the challenge of secularization to see precisely what its nature is and how it purports to impugn religious belief. Suppose the ceiling of a room in which you were sitting suddenly fell down. When you got over the shock and began to think about what had happened and what ought to be done about it, what kind of question would most naturally occur to you? I think it would be some such question as this : 'What went wrong with the laths or the plaster up there to account for this sudden collapse?' You might discover on investigation that the laths had rotted or the plaster deteriorated; or you might find that the effects of unusual vibration from passing traffic or some accumulation of water from a burst pipe had brought the ceiling down. That is the sort of thing which would answer your question. What you then did about your ceiling's collapse would be done in the light of that explanation. You would call in plasterers, joiners or plumbers to do what was necessary in order to put the ceiling back up again and make it secure. I call this kind of explanation and consequent action non-religious.

Now, the point which has to be taken here is this : what I have just described would be your natural reaction to a collapsed ceiling *whether you professed religious beliefs or not.* Even if you were a religious believer, it would not be a religious explanation or course of action which would most naturally occur to you in such circumstances. You would not ask yourself, for example, 'Why has God made my ceiling collapse?' Nor would you respond to the calamity by asking God to put it back for you. It may be, of course, that on reflection you would see some religious significance in your ceiling's collapse. But notice that, if you did so, it would almost certainly be a significance conditioned to some extent by the non-religious kind of explanation – e.g. you might feel that you had failed in your duty to your family or friends by not recognizing that your ceiling had become dangerous through deterioration of the laths or plaster and could therefore collapse upon them unexpectedly. If you saw the ceiling's collapse as a judgment of God upon you, that is to say, you would most likely see it as a judgment upon your failure to have appreciated the non-religious explanation of what had happened and to have taken the non-religious way of preventing it.

My example here has been a very simple one but I hope that it has served to make the point. In our time believers and unbelievers alike seek most naturally and immediately non-religious explanations of the events which occur in the course of their lives and they normally and characteristically come to terms with the world around them in the light of such explanations. Notice in this connection what I said a moment ago about the extent to which non-religious explanations condition religious explanations. This was one example of how religious belief has had to accommodate secularization in various ways. To take another example, if asked why it is inappropriate to pray that God will put one's ceiling back when it has collapsed, a contemporary believer might well say something to the effect that God has given us brains and hands so that we can do that sort of thing for ourselves – or better still for each other. I am not deriding such accommodation to non-religious explanations and the courses of action to which they give rise. It may well be that it is a process whereby religious belief is deepened and enriched. But that it is a process which goes on with what appears to be increasing momentum is further evidence of the second level of secularization.

It is important to recognize precisely how the second level of secularization amounts to more than the first level. The latter was simply the fact that some people believe in God but a large and increasing number do not. The second level of secularization is the fact that *both* those who do and those who do not believe in God normally think in non-religious terms over very wide areas of concern. It is doubtless an over-simplification to speak as if history could be divided into ages of faith and ages of unbelief; no age is monolithically either of these. But one feature of our own age as against former ages is the extent of the prevalence of this second level of secularization as I have chosen to call it.

In some ages and societies the concept of god has been closely integrated with other concepts which were essential to man's intellectual life at the time. An example of what is in my mind here is provided by Professor A. C. MacIntyre in his contribution to a discussion entitled 'Can One be a Believer Today?'. He wrote :

> . . . Christianity does not and never has depended on the truth of an Aristotelian physics in which the physical system requires a Prime Mover, and consequently many sceptics as well as many believers have treated the destruction of the Aristotelian argument in its Thomist form as something very little germane to the question of whether or not Christianity is true. But in fact the replacement of a physics which requires a Prime Mover by a physics which does not secularizes a whole area of enquiry. It weakens the hold of the concept of God on our intellectual life by showing that in this area we can dispense with descriptions which have any connection with the concept.[3]

Christian belief in God, that is to say, can logically exist apart from belief in a Prime Mover but it is more easily intelligible where the latter belief also exists. In such ways the prevailing world view always is either more or less *congenial* to prevailing religious belief. By saying that it is either more or less congenial I mean that the prevalent concept of god is either more or less relatable to those

concepts which provide the framework of the rest of man's intellectual life at the given time.

The challenge which defenders of religious belief have to face
in our own day is constituted by the fact that many, if not all, of the
concepts which provide the framework of man's intellectual life
appear to be in important respects uncongenial to religious belief.
I speak of this uncongeniality as a 'fact' and of religious belief as
though it were a homogeneous entity. Exception may be taken on
both counts. Whether or not the concepts which form the framework of our intellectual life today are so uncongenial to religious
belief is a question which must not be begged. Some would question
whether or not there is anything which can properly be called 'our
intellectual life today' if that expression presupposes that there is
in our day one logically unified world view. Some would want to
argue that, even if there is, religion is not – or not necessarily –
alien to it. They would at the least be entitled to point out that
religious belief is not 'a homogeneous entity', as I presuppose. We
shall see in the next section that 'secularized' forms of religious
belief seem to satisfy some believers in our day. Despite all such
qualifications, however, it must, I think, be recognized that there
are some grounds for speaking of an intelligibility gap between
religious belief and the rest of modern man's prevailing world
view.

MacIntyre goes so far as to say that, in order to make Christianity intelligible in our age we have 'to supply a social context
which is now lacking and abstract a social context which is now
present'.[4] That is to say we have, in effect, to modify the prevailing world view in order to see any point in what religious believers
say and do. Believers and unbelievers have in common a world
view which is logically ultimate so far as intelligibility is concerned.
It is only by reference to this world view that religious belief is
rendered intelligible to either party. Believers and unbelievers alike
have to see what needs to be added to, or taken from, the prevailing
world view in order to *understand* religion. Let me give two
examples of what I take to be the point here.

Suppose a theist brings God in to explain something which has
happened. 'What *caused* this?' he asks and his answer is 'God'.
Now, from his point of view as an orthodox theist, 'What caused
God?' is no doubt an illegitimate question. He *qua* theist excludes
the possibility of that question : in doing so he has to 'abstract a

social context'; that is, ordinary scientific or common sense enquiry, according to which that question would be legitimate. Given any other context of inquiry or discussion than religion, causal explanation would not have to be arrested in that arbitrary way.

Again; suppose in order to get something done a theist resorts to prayer. Well, there is nothing odd in asking other agents to do things for you. But *qua* theist he includes the possibility of a divine agent, i.e. an agent who has no body : he has to 'supply a social context', namely that of religious discourse, in which an agent can be spoken of who is not spatio-temporally identifiable. Such talk is, to say the least, unusual in any other context.

MacIntyre concludes :

If I am right, understanding Christianity is incompatible with believing in it, not because Christianity is vulnerable to sceptical objections, but because its peculiar invulnerability belongs to it as a form of belief which has lost the social context which once made it comprehensible.[5]

His conclusion is the somewhat startling one that *to understand Christianity is, in effect, to reject it*. To recapitulate, he arrives at it thus. In understanding anything one has to start from certain criteria of intelligibility and relate it to these. If the point of view in question is logically odd, then the only way of making sense of it is to work out what has to be abstracted from, or supplied to, it in order to bring it within the said criteria of intelligibility. The said criteria are normative. In our own day they are non-religious so, MacIntyre argues, the believer, in order to understand religion, has to accept non-religious criteria of intelligibility, to work out what needs to be added to, or taken from, his belief in order to make it intelligible by these criteria; and then, and only then, will he be able to make head or tail of it. To accept non-religious criteria of intelligibility is, in effect, to be an unbeliever; so, in order to understand his beliefs, the believer must reject them. He cannot be a conscious believer without understanding his beliefs and he cannot understand them without being an unbeliever.

In due course, I shall comment on MacIntyre's argument here and offer what I think are fair and valid reasons for rejecting it. But I have no desire to deny that there is a second level of secularization. It is not enough to say that in our time unbelief is on the increase. We must recognize that believers, as well as unbelievers, increasingly subscribe to a world view which owes little or nothing to the concept of god. This is the point which Bonhoeffer made when he said that God has become a 'God of the gaps'. God, that is to say, is dragged in to fill the interstices of our knowledge, to explain what natural science cannot explain; but these gaps grow all the time smaller and may for all practical purposes disappear in the end. Here again I shall have more to say about this in a moment. Suffice it for the present to recognize that the prevalent world view of believers and unbelievers alike is deeply secular.

The Philosophical Grounding of Secularization

The third level of secularization, as I call it, is the level at which the secular world view, to which I have just been referring, finds its philosophical grounding. It is not enough, I think, to conceive of secularization as consisting in the empirical fact that modern men subscribe to a world view which owes little or nothing to god. One must see why this is so. I am thinking not of empirical causation but of philosophical reasoning. What is the rationale of the secular world view? What logical justification is there for subscribing to it? I think these questions received an answer in the philosophical position called Logical Positivism. At its deepest level secularization, as I understand it, is grounded in a theory about *meaning*, about what it makes sense to say and what it does not. This brings us to the heart of philosophy and in particular I think to those philosophical developments in recent times which have brought mystery and metaphysics into deep discredit.

The leading British exponent of Logical Positivism was A. J. Ayer. His *Language, Truth and Logic* burst upon the scene in 1936 with enormous effect. Its first chapter is entitled 'The Rejection of Metaphysics'. This rejection was based entirely upon an argument to the effect that metaphysical propositions – amongst which Ayer included all talk of God – are meaningless. This argument went as follows :

What conditions must be fulfilled for a putative statement of fact to have literal meaning? It must be 'capable of being shown to be true or false'. A statement of fact which cannot be tested for truth or falsity is meaningless.

What conceivable ways are there of showing anything to be

true or false? There are two, namely logical analysis and empirical observation.

Before I explain what is meant by these terms, let me note a qualification which Ayer introduced. Some statements of fact, e.g. those in formal logic or mathematics, can be shown *for certain* to be either true or false. Their truth or falsity is, as we say, demonstrable. But other statements of fact, e.g. those made in natural science or history, are not demonstrably true or false. It is always conceivable that new evidence will be brought to light which disproves the scientific theories or historical records which at present are considered true. There is only a degree of *probability* that statements of scientific or historical fact are true, corresponding to the weight of evidence in their favour. In the light of such considerations, Ayer carefully phrased the question which he claimed determines whether or not statements of fact, other than those of logic or mathematics, are meaningful. It is not: Would any observations make its truth or falsehood logically certain, but simply: Would any observations be relevant to the determination of its truth or falsehood? And it is only if a negative answer is given to this second question that we conclude that the statement under consideration is nonsensical.[6]

I return from these remarks to the answer that there are two ways of testing for truth or falsity, namely logical analysis and empirical observation. Some statements of fact can be shown to be true or false simply by reference to the definitions of the terms used in them. If $X=2$ and $Y=4$, then $X+Y=6$. This is true simply because the expressions 'X' and 'Y' have the values given to them and other expressions in the statement, such as '$=$', '2', etc., mean what they do mean. Ayer calls this sort of proposition analytic. Analytic statements are, if true, tautologies; and if false, contradictions. '$2+2=4$' is a tautology; '$2+2=5$' is a contradiction. This is so because: $2=1+1$: $4=1+1+1+1$: $5=1+1+1+1+1$. And so '$2+2=4$' amounts to '$1+1+1+1$ is $1+1+1+1$', which is tautologous. '$2+2=5$' amounts to '$1+1+1+1$ is $1+1+1+1+1$' which is self-contradictory.

All other meaningful statements except analytic ones must be verifiable or falsifiable by empirical observation, i.e. within human experience. They are in effect hypotheses concerning such experience. If I say 'It is raining', I am predicting that any normal person will, if he goes outside, feel the rain. If I say 'It was raining yesterday', I am predicting what anyone would experience who set out to test this statement; if, for example, he did so by questioning people who were here yesterday, he would hear the reply, 'Yes, it was'. Statements in science, history and common sense are meaningful by this criterion.[7]

Ayer's position then is that: 'A statement is . . . literally meaningful if and only if it is either analytic or empirically verifiable'.[8]

Where does this leave metaphysical statements? They appear to be neither analytic nor empirically testable. Take for example, the controversy between monists, who say that reality is one substance, and pluralists, who say that reality is many substances. These statements of belief are not intended to be analytic. When the monist, for instance, says 'Reality is one substance', he does not purport to utter a tautology. If the word 'reality' meant 'one substance', then 'Reality is one substance' could be shown to be true by definition. But the monist is a monist, not because he holds certain beliefs about the word 'reality', but about reality. If we turn from definition or analysis to empirical observation, then, as Ayer says of monists, 'it is impossible to imagine any empirical situation which would be relevant to the solution of (the) dispute'.[9]

So this is Ayer's conclusion about metaphysics:

> We may accordingly define a metaphysical sentence as a sentence which purports to express a genuine proposition, but does, in fact, express neither a tautology nor an empirical hypothesis. And as tautologies and empirical hypotheses form the entire class of significant propositions, we are justified in concluding that all metaphysical assertions are nonsensical.[10]

Statements of religious belief seem to be in the same condemnation as metaphysical statements. They are not analytic. When a religious believer says 'God loves us', he does not purport to say that the word 'God' means 'one who loves us' so that 'God loves us' means 'One who loves us loves us'. He does not purport to utter a tautology. It is not the word 'God' about which he is speaking but the reality God, in whom he expresses belief. But neither do statements of religious belief appear to be empirically testable. Two features which characterize them lead to the conclusion that they are not. (i) Those who make them characteristically refuse to accept any empirical evidence as falsifying them. Some years ago Professor A. Flew issued a challenge to religious believers.

'What would have to occur or to have occurred to constitute for you a disproof of the love of, or of the existence of, God?'[11] The believer's answer does appear to be 'Nothing'. As a man of faith he characteristically holds his beliefs in spite of contrary evidence. 'Though he slay me yet will I trust in him'. But if nothing falsifies religious belief, then it cannot be tested for truth or falsity by empirical observation. (ii) Religious believers as such refuse to identify God as a spatio-temporal phenomenon. The God in whom they believe is by definition outside space and time. But if anything is empirically observable, then – a logical positivist at any rate would hold – it must be identifiable as a spatio-temporal phenomenon. It follows that God is not empirically observable and statements about him, not empirically testable. Statements of religious belief, therefore, are neither analytic nor empirically testable; and if the logical positivist's criterion of meaningfulness is correct, they are meaningless.

Logical Positivism is now somewhat out of date and in section iii, I will show why. But it was, I think, a most important element in the grounding of intellectual secularization.

We see then how deep the grounding of intellectual secularization is. It is a mistake to think that secularization simply means that many people have ceased to believe in God. We penetrate more deeply into the notion – and the fact – when we realize that methods of explanation and principles of action which owe nothing to the concept of god have become so widespread that they now inform and direct the entire intellectual life of modern man. But we arrive at the bedrock of secularization only when we see that it is fundamentally a notion of what does or does not make sense. The challenge of secularization is, in the end, not simply that religious beliefs are unpopular or out of date, but that they are meaningless.

(ii) THE RESPONSE TO THE CHALLENGE

One large and influential school of thought within Christianity has responded to the challenge of secularization by giving it an enthusiastic welcome. So far from seeing it as fatal to belief, this school of thought believes that it has brought, or will bring, modern men release from bondage to 'religion' and access into the freedom of 'faith'.

Bonhoeffer
Dietrich Bonhoeffer provides the classic example of the point of view to which I have just referred. In his now famous *Letters and Papers from Prison* (London, 1970) he heralded the dawn of 'religionless Christianity' and proclaimed the day of 'holy worldliness'. Religion, in the pejorative sense in which Bonhoeffer uses the word, compromises at least two elements. It speaks, to use his own words, 'metaphysically' and 'individualistically'. What it says under both heads is irrelevant to modern man.

When Bonhoeffer said that religion speaks *'metaphysically'* he meant that it offers God as the solution of those intellectual problems which remain when science, art, ethics, etc., have said all that they have to say. In so doing, however, it answers questions which man 'come of age' is no longer asking. Here Bonhoeffer seems to be feeling after the view that when religion speaks 'metaphysically' it is irrelevant for at least two reasons : (i) because the growth of scientific knowledge has been so great that there is less and less which the latter cannot explain; (ii) because 'metaphysical' questions are now seen to be pseudo-problems.

Bonhoeffer's *Letters and Papers from Prison* are written in a bewitchingly impressive style, rendered all the more impressive when one remembers that they were the work of a man who existed under the shadow of execution. But with regard to their critique of the 'metaphysical' in religion, the letters are often unclear in meaning. Consider these three passages for example :

> Weizsäcker's book *The World-View of Physics* is still keeping me very busy. It has again brought home to me quite clearly how wrong it is to use God as a stop-gap for the incompleteness of our knowledge. If in fact the frontiers of knowledge are being pushed further and further back (and that is bound to be the case), then God is being pushed back with them, and is therefore continually in retreat. We are to find God in what we know, not in what we don't know; God wants us to realize his presence, not in unsolved problems but in those that are solved.[12]

> The movement that began about the thirteenth century (I'm not going to get involved in any argument about the exact date) towards the autonomy of man (in which I should include the

discovery of the laws by which the world lives and deals with itself in science, social and political matters, art, ethics, and religion) has in our time reached an undoubted completion. Man has learnt to deal with himself in all questions of importance without recourse to the 'working hypothesis' called 'God'. In questions of science, art, and ethics this has become an understood thing at which one now hardly dares to tilt. But for the last hundred years or so it has also become increasingly true of religious questions; it is becoming evident that everything gets along without 'God' – and, in fact, just as well as before. As in the scientific field, so in human affairs generally, 'God' is being pushed more and more out of life, losing more and more ground.[13]

God as a working hypothesis in morals, politics, or science, has been surmounted and abolished; and the same thing has happened in philosophy and religion (Feuerbach!). For the sake of intellectual honesty, that working hypothesis should be dropped, or as far as possible eliminated. A scientist or physician who sets out to edify is a hybrid.[14]

What precise point, or points, is Bonhoeffer making in such passages? That is hard to answer.

It seems evident enough that he is recognizing a growth of knowledge which owes nothing to the concept of God but in what sense is he saying that 'metaphysical' questions in religion are pseudo-problems? Is he simply saying that modern man has lost all interest in talk of God? Or does he think that God can plausibly be reduced to a psychological projection of certain human needs or characteristics, as his reference to Feuerbach, who held such a view, would suggest? Bonhoeffer's main point is perhaps contained in what he says about our no longer needing God as a 'working hypothesis'. But if so, what precisely is this point? Is Bonhoeffer simply saying that science, art, ethics, to recall Laplace, 'have no need of that hypothesis' (i.e. God) in the sense that they are constituted logically by concepts other than that of God? If his point is that there is always a logical gap between talk of physical objects (science) or beauty (art) or goodness (ethics) and talk of God then it is a sound one, but I am not sure that this is his point.

Another remark which is doubtless important for an understanding of Bonhoeffer is that we 'should find God in what we know, not in what we don't . . . not in unsolved problems, but in those that are solved'. If this means that science, ethics, art, or whatever, will lead us to God, then it is at variance with what Bonhoeffer has just been saying. But it could mean either of two other things : (i) that every discovery which shows the wonder of the world enhances the believer's wonder at its Creator; or (ii) that everything which we know can (logically) be talked about within the theological universe of discourse, that for instances, there is a theology of art, science, morals, etc. Bonhoeffer's tone of voice, however, suggests that he was making some more unusual point than either of these. But if so, what point?

What now did Bonhoeffer mean when he said that religion speaks *'individualistically'*? Here I think his precise meaning is much easier to discern. Religion, he thought, offers man a personal salvation which consists in deliverance from the anxieties of guilt and death. It concentrates attention upon the weakness which these anxieties represent and the self-centredness of a desire for salvation which will deliver men from them. Bonhoeffer believed that man has 'come of age' in the sense that he no longer feels these anxieties and is no longer interested in this salvation – not, that is, unless or until religion plays the confidence trick of persuading him that he needs the salvation which only God can give. In the following passage, for example, Bonhoeffer indicates what religion does when it speaks individualistically, and then defines his attitude to it in three criticisms :

Efforts are made to prove to a world thus come of age that it cannot live without the tutelage of 'God'. Even though there has been surrender on all secular problems, there still remain the so-called 'ultimate questions' – death, guilt – to which only 'God' can give an answer, and because of which we need God and the church and the pastor. So we live, in some degree, on these so-called ultimate questions of humanity. But what if one day they no longer exist as such, if they too can be answered 'without God'? . . .

The attack by Christian apologetic on the adulthood of the world I consider to be in the first place pointless, in the second place ignoble, and in the third place unchristian. Pointless, because it seems to me like an attempt to put a grown-up man back into adolescence, i.e. to make him dependent on things on which he is, in fact, no longer dependent, and thrusting him into problems that are, in fact, no longer problems to him. Ignoble, because it amounts to an attempt to exploit man's weakness for purposes that are alien to him and to which he has not freely assented. Unchristian, because it confuses Christ with one particular stage in man's religiousness . . .[15]

It is of course, to say the least, an open question whether Bonhoeffer has the empirical facts right here. Do ordinary men feel no anxiety about sin and death? In certain states of life, true enough, men do not worry about such things; and perhaps many more people enjoy these carefree states of life nowadays than used to do so in the past. It may be true that secular man is, on the whole, healthy and happy, contented with what he can do and what he possesses. But is it true that, apart from the interference of religion, men continue in this condition all their days? Is it true that anxiety concerning guilt, death, or suffering, touches only 'a small number of intellectuals, of degenerates, of people who regard themselves as the most important thing in the world and therefore like to busy themselves with themselves' as Bonhoeffer thought?[16]

People who are morbidly preoccupied with themselves, their own sins, or their own mortality, are indeed a crashing bore. It is inappropriate that those who claim to have heard the good news of God should be so preoccupied; rather should they rejoice that God has freely given them all things. But is Bonhoeffer's attack on degenerate intellectuals justified? He exalts the ordinary man – the ordinary man who spends his everyday life at work, and with his family, and of course with all kinds of hobbies and other interests too, is not affected by any existential anxieties. He has neither time nor inclination for thinking about his intellectual despair and regarding his modest share of happiness as a trial, a trouble, or a disaster.[17] But such ordinary men do not produce the great art or literature of the world, nor did they extend the frontiers of scientific knowledge. In a sense intellectuals *are* 'themselves the most important thing in the world' if this means that their preoccupation with themselves is a preoccupation with the interior world of human ideas, hopes, discontents and dreams. It is a kind of philistinism to think otherwise.

Recognizing that many people will think that without its 'metaphysical' and 'individualistic' elements Christianity would be moribund, Bonhoeffer in passages such as the following argues that this is not so. Nothing of importance is lost.

> Anxious souls will ask what room there is left for God now; and as they know of no answer to the question, they condemn the whole development that has brought them to such straits . . . a return to that can be a counsel of despair, and it would be at the cost of intellectual honesty. It's a dream that reminds one of the song *O wüsst' ich doch den Weg zurück, den weiten Weg ins Kinderland.* There is no such way – at any rate not if it means deliberately abandoning our mental integrity; the only way is that of Matt. 18.3, i.e. through repentance, through *ultimate* honesty.
>
> And we cannot be honest unless we recognize that we have to live in the world *etsi deus non daretur.* And this is just what we do recognize – before God! God himself compels us to recognize it. So our coming of age leads us to a true recognition of our situation before God. God would have us know that we must live as men who manage our lives without him. The God who is with us is the God who forsakes us (Mark 15.34). The God who lets us live in the world without the working hypothesis of God is the God before whom we stand continually. Before God and with God we live without God.[18]

Notice how here God is, as it were, both retained and rejected; and compare it with what Bonhoeffer says immediately prior to his definition of 'religion' as 'individualistic' and 'metaphysical'. There he refers to Rudolph Bultmann's attempt to demythologize the New Testament. Bultmann, it will be remembered, tried to accommodate Christianity to a modern world view by translating the New Testament concept of salvation into the existentialist concept of 'authentic existence', that is into terms of human experience rather than divine action. In a word, to demythologize Christianity. The New Testament narratives, Bultmann believed, embody mythologically a certain conception of human existence; to have *faith* is to attain this understanding of one's own existence. Bonhoeffer offered this remark on Bultmann:

> A few more words about 'religionlessness'. I expect you remember Bultmann's essay on the 'demythologizing' of the New Testament? My view of it today would be, not that he

went 'too far', as most people thought, but that he didn't go far enough. It's not only the 'mythological' concepts, such as miracle, ascension and so on (which are not in principle separable from the concepts of God, faith, etc.), but 'religious' concepts generally, which are problematic. You can't, as Bultmann supposes, separate God and miracle, but you must be able to interpret and proclaim *both* in a 'non-religious' sense. Bultmann's approach is fundamentally still a liberal one (i.e. abridging the gospel), whereas I'm trying to think theologically.[19]

What did Bonhoeffer mean when he said that he sought to think 'theologically'? Presumably, that he wished to meet the challenge of intellectual secularization, not by substituting Existentialist philosophy for Christian theology *à la* Bultmann, but by somehow or other talking in terms of God; yet the theology that he wanted to do was theology without the God who is the solution of metaphysical problems and the saviour of individuals from guilt and death. His central doctrine was this: God is teaching us that we must live as men who can get along very well without Him.[20] But what precisely does this mean? Two questions are of interest to us here : (i) Can Bonhoeffer's theological position be held? (ii) If it can, is it compatible with intellectual secularization? I will consider them in turn.

(i) Is it logically possible to think theologically without thinking in terms of god? Can (logically) a theologian both retain and reject the concept of God as Bonhoeffer wished to do? It is perfectly possible for a theologian to give up theism for some other theological position, say, pantheism, but that is simply to give the concept of god a different content. Again, it is possible within theism to reject some conceptions of God for the sake of others, to prefer, say, that in the New Testament to that in the Old. Bonhoeffer, however, does not appear to have been making any such moves. He does not seem to have been advocating a substitution of pantheism, or whatever, for theism. Nor does he seem to have been simply substituting within theism one conception of God for another. It is true of course that he wanted to get rid of 'metaphysical' or 'individualistic' conceptions of God, i.e. of the 'God of the gaps' and the *deus ex machina* but in so far as God is teaching us that we must live as men who can get along very well without Him it is the *same* God who is teaching us and whom we are to get along without. I know, of course, that this remark may be intentionally paradoxical. But some paradoxes are intolerable. They make their point with a degree of oddness which amounts to meaninglessness in any context but a poetical one. Perhaps Bonhoeffer's remark is intended to be poetical; that is, simply to induce a mood or inspire an attitude. But if it is intended to be theologically significant, where does its significance lie?

It is true that fathers can teach their children to get along without them, a process which is complete when the children come of age and are entirely independent. After this analogy it is no doubt conceivable that God should teach men to manage without him, either as a stop-gap for the incompleteness of their knowledge or as a *deus ex machina.* There is nothing self-contradictory in the thought of men managing without God in that sense and in God himself showing them how to do so. Men, that is to say, could (logically) manage without God as a practical aid in life (*deus ex machina*) or as a theoretical entity (a working hypothesis) in certain kinds of enquiry (science, ethics, etc.). But it is quite a different matter to suggest that Christian theologians, as such, could (logically) manage without God as the constitutive concept of their universe of discourse. They certainly could not. This would be like science managing without the concept of a physical object or moralists without that of moral obligation.

My answer then, to the first of the two questions posed above, namely 'Can Bonhoeffer's theological position be held?' is that it can *provided* he did *not* mean that it is possible to think theologically without thinking in terms of god. Not even God himself could do that. Nonsense would not cease to be nonsense simply because it was talked by God.

(ii) So we come to the second of the two questions posed above, 'If Bonhoeffer's theological position can be held, is it compatible with intellectual secularization?' The answer to this question is that in the only way it can (logically) be held, Bonhoeffer's position is *not* compatible with intellectual secularization. Intellectual secularization to the degree that it is thorough-going excludes the possibility of god-talk, however sophisticated the latter may have become.

Have any other theologians been more successful than Bonhoeffer in working out a clear and consistent position which is logically compatible with intellectual secularization? I think in some recent theological writing one can see the attempt to do this being made in two main ways which sometimes overlap. One of these ways attempts to 'cash' Christianity in terms of human experience. The other endeavours to eliminate the logical distinction between theism and atheism. I will take R. B. Braithwaite and P. van Buren as representative of the former attempt, and Paul Tillich and Harvey Cox of the latter.

Braithwaite
Professor R. B. Braithwaite in his ingenious and widely discussed Eddington Memorial lecture, *An Empiricist's View of the Nature of Religious Belief* (1955), presented a sophisticated account of how Christianity can be 'cashed' in terms of human experience. 'The kernel for an empiricist of the problem of the nature of religious belief is to explain, in empirical terms, how a religious statement is used by a man who asserts it in order to express his religious conviction'.[21] In his attempt to solve this problem, Braithwaite argued that the primary use of the religious assertion is as a moral assertion. It expresses a pro-attitude towards, and an intention to follow, a Christian − i.e., as Braithwaite has it, an 'agapeistic' − way of life. Each individual religious assertion must be regarded as the representative of a large body of assertions which, Braithwaite claims, taken together implicitly specify a way of life. It may well be objected that this is to treat religious assertions as though they were indistinguishable from moral assertions. Religious assertions do not *prima facie* look like moral assertions and Braithwaite is aware of this. Some are straightforward historical statements, e.g. 'Jesus was crucified'. Others are partly or wholly meta-historical, e.g. (partly) 'Jesus was conceived by the Holy Ghost' or (wholly) 'God created the heavens and the earth'. Now, these meta-historical assertions are, said Braithwaite, *'stories'* of which two things must be noted : (a) they consist of a proposition (or propositions) 'capable of empirical test'; and (b) they 'are thought by the religious man in connection with his resolution to follow the way of life advocated by his religion'.[22]

With regard to (a) it is important to see just what Braithwaite was saying. The assertion 'God created the heavens and the earth' is not as it stands, empirically testable. But the 'story' of a great being making a big thing would be empirically testable − in the sense that we should know what it was like for such a story to be shown to be true or false by empirical observation. On Braithwaite's analysis, the doctrine of creation can be thought of as a 'story' about a great being (God) making a big thing (the heavens and the earth) and in so far as it can be so thought of, it is from his point of view meaningful.

With regard to (b), it is important to notice what the connection is between the 'stories' and the agapeistic way of life according to Braithwaite. They support the latter psychologically, not logically. The stories encourage and inspire the religious man in his efforts to live agapeistically. They do not logically justify his doing so.[23]

What is to be said of this account of religious belief?

Braithwaite's position seems to be successful from his own point of view at first sight. Starting out as both an empiricist and a believer he propounds an account of religious belief which (a) saves the meaningfulness of religious propositions which it is essential for him as a believer to do and (b) saves it in terms of an account of meaning which is in accordance with his philosophical empiricism. Again : as an attempt to accommodate theistic beliefs such as those which Christians hold to intellectual secularization, Braithwaite's account of religious belief is successful at any rate to the extent that (unlike Bonhoeffer's) it *is* compatible with intellectual secularization.

The crucial question seems to me to be whether or not a religious believer as such could (logically) subscribe to the account of religious belief which Braithwaite offers.

But to do Braithwaite full justice let us consider first a somewhat different question : is what he understands by religious belief what is generally understood by it or has he placed his own stipulative definition upon it? I am thinking of course, in particular, of Christian belief.

Many Christians find his account of belief unacceptable. For example, F. R. Barry wrote in *The Times,* 28 November 1970, as follows about interpretations of religion such as Braithwaite's (though he does not mention the latter) :

The question that men are asking today is far more radical than any by which our grandparents were assailed. They are asking whether 'God' is substantive reality, or whether the word is no more than a verbal symbol for a religious attitude to life – in the end, for something happening in our own minds. This is obviously a question of life or death for Christians whose religious assertions claim, at the very least, to be saying that something is the case. That God should be ontologically there is indispensable to Christianity.

In defence of Braithwaite, it can be said that his account of religious belief would not necessarily inhibit a religious believer from thinking, saying or doing, most things which *qua* religious believer he must (logically) think, say or do. A believer could (logically) theologize, i.e. *think* and *say* in terms of the story whatever believers as such do think and say. He could work out what is, and what is not, entailed by whatever is said in the story. For instance, he could ask what account of the evils which occur in the world is compatible with the story of God creating it. Again; a believer could play his own part in the story by liturgical or practical activities. He could, that is, do whatever believers as such are required to do in order to qualify as believers. He could, for instance, see himself as created to serve God and his fellow men, and therefore attempt to act in ways which were consistent with this view.

On Braithwaite's behalf, it may also be said that there is a difference between first-order religious discourse and second-order philosophical accounts of it, which must not be ignored. A comparison with morality is apposite here. On the first-order level of moral discourse people argue or act in the light of their opinions about what is right or wrong. They do this just as seriously regardless of whether, on the second-order level of moral philosophy, they are intuitionists, emotivists, prescriptivists, neo-naturalists, or whatever. They can (logically and psychologically) hold, and indeed change, their philosophical position about moral discourse without this making the slightest difference to their first-order moral thinking or activity. It has sometimes been said that if a man becomes an emotivist, then he will not take moral issues as seriously as he would if he were an intuitionist; but emotivists like Ayer give the lie to this by the strong lines which they have taken on moral issues such as apartheid, etc. Now, it is tempting to argue that exactly the same kind of thing is true where religion is concerned. If it is possible to theologize or to accept a role of practical service within the Christian story, then surely first-order participation in religious belief is unaffected by the fact that, on the second-order level of empiricist philosophy, ordinary religious beliefs are thought of as stories !

But I am afraid that attractive as it appears this position cannot be sustained, or at least not without some further comment. The rub in Braithwaite's account of religious belief comes when we recognize that, in Christianity at any rate, the believer as such must (logically) think of his belief as *more than a story* in the sense in which Braithwaite appears to use 'story'. So used, whatever is called a story is thereby contrasted with whatever is in accordance with real and objective fact. For instance, *The Scarlet Pimpernel* is a story, but an accurate account of the French Revolution is more than a story. Whatever is in accordance with real and objective fact is whatever really exists or has existed. In Chapter 4 I argued that whilst the question 'What really exists?' makes sense, it is not for anyone to claim that he knows in a final and absolute way the answer to it. There is an openness to this question. Every man has to make his own ultimate ontological choice. But the point which must now be taken is that this question is *not* open so far as the believer is concerned. He has *made* a choice. It must (logically) be in accordance with the ultimate ontological choice of the believer as such that God really exists. In calling him a believer, we imply that. That is one thing which the word 'believer' means. When Braithwaite speaks of religious beliefs as 'stories', is he in effect saying that it need not be in accordance with a believer's ultimate ontological choice that God exists? The suspicion that he must be doing so is the rub.

It would of course be possible for Braithwaite to point out that, since the God in whom Christians believe is by definition not a spatio-temporally identifiable individual, he cannot (logically) exist in the way that physical objects exist; and since propositions about God are, by definition, not simply analytically true, God cannot (logically) exist as the truths of mathematics or logic do. And if all that were meant by calling religious beliefs 'stories' were that they are neither analytic nor empirically testable, then there is no reason at all why a religious believer should not subscribe to that view. But if that view is coupled with positivism – i.e. with the belief that *whatever really exists* is either analytic or empirically testable – then it follows that religious beliefs are 'stories' in the sense that they are *not* about what really exists. This seems to be Braithwaite's position in the end. I claim that it is a view which a religious believer as such cannot (logically) accept. It is contrary to the meaning of 'religious believer'. A defining characteristic of that expression is that anyone to whom it applies believes that God really exists.

Van Buren

Paul van Buren's attempt to discover what he calls the secular meaning of the Gospel is very reminiscent of Braithwaite's empiricist view of religious belief. Van Buren acknowledges his indebtedness to Braithwaite but criticizes the latter on two grounds: (i) Braithwaite has not done justice to the historical aspect of the Gospel and has completely neglected the peculiar 'story' of Easter; and in consequence (ii) Braithwaite's presentation of the relationship between entertaining the Christian stories and the intention to behave agapeistically is not adequate to the language of the Gospel of Easter.[24] I will comment on these in turn.

(i) It is important to van Buren to bring out that *something happened* at Easter. We cannot press the historical investigation beyond what happened to the disciples but we do know that something happened to them and this is an essential part of the meaning of the Gospel.

> On the other side of Easter we can say that the disciples were changed men. They apparently found themselves caught up in something like the freedom of Jesus himself, having become men who were free to face even death without fear. Whatever it was that lay in between, and which might account for this change, is not open to our historical investigation. The evidence is insufficient. All we can say is that something happened.[25]

Van Buren goes a little further at some points and is more precise about what must – or at least must *not* – have happened:

> If historians could establish, to suppose an extreme case, that Jesus had made an agreement with the authorities to spend his remaining days in the wilderness in silence and let some other person be crucified in his place, thereby revealing that he was as insecure and self-interested as his enemies, Christian faith as the New Testament presents it would cease to be tenable.[26]

Here he appears to be saying that it is essential that Jesus should *as a matter of historical fact* have been what the disciples thought him to be. But as we now turn to van Buren's account of the connection between what the disciples discerned in Jesus and what this inspired them to be, I think we shall see that if they had simply been imagining Jesus to be what they took him to be they nevertheless could (logically) have had their saving discernment just the same.

(ii) Between entertaining the story of Jesus and forming the intention to live agapeistically, as Braithwaite has it, or in the freedom of Easter, as van Buren puts it, comes, according to the latter, discernment and commitment. Van Buren describes these two conditions thus :

> It seems appropriate to say that a situation of discernment occurred to Peter and the other disciples on Easter, in which, against the background of their memory of Jesus they suddenly saw Jesus in a new and unexpected way. 'The light dawned'. The history of Jesus, which seemed to have been failure, took on a new importance as a key to the meaning of history. Out of this discernment arose a commitment to the way of life which Jesus had followed. The validation of Peter's Easter assertion is to be found in the fact that Peter too, according to an old and probably reliable tradition, died on a cross.[27]

The important question, I think, is : do van Buren's notions of discernment and commitment here add anything to Braithwaite's empiricist account of religious belief? Is van Buren saying more than that the Christian stories are psychologically very effective in inspiring the resolution to live an agapeistic kind of life? If not, then he goes no further than Braithwaite. Both he and Braithwaite have the problem of justifying their view that the stories are effective as a matter of psychological fact, but that is a subject for empirical investigation and not a philosophical problem. Since van Buren evidently thinks that he is adding something to Braithwaite's analysis by calling attention to the discernment and consequent commitment which Christian stories inspire, what can this something conceivably be? The natural question to ask when any claim that a discernment has occurred is made is : a discernment *of what*? Van Buren's reply is 'of the key to history' in the present case. What does that mean? Presumably either (a) that

Jesus somehow *explains* history or (b) that Jesus constitutes a *norm* by which to judge history – or both. (The former is the more natural meaning, but I think 'the key to history' could be taken to mean something which provides a norm by which to judge history.)

To say that the life and death of Jesus explain history could presumably mean something to the effect that certain purposes were realized in those events, which purposes all history is either promoting or frustrating. To say that the life and death of Jesus provide a norm by which to judge history would presumably mean that when men have acted as he did, they deserve approval, when not, disapproval. Understood in either way the remark that Jesus is the key to history is quite intelligible : it would make sense to say that he is. But what is added if one says that one *discerns* that he is? A claim to knowledge is added. To discern something to be the case is to do more than simply believe or suppose that it is. When a claim to know that something is the case is made, some ground must be given for it which takes us beyond the mere belief that it is so. The trouble with claims to know by what van Buren calls discernment is that they do not really take us beyond belief. They have no answer to the question : what is the difference between discerning that X and merely supposing that X? Van Buren speaks of discernment 'grasping' and 'holding' the believer. But all he seems to mean is that the believer believes very firmly. That is a misuse of the word 'discernment'. The claim to know by such discernment is open to all the objections to the claim to know by intuition.[20]

Braithwaite and van Buren then, attempt to 'cash' Christianity purely in terms of human experience as a way of meeting the challenge of secularization. Braithwaite's attempt is the more effectively argued and philosophically the more respectable. But doubts remain as to whether it is compatible with what is meant by being a religious believer.

Tillich and Cox

A second way of attempting to reconcile Christian belief and intellectual secularization has been by eliminating the logical distinction between theism and atheism. I will refer briefly to two authors who have made this attempt, Paul Tillich and Harvey Cox.

Tillich, with a wealth of rhetoric, identified God with man's ultimate concern – or perhaps better with the resolving of man's ultimate concern. ' "God" ', said Tillich 'is the answer to the question implied in man's finitude; he is the name for that which concerns man ultimately'. He explains further : 'This does not mean that first there is a being called God and then the demand that man should be ultimately concerned about him. It means that whatever concerns man ultimately becomes god for him, and, conversely, it means that a man can be concerned ultimately only about that which is god for him.'[29] As a finite being man is subjected to three kinds of existential anxiety – the fear respectively of death, meaninglessness, and condemnation.[30] To overcome these anxieties is to have what Tillich calls 'the courage to be'. Such courage to be is faith in God.[31] It follows (a) that all men are in touch with God since all are subject to ultimate concern; (b) that any man who evinces the courage to be thereby evinces faith in God. Tillich differentiates the 'divine', the 'holy' and the 'secular'. The divine is God. The holy is 'the *quality* of that which concerns man ultimately'. The secular is 'the realm of preliminary concerns'. However, 'everything secular is implicitly related to the holy. It can become the bearer of the holy. The divine can become manifest in it'.[32] Men may flee from ultimate concern into complacency.[33] But this is shallowness of life not religious disbelief. And wherever men are immersed in secular concerns without complacency, the holy and the divine either break through or are on the point of doing so.

Harvey Cox, at the end of his book *The Secular City* (London, 1965) discusses what it is 'to speak in a secular fashion of God'. He begins by condemning the efforts of those theologians who have tried to sidestep the problem of God's existence. Whether or not God exists, he says, *is* a desperately serious issue. But he argues that 'God' is a name which each man has to decide for himself whether or not he will use. Eventually we find Cox saying this :

> The difference between men of biblical faith and serious non-theists is not that we do not encounter the same reality. The difference is that we give that reality a different *name*, and in naming it differently, we differ seriously in the way we respond.[34]

God, says Cox, is not interested in our 'religious' practices, such as liturgical adoration, etc. But we do encounter him sometimes in the work of artists. God no longer encounters us as a 'Thou' who has authority over our 'I'. Cox conceives of our encounter with God in terms of a new sort of human relationship which he sees as having emerged in our urban society. It is one which is just as human as I-Thou but qualitatively different. He calls it 'alongsideness'. It often occurs, he says, in team work, in research projects, even in painting a house with other people. He sees it as participation in God. Cox's view is evidently that a theist is one who gives such relationships of alongsideness the name of God. Theists and atheists both participate in such relationships. Therefore the atheist, even though he may not be aware of it, participates in God.

The basic question, I think, which arises with regard to views such as those of Tillich and Cox is: what *more* have you said when you have said 'God'? When you have called man's ultimate concern God, what have you added to the understanding of it? When you have given the name God to alongsideness, what more have you told anybody about it? If you cash the word 'God' in terms of certain human experiences, and insist that there is no more to it than that, then why not speak simply in terms of those human experiences and drop all references to God?

Writers such as Tillich and Cox seem to me to offer two different answers to this question. The first is that in calling ultimate concern, or alongsideness, or whatever, God, we are evincing a certain attitude towards it. This answer makes quite good sense. The names which we give to things can, and frequently do, express our attitude towards them. For example, a man who calls his car by a proper name – 'I call her Clara' – is expressing an attitude of affection towards the vehicle. Similarly, someone who refers to certain experiences, e.g. the longings in his own heart or the fellowship which he has with other people, as God, is doubtless expressing an attitude of reverence towards them. But, to say the least, it is an unusual interpretation of Christianity which sees faith in God, not as putting one in touch with some putatively distinct and objective reality, but simply as inspiring one with a distinctive attitude towards certain things in one's experience.

The other answer to the question, 'What more have you said when you have said 'God'?, which is found in Tillich at any rate,

is that when you call ultimate concern or alongsideness 'God', you
are thereby pointing to 'the God above God'. This 'God above
God' Tillich deemed to be a necessity because of the paradoxes
inherent in theism. He wrote :

> The God above the God of theism is present, although hidden,
> in every divine-human encounter. Biblical religion as well as
> Protestant theology are aware of the paradoxical character of
> this encounter. They are aware that if God encounters man
> God is neither object nor subject and is therefore above the
> scheme into which theism has forced him. They are aware that
> personalism with respect to God is balanced by a trans-personal
> presence of the divine. They are aware that forgiveness can be
> accepted only if the power of acceptance is effective in man
> – biblically speaking if the power of grace is effective in man.
> They are aware of the paradoxical character of every prayer, of
> speaking to somebody to whom you cannot speak because he is
> not 'somebody', of asking somebody of whom you cannot ask
> anything because he gives or gives not before you ask, of saying
> 'Thou' to somebody who is nearer to the I than the I is to
> itself. Each of these paradoxes drives the religious consciousness
> towards a God above the God of theism.[35]

What is the difference between the God of theism and this 'God
above God'? Tillich speaks here of the religious consciousness
being driven by contradictions (for which paradoxes in the context appears to be simply a polite synonym) in the concept of God
to the concept of the 'God above God'? Presumably, therefore,
the driving force must be the desire for coherence and consistency
in the concept of God. But when Tillich goes on to define 'absolute
faith' which is his expression for faith in the 'God above God',
coherence and consistency are the last things which could be said
to characterize it. He wrote :

> Absolute faith, or the state of being grasped by the God beyond
> God . . . never is something separated and definite, an event
> which could be isolated and described. It is always a movement
> in, with, and under states of the mind. It is the situation on the
> boundary of man's possibilities. It *is* this boundary. And there-
> fore, it is both the courage of despair and the courage in and
> above every courage. It is not a place where one can live, it is

·without the safety of words and concepts, it is without a name, a church, a cult, a theology. But it is moving in the depth of all of them. It is the power of being, in which they participate and of which they are fragmentary expressions.[36]

Rhetorically this is impressive but whatever does it mean? Tillich's talk of things which are 'without the safety of words and concepts' here suggests that there are two sorts of belief which can have meaning, namely (i) one kind which pusillanimously hides within the safety of words; and (ii) another kind which ventures courageously out of the funk-hole of being able to say what you mean into an adventurous world of being able to mean what you cannot say. No doubt it can make sense to speak of meaning what one cannot say in some contexts. A gift – 'Say it with flowers' – or an action – the kiss of greeting or farewell, the passionate embrace, etc., – could be bearers of meaning which is in some sense not expressible in words. The flowers say it so much more completely etc. But it is another matter to assert, as Tillich seems to be asserting, that contradictions which reduce ordinary theism to meaninglessness point beyond themselves to a theism above theism in which the contradictions are resolved, *not* by replacing them with self-consistent propositions, but with the inexpressible which nevertheless has meaning. Tillich in effect said simply that the inexpressible *must* have such meaning but he did nothing to show how it can.

Of the attempts to respond to the challenge of secularization which I have considered in this section, fashionable though they are or recently were, the only one which seems to me interesting or coherent is Braithwaite's. However, what validity there is in his account of religious belief seems to me to reside more cogently and clearly in Wittgenstein's account of religious belief as using a picture, which we considered in Chapter I.

(iii) THE LEVELS OF SECULARIZATION RECONSIDERED

I turn then from such attempts of others to deal with the challenge of secularization to an attempt of my own. I will make this attempt by reconsidering briefly each of the levels of secularization which were referred to in the first section of this chapter and showing, if I can, why each of them in turn fails to provide unshakeable ground for the rejection of religious belief.

The Decline of Belief

I made the point, when dealing with the first level of secularization that the mere fact, if it is a fact, that fewer people now believe in God than disbelieve in him does not render such belief intellectually disreputable. The factors which have led to this decline in belief could be – probably are – many and various. The decline may not be due simply to the fact that religious belief has appeared to many when they reflected upon it carefully and objectively to be incredible. It could be due to the fact, for example, that the moral demands of religion are irksome to modern men, or the authoritarian ethos of most churches, uncongenial; and the reasons which men give for their rejection of religion, be in consequence rationalizations of their desire to escape with a good conscience from the moral demands which religion makes. But leaving aside all this and assuming that, after rational consideration, most people in our society do find it impossible to believe in God this fact in itself would not discredit religion. It is only too easy for men to be mistaken; not least in their most carefully considered opinions. The rational acceptability of religion cannot be settled by counting heads. God is not Tinker Bell. His existence does not hang upon how many believe in it.

The Secular World-View

The second level of secularization I took to be constituted by the fact that the norms of intelligibility to which modern men subscribe, whether they are religious believers or not, are alien to religious belief. In particular, I considered MacIntyre's contention that because this is so, even a believer has to see how religion appears from a secular standpoint in order to make sense of it. He has to see what needs to be added to, or taken from, our normal ways of interpreting and explaining our experience in order to make religious interpretation or explanation intelligible. So, according to MacIntyre, in order to understand religion a modern man must (logically) disbelieve it. That is to say he must take up the position of the unbeliever before he can move to that of the believer with any comprehension of what this latter position is. He must be an unbeliever in order to be a believer.

On this two comments seem to me appropriate.

I do not think that the prevailing world view is as thoroughly secular as MacIntyre makes it out to be. It is true of course that scientific explanations and the courses of action to which they give rise seem to grow ever more comprehensive and successful. But religious ways of thinking are not so alien to modern men as all that. One has only to remark the widespread profanity in ordinary conversation to recognize that 'God' is a word still in use! True, its use for profane purposes may witness to decline in religious belief; men, it may well be, no longer hesitate to take the name of God 'in vain', as they did in ages of faith, because they do not now believe in him. But loss of respect for, or belief in, God is one thing; inability to make head or tail of remarks about him is another. Men have not forgotten, so to speak, how to play the religious language-game even if they no longer play it for real. The man who replied to the Salvation Army girl's question, 'Are you saved?' with 'No, I'm an atheist, thank God!' witnessed to the prevalence of religious attitudes, if not belief, in our secular society.

A more important comment on MacIntyre's argument is this. It is perfectly true that one must understand religious *un*belief in order to understand religious belief. But, then, one must understand, for examples, Socialism in order to understand Conservatism, or Newtonian physics in order to understand Einsteinian. Understanding any system of belief is a matter of understanding the difference which it makes to hold those beliefs. That is to say, how belief in the relevant respects differs from unbelief. But it would be sophistry to say that therefore in order to be a Conservative one must (logically) be a Socialist (or *vice versa*) or that in order to subscribe to Einstein's views one must hold Newton's, etc. It is similar sophistry when MacIntyre claims that in order to understand religious belief one must (logically) be an unbeliever. Modern religious believers may well be torn from time to time – perhaps all the time – between their secular and their religious world-views; there may be considerable psychological conflict between the way they see things in Church and the way they see them in the laboratory or the market-place. Modern believers may, moreover, feel increasingly at home in these latter venues and less and less at ease in the dim religious light. But all this, even if it is the case, does not support MacIntyre's evident intention of showing that the modern believer is in the position that he must (logically) disbelieve in order to understand. Such logical truth as

there is in MacIntyre's point derives from the fact that any assertion, in order to assert, must implicitly deny. To say that X is the
case is to say that whatever is not X is not the case. Unless one
understands what it is for something to be not X, one cannot
understand what it is for it to be X. *All* understanding of assertions involves some recognition of what is being denied as well
as what is being affirmed. It is sophistry to talk as if this were
true only of the assertion of religious belief and constituted some
defect of intelligibility in the latter.

The Philosophical Grounding
The third level of secularization, I said above, is constituted by a
philosophical theory of meaning according to which religious beliefs are meaningless because they are neither analytic nor empirically verifiable. This philosophical theory is now discredited, I
think for two main reasons to which I will briefly refer.

First, the so called 'verification principle' upon which this
logical positivist theory of meaning was based has eluded all
attempts to give it satisfactory formulation. The difficulty has been
to arrive at a formulation which is neither too exclusive nor too
inclusive. In order to verify a scientific law – such laws being uni-
versally of the form, 'All A's are B' – one would need to have
observed all the A's in the universe. But it is logically impossible
ever to be sure that one has done so; there may always be an A
somewhere which is not B. So scientific laws are unverifiable
and therefore meaningless. If, in this theory of meaning, falsifiability is substituted for verifiability as the test, then it seems to
play havoc with common sense. 'All A's are B' is falsifiable if we
find one A which is not B; and if all scientific laws are universals
of the form 'All A's are B', then they are all falsifiable and therefore meaningful. But what of common sense remarks of the form
'Some A's are B'? They cannot be falsified; however many A's
we found which are not B, it might always be the case that there
are some which are B. So, by the falsifiability test, common sense
remarks of the form 'Some A's are B' will be meaningless.

It ran dead against the aim of the logical positivists to exclude
either science or common sense from meaningfulness. To avoid
this conclusion therefore the verification principle was recast thus :
a statement is meaningful if some empirically testable statement
can be deduced from it in conjunction with certain other premises,

without being deducible from these other premises alone. The trouble with this reformulation, however, is that it would *include* metaphysical statements. From (i) 'The Absolute is spirit' together with (ii) 'If the Absolute is spirit, then all cats are black' we can deduce 'All cats are black' which is empirically testable and which cannot be deduced from (ii) alone. Therefore by the verification principle, as just reformulated, it follows that 'The Absolute is spirit' is meaningful. But it ran against the logical positivists' whole intention to include metaphysical statements amongst those which are meaningful. This philosophical standpoint, in which intellectual secularization on the view taken above is fundamentally grounded, is one which purports to discredit all propositions about that which is not empirically observable, including God, and to exalt science and common sense alone as meaningful. We see that by its own terms it failed to achieve this.[37]

The second of my two reasons for rejecting this philosophical grounding of intellectual secularization is that, even if it could be formulated satisfactorily, its theory of meaning is too narrow. Empirical falsifiability is a criterion of demarcation, but not of meaning.[38] It defines natural science and possibly certain other universes of discourse. If a statement is not testable by empirical observation of some kind then it is of no interest to natural scientists. It is not, so to speak, a possible move in their language-game and so from their point of view, meaningless. But it does not follow that natural science and allied universes of discourse alone are meaningful. Of course, a religious believer cannot have it both ways. He cannot maintain that the expression of his religious belief is logically the same sort of thing as a scientific statement would be – for instance, that it expresses the same sort of claim to knowledge – and at the same time maintain that it does not have to fulfil the same conditions as scientific statements do. I criticized some exponents of religion for thus attempting to have it both ways when I was considering in Chapter 3 whether or not the existence of God can be established by appeal to empirical evidence. But provided that such attempts are avoided, religious belief can be considered as a universe of discourse, distinct from natural science. Its logical frontiers can be mapped and its fundamental presuppositions discovered as they were in Chapter 1 of this book.

The most important discovery in philosophy since the heyday of

logical positivism has been that language may have many different
kinds of meaning. Wittgenstein and Austin are the two main in-
fluences which have been at work in recent analytical philosophy
to this effect.[39] As we saw in Chapter 1, Wittgenstein, in his later
writings, rejected the theory of meaning in his *Tractatus Logico
Philosophicus* (English translation, London, 1922), which had
deeply influenced the logical positivists, because he now saw that it
was too narrow. We saw in the quotation from *Philosophical Investigations* on pages 5–6 above his emphasis upon the variety of
meanings which language can have.[40] J. L. Austin, though he evidently owed little or nothing to Wittgenstein, also emphasized,
to use his own terms, how many different things we can 'do with
words'. He listed the following as examples :

asking or answering a question,
giving some information or an assurance or a warning,
announcing a verdict of an intention,
pronouncing a sentence,
making an appointment or an appeal or a criticism,
making an identification or giving a description.[41]

I am not suggesting of course that the work of Wittgenstein or
Austin knocks the bottom out of intellectual secularization in any
absolute sense. There may still be good reasons for rejecting religious belief as unintelligible even if Logical Positivism's theory of
meaning does not constitute them. It may, for instance, be the
case that we cannot meaningfully talk about god because the
concept of god is inherently self-contradictory. I shall deal with
this possibility in the next chapter and hope to dispose of it. But
I have not disposed of it here. Here all I could claim to have done
is to have indicated why the view that it does not make sense to
talk about god *because* of the logical differences between such
talk and natural science or mathematics is not good enough philosophical ground for intellectual secularization. I have argued that
such a view of what does and what does not make sense cannot
be satisfactorily formulated and even if it could, it would be too
narrow to fit the facts.

I conclude then that on each of the three levels of intellectual
secularization to which I have referred in this chapter, religious
belief can be defended against the attack which has been mounted
against it on that level.

6 The Question of Rationality

The religious language-game is played : but is it rational to play this game? That is the question which I must now attempt to answer. The account of religious belief which I offered in Chapter 1 attempted to show that the religious language-game is not too dissimilar to other major language-games in its basic logical structure. It is constituted by a concept which is tacitly presupposed in every move which is made within it. It 'uses a picture' in accordance with a technique which has to be learned. In its case the constitutive concept, the fundamental picture, is that of god. But, of course, the mere fact, if it is a fact, that to speak in terms of god is in certain respects not unlike speaking in terms of physical objectivity or moral obligation or whatever does not establish that it is as rational to be religious as it is to be scientific or moral, etc.

'Rational' is a difficult word to define. It is one of those words which have both an emotive and a descriptive meaning.[1] Its emotive meaning is constant : to describe a being or an activity as rational is invariably in normal use to express approval of it. But the descriptive meaning of 'rational' may vary from speaker to speaker, for what constitutes rationality is a subject about which there has been, and still is, no small difference of opinion. With the best will in the world therefore, I do not think that I can supply a single, straightforward definition of rationality and I shall not attempt to do so. Rather, I intend in this chapter to consider five possible definitions of what it is to be rational and to relate each of them to religious belief by means of the question : could a religious man as such be rational in this sense? The five definitions must not be taken as alternatives which exclude one another. They represent what appear to me to be the main uses of the word 'rational' (and its cognates) nowadays. Any adequate definition of the word would, I think, have to take account of all of them. In the case of each, my answer to the question posed,

'Could a religious man be rational in this sense?', will be a tentative yes.

I must make it clear, however, that I shall not be arguing that everything which passes for religious belief, or even everything which passes for theism, is rational. Christian theism is the form of religious belief with which my readers are most likely to be familiar and so it is that form which I shall have mainly in mind throughout this chapter. But though I shall try to show that it is logically possible to be a Christian theist and at the same time to be rational in each of the five senses of the word to be considered, this does not mean of course that I have to defend any and every belief about God which occurs within such theism. All I shall take myself to have to do will be to show that the theistic concept of God – say in its broad Judaeo-Christian outlines – can constitute a language-game in which it is not obviously irrational to participate. If I can successfully achieve this limited objective I shall be more than satisfied.

Proportioning Belief to the Evidence

The first conception of rationality to which I shall refer is that to be found in David Hume's famous discussion of miracles in Chapter x of his *Enquiry concerning Human Understanding* : 'A wise man ... proportions his belief to the evidence'.[2] It is clear that by a 'wise' man Hume meant a 'rational' man since the argument which follows appeals to what is evident – I quote Hume again – 'in the eyes of all reasonable people'.[3]

Hume's attack on miracles in the chapter to which I have just referred is a paradigm case of what he meant by proportioning belief to the evidence and it raises all the relevant questions concerning the application of this criterion of rationality to religious belief. I will first outline the argument against miracles and then turn to religious belief as a whole.

Hume starts from a general point about historical probability. As regards the claim that any event has occurred, there are always two possibilities : (i) that what is said to have happened really did so; (ii) that those who have said that it happened were (intentionally or unintentionally) lying. What have we to go on in deciding which of these two possibilities is realized in any given case? Only our experience, says Hume. On one side of the scales, so to speak, we must put our experience of the undoubted occurrence of events similar to that which is said to have happened; and on the other side, our experience of such events being falsely reported to have happened. The question then is: on which side do the scales come down? Have we more experience of the former sort or of the latter? Such comparison of our experience of these respective kinds of occurrence (i.e. this kind of event happening and this kind of event being falsely reported to have happened) gives the degree of *probability* either that the miracle in question really occurred and was not falsely reported to have done so, or vice versa.

Turning specifically to miracles, Hume defines a miracle as 'a violation of the laws of nature'. He does not of course conceive of such 'laws' as commands which the universe is compelled to obey nor of our present knowledge of them as complete and beyond all question. He simply makes the point that 'a firm and unalterable experience has established these laws'. He is well aware that so called laws of nature are simply generalizations which have hitherto not been empirically falsified. A miracle is a violation of these laws, says Hume, in the sense that 'nothing is esteemed a miracle, if it ever happened in the common course of nature'. That is to say a miracle is an event which runs counter to what we have consistently experienced apart from it. This definition is in accordance with the ordinary use of the word 'miracle'. An event is not normally called a miracle unless it is exceptional. Two qualifications may be readily conceded : (i) There is normally a great deal more than that to a miracle : an event is not called a miracle in the great religions unless it is deemed to manifest the justice or goodness, etc. of God. (ii) In some cases a miracle may resemble a phenomenon which commonly occurs – it may be, for instance, a downpour of rain or a flash of lightning – but in such cases there is always an additional element of some kind which makes it a miracle – the rain or lightning occur at some person's command or at an especially advantageous time, for examples. However, such qualifications, it will be clear, do not alter the fact that a miracle is, in Hume's sense of the word, a violation of the laws of nature.

Now, if we ask 'What is the probability that any miracle has, as a matter of historical fact, occurred?', we are faced with the fact, to quote Hume, that 'no testimony is sufficient to establish a miracle, unless the testimony be of such a kind that its falsehood would be more miraculous, than the fact, which it endeavours to establish'. Remember that the historical probability of an event is determined by weighing (a) our experience of that kind of event really occurring against (b) our experience of its being falsely reported to have occurred. In the case of a miracle, (a) is nil. 'There must ... be a *uniform experience against* every miraculous event, otherwise the event would not merit that appellation' (italics mine), as Hume reminds us. What of (b) – i.e. false reporting – in the case of miracles? Hume lists a number of considerations which seem to him to bring the scales down heavily on this side, amongst them the following. He considers that there is not to be found in all history a miracle attested by 'a sufficient number' of men of such intelligence and integrity as 'to place them beyond all suspicion of any design to deceive others'. Again : it cannot be denied that gullibility is characteristic of human nature and men are only too ready to credit 'utterly absurd' stories which gratify 'the passion of *surprise* and *wonder*' (italics Hume's). Mendacity is no less common : 'it is nothing strange ... that men should lie in all ages'. To such considerations is added 'a strong presumption against' miracles by the fact that stories of their occurrence are commonest amongst 'ignorant and barbarous nations'. In Hume's view all this weight of experience tips the scales decisively against the probability of any miracle having occurred as a matter of historical fact.

Hume adds a rather neat argument to these considerations. Adherents of any religion, he says, necessarily believe two things : (i) that the miracles reported in their religion really occurred, and (ii) that similar miracles reported in other religions, did not. Now, by calling any event a miracle in their religion adherents signify that they have *no* experience apart from it of this kind of event really occurring, otherwise they would not describe it as a miracle. But by regarding similar miracles in other religions as false they signify that they have *some* experience of this kind of event being falsely reported to have occurred. Therefore the balance of probability must (logically) always be against the miracle in question.

How effective is Hume's main argument? At the time when Hume was writing, miracles were commonly adduced as evidence of the truth of religion. The argument was from the fact that certain miracles had occurred to the existence of God as their only reasonable explanation. Against any such line of argument,

Hume's counter-argument is completely effective. If there is a strong probability that a certain event has not occurred, a rational man will recognize that it is, other things being equal, equally improbable that the God who is involved as necessary to explain it, exists. It is not therefore rational to hold religious beliefs solely on the strength of certain putative miracles. Today, however, it would be unusual for sophisticated advocates of religious belief to argue that miracles prove the existence of God. Indeed, so out of fashion is any such move, that some modern Christian apologists eliminate supernatural occurrences altogether from their account of Christianity. For instance, they reduce the claim that Christ rose from the dead to the claim that the disciples simply had visions of him after his death[4] or even that they just stopped worrying about their personal survival or well-being.[5]

If a more traditional view is taken and it is believed that Christ literally came back to life after he had been dead, it is recognized by modern Christians that there is a high degree of probability against this, regarded simply as a historical event; but they would argue that *if you already believe in God* it is not irrational to believe him capable of doing something unique such as bringing Christ back to life again. Here the miracle of the Resurrection is not thought of as something which has indisputably occurred and requires God for its explanation; it is regarded as an event which cannot be believed to have occurred apart from a logically prior belief in God. Of course, the theological proposition 'God raised Christ from the dead', taken literally, could not (logically) be true unless the historical proposition 'Jesus was raised from the dead' were also true. But Hume's argument must *not* be taken to have shown that the historical proposition cannot be true *and therefore* neither can the theological. It shows no such thing. It simply shows that an event which theists would attribute to God, if considered purely as a historical event apart from divine agency would be highly improbable. No theist is going to be unduly dismayed by that.

But of course the question which arises is : what evidence has the theist for attributing miracles to God? A moment ago I introduced the condition, 'if you already believe in God' and suggested that *given* such belief it might not be irrational to believe in miracles also. But what grounds are there for fulfilling the condition? If a rational man is one who proportions his belief to the

evidence, what is the evidence to which a rational theist will proportion his belief in God? The demand for evidence seems simply
to have been put one stage further back – not now evidence of
miracles but of God's existence. Those who in Hume's day argued
from miracles to God were at least trying to find some evidence
to which to proportion their belief. What can a modern theist,
who wishes to be rational, offer in place of the discredited evidence
of miracles?

As I have already suggested, at first blush this looks like a perfectly proper question to ask. But in Chapter 4 I tried to show that
in the last analysis it is not. I argued there that the question 'Does
God really exist?' is not one which can be settled by appeal to the
kind of evidence which verifies a scientific hypothesis, substantiates
a moral judgment or settles any non-religious question; and
furthermore it cannot be treated as a religious question either, because everything which is said in religious terms presupposes the
existence of god. What the question calls for, I claimed, is an
ontological choice, not a conclusion supported by evidence.

In reply it may be contended that if such is the case, if religion's
basic presupposition is not susceptible of evidence for or against,
then the necessary condition of being rational – i.e. proportioning
belief to the evidence – cannot (logically) be fulfilled where religion
is concerned. In which case the answer to the question 'Can a
religious man be rational according to that criterion of rationality?'
must be no. But then, how am I going to reconcile my view that
the fundamental premise of all religious belief is one for which
evidence cannot be adduced with my view that the answer to the
question 'Can a religious man be rational by the present criterion?'
is yes? I think I can do so by making two points.

First, it must not be assumed that there is some homogeneous
commodity, evidence, which weighs for or against beliefs. What
counts as evidence differs from one universe of discourse to
another. Compare, for instance, the appeal to axioms, or definitions of signs, by means of which a geometrical proof proceeds,
with the appeal to facts about the physical world by which a
scientific theory is tested. Just as within mathematics or science,
argument proceeds by appeal to *a certain kind* of evidence so in
religion discussions about the true nature of god occur and are
settled, sometimes at any rate, by appeal to *a certain kind* of
evidence. This is true whether one thinks of discussions between

adherents of differing religions or of controversy within any particular creed. Sometimes the religious evidence looks odd if one
thinks of a religious belief as though it were some kind of scientific or historical hypothesis. Wittgenstein, for example, remarked on
the oddness of a man, who believed that there would be a Last
Judgment because he had dreamed about it;[6] and that is certainly
most odd if the man in question was thinking of the Last Judgment as a spatio-temporal event which could be predicted. But,
of course, it is perfectly possible for there to be something called a
Last Judgment, for which those who conceive of it take dreams
to be evidence; and though such people may be very odd, in some
sense of that word, their move from dreams to Last Judgment
will not be odd given their presuppositions. It will be the move
to make if you are thinking in their way. I am not concerned to
argue for dreams or Last Judgments of course, but simply to point
out that *only when it is clear what counts as evidence in religion*
can a rational man here as elsewhere proportion his belief to the
evidence. Every thoughtful and sincere religious believer in fact
does precisely that : he participates in the religious language-game
by holding beliefs for which he has, or thinks he has, the kind of
evidence which counts in that game. The *kind* of evidence which
counts is given. A religious man has not made up his own evidence
in the sense of deciding for himself what shall count as evidence.
It is determined by the nature of the language-game in which he
has chosen to participate.

I turn to the second point which I wish to make. The question
now comes up : does it make sense to insist that if a religious believer cannot point to some sort of evidence, which makes his
participation in religion itself rational, then he can only be rational
by ceasing to participate? I wish to say no. I think there comes a
point where proportioning belief to evidence has to stop. But this
does not mean that what then occurs is necessarily irrational. For,
just as the question 'Does god really exist?' calls for an ontological choice, so, as I tried to show in Chapter 4, do such questions
as 'Do physical objects really exist?', 'Does moral obligation really
exist?', etc. One cannot adduce evidence for one's answer to such
questions. It would not make sense to say that one had done so. So
if a religious believer cannot adduce evidence for his participation in the religious language-game he need not feel more irrational in being religious than a scientist in being scientific or a

moralist in being moral. It is no discredit to religious belief that
it cannot meet the requirements of a criterion of rationality at
the point where the demands of the latter would cease to make
sense.

Avoiding Self-Contradiction

A belief is irrational if the statement of it is self-contradictory. To
utter a contradiction is, of course, to make noises or to put marks
on paper. But not all noises or marks have meaning. Therefore
the mere fact that self-contradictory remarks can be uttered does
not give them meaning. It is true that some contradictions may
amount to more than meaningless noises or marks. They may have
what is called emotive meaning : i.e. they may express the speaker's
emotion or induce emotion in the hearer. But emotive meaning
must be differentiated clearly from cognitive meaning. An
utterance has cognitive meaning in so far as it can contribute to
our knowledge of what is, or is not, the case as a matter of objective
fact.

The defect of contradictions is that they are always self-stultifying so far as cognitive meaning is concerned; that is, in so far as
they purport to state that something is, or is not, the case. To state
a contradiction is logically tantamount to stating nothing at all.
We can say that something *is* the case only by marking it off from
what is *not*. To say that X (or not-X) *is* the case is to say by implication that not-X (or X) is *not* the case. The statement 'It is raining', for instance, refers to a state of the weather which is distinct
from all other conceivable states and asserts that this state, and
none of the others, exists here and now. 'It is not raining', refers
to those other conceivable weather conditions and states that one
of them, and not rain, obtains at the present time and place. Now,
suppose we invented a word which referred to *all* conceivable
weather conditions, the word 'naining' let us say. And suppose
that someone was confined in a room with drawn curtains and
asked us, when we visited him, what the weather was like outside. We reply, 'It's naining' (using that word as I have just
defined it). This reply will give him no idea at all of what the
weather is like outside. Because it refers by definition to *all* conceivable weather conditions it is logically impossible to use the
word 'naining' to state that *any specific* weather condition obtains.
The self-contradictory statement 'It is raining and it is not raining'

is logically exactly like 'It is naining'. It refers to all conceivable weather conditions and so cannot be used to state that any specific weather condition obtains.

Another way of expressing the logical objection to self-contradictory statements is this : any conclusion whatever can be deduced validly from any contradiction whatever. The following piece of reasoning is logically sound whatever values are given to the variables A and X :

A and not-A
If A then either A or X
But not-A
Therefore X.

For example :

It is raining and it is not raining.
If it is raining, then either it is raining or I am 1,000 years old.
But it is not raining.
Therefore I am 1,000 years old.

Any contradiction whatever could be substituted for 'It is raining and it is not raining' and the conclusion 'I am 1,000 years old' would follow. Similarly, any conclusion whatever could be substituted for 'I am 1,000 years old' and then deduced validly from 'It is raining and it is not raining'. From any and every contradiction every and any conclusion follows validly. This is why a contradiction is always useless as a contribution to rational argument or discussion. In such argument or discussion the whole significance of an utterance lies in the fact that it is logically compatible only with certain other utterances. An utterance which is logically compatible with all other utterances gets us nowhere. To say something which is logically compatible with saying anything else whatever is, from the point of view of rational argument or discussion, tantamount to saying nothing at all.

The communicative function of language has been analysed into four elements[7] : (i) the *expressive* function, and (ii) the signalling or *stimulative* function; (iii) the *descriptive* function, and (iv) the *argumentative* function. I had the two former of these functions in mind when I said that self-contradiction can be used to express or induce emotion; but my main argument has been that neither of the two latter functions, i.e. the descriptive and the argumentative, can be fulfilled where there is contradiction. To allow self-contradiction is to permit all attributes to be ascribed to a subject at once and to admit all claims to be made at once. But description is only logically possible where certain attributes which a thing has are clearly marked off from others which it lacks. And argument is only logically possible where two claims can be shown to be incompatible. Contradiction, therefore, robs us of all power to describe or to argue, that is, to say what is the case as a matter of either empirical, or of logical, fact. To allow self-contradiction in religious discourse, for example, is to reduce the latter, at best, to the expression or stimulation of emotion. In a word, to poetry.

Within theism self-contradictory utterances frequently purport to have cognitive meaning; that is, they are intended to inform us as to what is, or is not, the case. I turn then to the particular case of self-contradictory beliefs about God. Many theistic thinkers appear to be under the illusion that the logical objections to self-contradictory statements which I have set out above disappear provided that the statements concerned are about God. It may mean nothing to say 'It is raining and it is not raining', but, they hold, contradictions concerning God can be full of significance. I have already conceded that within religious discourse contradictions may sometimes have emotive meaning. But if such contradictions purport to have cognitive meaning, then I contend that they are open to exactly the same objections as those which we have seen apply to 'It is raining and it is not raining'. Nonsense does not cease to be nonsense simply because it is talked about God.

Does what I have just said impose any kind of limitation on God? Religious thinkers sometimes speak as if it did; and they hold that God would not be a fitting object of worship if the law of non-contradiction applied with respect to beliefs about him as I have argued that it does. They draw a distinction between so-called divine and human reason and hold that, whilst human reason may not be able to cope with contradictions, divine reason can. It is not always clear precisely what is meant by 'divine reason can' in this context. Sometimes the essence of the claim appears to be that God is so intelligent that he can make sense of contradictions even when men cannot; sometimes, that God is such a remarkable subject that the contradictions which men utter about him can be meaningful though they would not be if uttered about any other subject. But, either way, what the contention amounts to is that God is infinite or mysterious and therefore 'above' logic. What must be said in reply?

Notice that the law of non-contradiction imposes a limitation *only* upon what can be said. To claim, as I have done, that God cannot be (or do) X and not-X is simply to point out that if anyone said that God was (or did) X and not-X, that remark would be uninformative for the reasons given above. It would lack any cognitive meaning. This is not like saying that God cannot be (or do) X (whatever X may be) because he lacks the requisite power, or wisdom, or whatever. The impossibility of God being (or doing) X and not-X is a logical impossibility. Logical impossibility does not argue any weakness or limitation in that to which it applies. It simply means that if what is logically impossible were uttered, no one would be able to make any sense of that utterance. The theistic thinkers to whom I have referred seem to think that God could not be God unless he were, to use the expression used a moment ago, 'above logic'. Being 'above logic' is conceived here as if it were a condition of existence entitling one who enjoyed it to our utmost reverence. But, so far as I can see, the only meaning which can be given to this expression 'above logic' is that anything so described is a subject about which nonsense is, or may be, talked. I see no reason whatever to think that it constitutes any limitation on God if I deny, as I wish to do, that he is such a subject. And why anyone should suppose that unless God is such a subject he is not a fitting object of worship entirely escapes me.

Some modern theologians, however, seem to suffer from an irrepressible desire to speak of God in self-contradictory terms as both the conceivable and the inconceivable, the definable and the indefinable, etc. Paul Tillich provides a particularly blatant example of this tendency in the paper entitled 'The Meaning and Justification of Religious Symbols', which he read to the fourth annual meeting of the New York University Institute of Philosophy. Religious symbols, said Tillich, are 'a representation of that which is unconditionally beyond the conceptual sphere'.[9] The word 'God', he contended, is such a symbol.

In the word 'God' is contained at the same time that which actually functions as a representation and also the idea that it is *only* a representation. It has the peculiarity of transcending its own conceptual content – upon this depends the numinous character which the word has . . .¹⁰

But how can we conceive of anything which is beyond conception? How can a symbol point us to its symbolizandum if it is impossible for us to conceive of the latter? The 'cans' in these questions are logical and the answers are that we – or it – *cannot.* Tillich evidently recognized this logical impossibility, yet gloried in it. The test of the truth of the symbol 'God', he averred, '*cannot* be the comparison of it with the reality to which it refers, just because this reality is absolutely beyond human comprehension' (italics mine). And he does not mean here that, as a matter of empirical fact, people are not clever enough to comprehend it, but, to quote him again, that the word 'God' 'produces a contradiction in the consciousness'.¹¹ He appears to think that it is perfectly all right for the word 'God' to do this, but he gives no reason for thinking so. We have seen that anything is deducible from a contradiction and so if Tillich is right any nonsense whatever is deducible from talk about God because the latter always 'produces a contradiction'.

This account of God-talk is, as a factual description of the latter, in my opinion quite mistaken. I concede that there is much in the writings of mystics and theologians which lends it some support; they have often talked about God as if they took themselves to be conceiving of the inconceivable. However, Tillich writes, in the paper referred to, as though no utterance concerning God makes sense unless it purports to conceive of the inconceivable. Presumably, he takes it that, for good or ill, that is how God is conceived by those within theism who profess belief in him. If Tillich were right about this, and if I am right in what I have said above about the logical character of contradictions, it would follow that theism is just nonsense. But I do not think that Tillich is right. Whatever theologians or mystics may have done with language in their talk of God, very many theists manage to think and speak of God in ways which do not have to be described as attempts to conceive of the inconceivable. God is thought of as almighty, omniscient, surpassingly holy, etc. etc., but such concepts are not inherently self-contradictory. Talk of God does not have to be cast in contradictions in order to qualify as talk of God.

When theologians speak of the word 'God' as, to recall Tillich, 'transcending its own conceptual content', or when they say things like : 'not the most concentrated attention can elucidate the object to which this (sc. numinous) state of mind refers, bringing it out of the impenetrable obscurity of feeling into the domain of the conceptual understanding', as Otto did in his *The Idea of the Holy*[12], I suppose that what they wish to indicate is the infinity or mysteriousness of God. Let me make it quite clear that by all my strictures on self-contradiction in religion, I do not wish to imply that expressions such as 'infinite' or 'mysterious' cannot be ascribed to God in any meaningful sense. If anyone purports to mean by these expressions that God is 'beyond definition' or 'beyond conception' and *having said that* then goes on to speak of him as if he were definable or conceivable, that is self-contradictory and I have been concerned to emphasize that the mere fact that it has to do with God does not redeem such self-contradiction from absurdity. If, however, by calling God infinite or mysterious anyone means that there is *more to God* than he has hitherto experienced or understood, that is an entirely different matter. This is a perfectly intelligible thing to say about God or indeed anything else. The word 'more' is one that can be clearly defined and coherently used; and the expression 'what he has hitherto experienced or understood' is not in the least opaque and is significant by contrast with 'what he has *not* hitherto experienced or understood'. When Newton, with his scientific discoveries in mind, said that he felt like a child who had picked up a few pebbles on the shores of the ocean of truth, he was expressing his sense of the mystery of things and of how much more there might be to know than he knew. It makes perfectly good sense to say that he was voicing his sense of the infinite bounds of the mysterious world which science has to explore. But notice that he was not claiming a licence to say self-contradictory things about that world and get away with it. Many religious believers might echo Newton's words with reference to God. They feel that what they have experienced or understood of God is an infinitesimal part of what there is to be experienced or understood. There is nothing self-contradictory in their saying that they do so.

It is not, I suppose, absolutely essential for a scientist, as such, to share Newton's sense of mystery (though I suspect that no one could be a good scientist without having some feeling for the fascination of the unknown); but so far as the religious believer is concerned some sense of the *mysterium tremendum et fascinans*

with which he is confronted in God is, I would think, a necessary
condition of his being what we normally mean by a religious
believer. If so and if this had been what Otto meant by his insistence that a feeling for the numinous is essential to religion, or
what Tillich meant by the word 'God' being a symbol with a
transcendent content, then we might readily have agreed with
them. To do so would certainly make good sense. There could
(logically) be far more to God than we have experienced or understood. But to recognize this is different from claiming the logical
right to make self-contradictory statements where God is concerned.

No doubt it will be objected in some quarters that the sort of
thing which I have been saying so far in this section completely
ignores the essential role played by paradox in religion. By 'paradox' I mean the sort of statement which is self-contradictory in
form yet says something significant. 'The greatest of realities is
the greatest of paradoxes', religious thinkers have sometimes con-
fidently affirmed.[13] Human thinking, they insist, frequently runs
out at last into paradox. Man and the world which he inhibits are
so mysterious that reflection upon them inevitably leads to un-
resolved paradoxes; for examples, the wave-particles paradox in
sub-atomic physics or the body-mind problem in philosophical
psychology. This being so, we should not be surprised to find that
religious thinking runs out into the most irresoluble of paradoxes.
God, the greatest of realities, is necessarily the greatest of paradoxes.

Paradox, of course, is a familiar linguistic device and it has
some perfectly legitimate uses. For instance, a paradox may be
employed to express or to create puzzlement, a use reminiscent
of what I was saying earlier about the emotive meaning which a
self-contradiction may have. Paradox may also be used with cognitive meaning to indicate the unique and complicated character
of its subject-matter.

'Is X a Y?'
'It is and it isn't' (or 'Yes and No').

Given many values of the variables X and Y, this snatch of dialogue would make perfectly good sense. The alternative replies,
'It is and it isn't' or 'Yes and No' indicate that the X referred to is
like Y in certain respects but not in others: and it undoubtedly

tells you something about X to learn this. Take the following examples. To each of these questions the reply, 'It is and it isn't' (or 'Yes and No'), could be given.

'Is Frankenstein's creature a man?'
'Is Victor Borge a comedian?'
'Is the Loch Ness monster just a joke?'

And so on. The point to take is that in every such case the paradoxical reply 'Yes and No' or 'It (he) is and it (he) isn't' is simply a conventional shorthand way of saying that the particular subject-matter referred to is in some respects like members of the class referred to, but not in others. Frankenstein's monster has a body and moves like a man, but does not come into being like one; Victor Borge cracks a very good joke like a comedian but he is also a professional pianist; the Loch Ness monster is a subject of much ridicule and merriment but large sums of money have recently been spent by universities in investigating scientifically whether or not it exists. None of these remarks which I have just made about Frankenstein's monster and the rest is essentially self-contradictory. It is possible, that is to say, to get rid of any apparent self-contradiction in the above examples of paradox and still say what one means. Given time and care one can replace 'It (he) is and it (he) isn't' or 'Yes and No' by replies which are entirely free from self-contradiction. The replies 'It (he) is and it (he) isn't' and 'Yes and No' are simply colourful, dramatic ways of saying something which is perfectly self-consistent. The legitimacy of paradoxes in cases such as these does nothing to legitimatize contradictions which are irresoluble.

Nevertheless, it may be said, do we not have to rest content sometimes with paradoxes which cannot be thus resolved? Reference was made a moment ago to apparent paradoxes in sub-atomic physics and philosophical psychology. In sub-atomic physics the problem is that the same subject-matter, namely light, seems to call for description, now in terms of waves, now of particles, and there does not appear to be any satisfactory way of harmonizing the one description with the other. In the description of human behaviour we seem to be necessarily involved in two 'language-games', that of free agency and that of bodily movement, because there is no satisfactory way of reducing the one to the other or both to some third 'language-game'.

The latter is the less worrying problem of the two from the point of view which I have adopted. It may be unsatisfactory to end the investigation of human behaviour with a Cartesian dualism of body and mind, but at least, that is not a self-contradictory position. It offends 'the philosophical craving for unity' no doubt, and we may hope to see the dualism resolved. But to say that two things are going on, one in the body and another in the mind, is not the same as to say that the same thing both is and is not going on. In the present state of our philosophical knowledge it may be that we cannot achieve the desired unity in our description of human conduct. But all that this necessarily entails is that the subject-matter with which we are dealing is so complex or mysterious that we do not fully understand it.[14]

The wave-particle paradox is perhaps more difficult for anyone who tries, as I have been doing, to dispose of the claim that self-contradiction is essential in religion as in science. Does not the wave-particle paradox entail that, in order to talk about physical reality, we must engage, in the last analysis, in irresoluble self-contradiction? I am not competent to discuss sub-atomic physics in any detail but, so far as I understand the matter, physicists do apparently now find themselves in a position where they have to say that the same entity both is and is not either a number of particles, or a wave. Notice, however, that even if this is so they do not rest content with the position, much less glory in it or regard it as a remarkably significant position to be in. Their best efforts are spent in trying to get out of it for they recognize that unless they do so they cannot make further progress in understanding the physical world. As A. N. Whitehead said in *Science and the Modern World,* (Cambridge, 1946):

> The two theories (sc. the wave and particle theories of light) are contradictory. In the eighteenth century Newton's theory was believed, in the nineteenth century Huyghens's theory was believed. Today there is one large group of phenomena which can be explained only on the wave theory, and another large group which can be explained only on the corpuscular theory. Scientists have to leave it at that and wait for the future, in the hope of attaining some wider vision which reconciles both.[15]

Contrast all this with the attitude of the kind of religious thinker about whom I was speaking earlier to his contradictions concerning God. He thinks the latter profoundly significant. He shows no inclination at all to get away from them. He thinks that he has made a new and highly important theological discovery, namely, that God can only be talked about in paradoxes or contradictions. In support of this point of view reference is sometimes made to the writings of Professor John Wisdom, the Cambridge philosopher.[16] Wisdom did show that paradoxes may be cognitively significant as well as emotively expressive. They may, that is, enable us in the long run to see more clearly what is, or is not, the case. Wisdom draws a distinction between what he calls the 'domestic' logic of statements of any given type and their 'fundamental' logic. The pure logician, says Wisdom, is concerned with domestic logic. That is to say he is not concerned with whether or how far a statement of any given type is true but with how one would know the truth of one statement of one of these types given another of the same type. The metaphysician is concerned with fundamental logic. He is concerned, that is to say, with how one could know the truth of a statement of a given type, not from other statements of the same type, but from the sort of thing which in the end is the ground for any statement of the type in question. Einstein, for example, effected a change in ultimate logic so far as physics is concerned. Einstein's theories gave rise to what, from the point of view of the physics which preceded them, were paradoxical ideas as to 'the procedure proper to the proof of statements as to the dates and places at which events occur'.[17] But his theories gave us thereby a fuller understanding of the ultimate logic of such statements. Wisdom recognizes that the paradoxes of religious belief may similarly have cognitive significance. He writes :

One might have expected that in the sphere of religion everyone would have learned by now to move carefully and neither at once to accept nor hastily to reject what sounds bewildering. But no, even here we still find a tendency to reject strange statements with impatience, to turn from them as absurd or unprovable or to write them down as metaphor – deceptive, or at best, merely picturesque. Only a few months ago someone came to me troubled about the old but bewildering statement that Christ was both God and man..He has asked those who taught him theology how this *could* be true. Their answers had not

satisfied him. I was not able to tell him what the doctrine means.
But I did remind him that though some statements which seem
contradictory are self-contradictory, others are *not,* that indeed
some of the most preposterous statements ever made have turned
out to convey the most tremendous discoveries.[18] (italics mine)

I have no quarrel with all that. But I am rather worried by what
some theologians seem to want to make of it. There appears to me
to be a dangerous ambivalence in what Professor T. F. Torrance,
for example, makes of Wisdom's arguments when applied to theology. Torrance writes :

> . . . the task of a living and constructive theology, [is] to discover
> and work out the interior logic of our knowledge of God, but
> in the nature of the case it will not be able to avoid constant
> tension between the material logic thrusts upon it from the side
> of the creative and redeeming operations of God in Christ, and
> the logico-verbal atoms of our thought and speech that are
> already schematized to this world, for the Truth of God as it is
> in Christ Jesus breaks through all our linguistic and logical
> forms. While God has made His Word audible and apprehen-
> sible with our human speech and thought, refusing to be limited
> by their inadequacy in making himself known to us, He never-
> theless refuses to be understood merely from within the con-
> ceptual framework of our natural thought and language but
> demands of that framework a logical reconstruction in accord-
> ance with His Word. Hence a theology faithful to what God has
> revealed and done in Jesus Christ must involve a powerful
> element of apocalyptic, that is epistemologically speaking, an
> eschatological suspension of logical form in order to keep our
> thought ever open to what is radically new.[19]

If the reader looks back to the words which I quoted a moment or
two ago from Wisdom, he will see that, on Wisdom's view, the
fruitful paradoxes are those which are *not* self-contradictory. I am
not sure that Torrance is saying simply that. What are we to make
of his remark that 'the Truth of God as it is in Christ Jesus breaks
through *all our linguistic and logical forms*' ? (italics mine). Does
this simply mean that what at first sight appear to be self-contradictory statements about God may turn out on closer inspection
to be not self-contradictory? If so, fair enough. But is he, on the

other hand, saying that in the very nature of the case, if God is to be spoken about at all, he must be spoken about in self-contradictory terms? If so, then I do not think Wisdom meant that and, if he did, it would make nonsense of God-talk.

I have, then, two final comments to make on self-contradiction in religious belief. (i) The existence of paradoxes such as the body-mind or wave-particle paradoxes does nothing to justify the attitude some religious thinkers like Tillich adopt towards their contradictions about God. (ii) It is, of course, logically possible to hold like Otto, the view that reason cannot take us any further to a knowledge of God and so we should be guided by non-rational considerations where religion is concerned. But if anyone adopts that position, it is important that he recognize the price which has to be paid for so doing. If you call a halt to rational discussion, you call a halt to it. You are not entitled to go on turning out what purport to be rational arguments concerning God, but each time these arguments appear invalid retreating to the position that since God cannot be rationally discussed arguments concerning him do not have to be valid. That is a form of one-upmanship not unknown among religious thinkers. If religion is a matter of expressing or inducing a distinctive kind of experience through art-forms of one sort or another, so be it. But one is not justified in calling the deepening of such experience fuller knowledge of God unless one makes it perfectly clear that the word 'knowledge' is being used here in a sense quite unlike that in which it is normally used.

Using Language Intelligibly

The conception of rationality which I shall next consider is that to be rational is to use language in accordance with the normal rules for its use, that is, *intelligibly*. It is true of course that these rules are sometimes imprecise and that they may certainly change from time to time or place to place. Nevertheless at any given point in time and space generally accepted rules for the use of language exist and there is always the possibility of their being violated to the point of unintelligibility. Anyone who does so violate them has, in effect, opted out of the rational community which they constitute. The charge which some bring against religious believers, and theists in particular is that they are irrational in this way. In their mouths, when they talk of God, language 'dies by a thousand qualifications'.[20] That is to say, words are used in ways so far removed from their normal use that they lose all meaning.

I do not deny that this can happen and sometimes does. But I am not prepared to accept that theistic belief is necessarily unintelligible any more than I was, that it is of necessity self-contradictory. To make more clear precisely what the charge of unintelligibility amounts to, and in an attempt to show how talk of God can be defended against such a charge, I intend to consider one or two examples. First I shall say a little about the theistic belief that God is *good*. Then I shall pass to the equally fundamental beliefs that God *acts* in the world and *encounters* men in some way or other. In each case I will try to show why there is some force in the charge that the belief in question is unintelligible. Nevertheless I shall then attempt to defend the language of theism at the point in question against the charge of unintelligibility. I do not have space, even if I had skill, to conduct a full-scale defence of the whole language of theism. But if I can defend the characteristically theistic beliefs that God encounters men, acts in their world and in all that he is or does is good against the charge of unintelligibility, then that may give reason to hope that some sense can be made of the rest of theism.

The difficulty in speaking of God as *good* is that activity, or rather inactivity, is attributed to God which if it were attributed to a man would disqualify him for the description 'good'. If a man could, but did not, relieve the suffering of someone else who was wracked with pain or wasted with deprivation, then we would not call that man 'good'. What sense then does it make to speak of almighty God as good when he could prevent the suffering which is so rife in his creation? This is the age-old problem of evil. What I want to bring out is that the root of it is the apparent unintelligibility of the language traditionally used of God. The problem of evil arises within theism just because, on the one hand, it is part of theism to conceive of God as good, but, on the other, to conceive of him in ways which are incompatible with his being good in accordance with the normal rules for the use of that word.

There are only two ways of dealing with the problem. Either the rules for the use of 'good' must be stretched to accommodate the belief that God is omnipotent; or the concept of omnipotence must be interpreted in a way which is compatible with the normal use of 'good'.

I think that the former of these two ways is abortive. It is followed by I. T. Ramsey in his *Religious Language* (London, 1957). If I may say so, I greatly admired Ramsey for his pioneering attempts to provide a contemporary account of Christian belief which was philosophically respectable, but I think this is one of the points at which he went astray. Ramsey constructs a table of degrees of goodness. Ferdinand Lopez is *hardly* good, Long John Silver *fairly* good, and so by degrees to St Francis who is *intensely* good. After marking a gap at this point, Ramsey adds to his list God, who is *infinitely* good. The gap marked by the word 'infinitely', he argues, stimulates us to develop the model of goodness in a certain direction. But it also points us to *'something outside "good" language altogether'*.[21] He compares this use of 'infinitely' with its use in mathematics. A succession of signs can be constructed which progresses infinitely towards 2 without ever reaching it, 2 being a limit word to this series, but standing outside it and being of a different logical status. So when God is defined as infinitely good, there is a logical gap between what 'good' means in the case even of a St Francis and what it means in the case of God. So far so good. But trouble starts when Ramsey suggests that this logical gap allows the theist to dismiss such troublesome questions as, 'If God is good, why does he permit evils which good men would not permit if they had his power?'. According to Ramsey this question confuses a *logical oddity,* namely goodness in God, with a *logical commonplace,* namely goodness in man.[22] He evidently thinks it no contradiction to say that God is *infinitely* good and permits evils to occur, though it would be self-contradictory to say that God is *very* good and permits the occurrence of evils. Notice what a high price the theist has to pay for this manœuvre. If 'God' in 'God is good' is, as Ramsey says, something outside 'good' language altogether, what does this amount to in the end, if not an admission that God is *not* good in any intelligible sense of the word? Ramsey would no doubt have replied that 'good' in 'God is good' both *is* and *is not* outside 'good' language. But what are we to make of that? It amounts to nothing more than a special plea to be allowed to use language unintelligibly where God is concerned.

For my own part I take the other way : the problem of evil is to be solved by careful interpretation of the omnipotence attributed to God. In a paper entitled 'An Attempt to Defend Theism' (*Philosophy,* 1964) I tried to show that God's omnipotence can, and should, be interpreted, at least within Christian theism, as the omnipotence *of love.* I have space to do no more than outline the argument in the briefest terms. A world in which there are personal beings possessed of free will is, other things being equal, better than one in which there are not. God, being good, chose to create a world in which there are such personal beings. They can, and do exercise their free will to do evil. It is conceivable that their evil doing and its consequences should reach such proportions that a good God could no longer tolerate it. But it is also conceivable that a good God should, by sustained and unrestricted love, win from free personal beings a response which would lead them to turn from evil to do good. We do not strain the ordinary meaning of 'good' in 'a good God' here, nor the ordinary meaning of 'love' in the thought of 'sustained and unrestricted love' winning such a response. In so acting God would exercise the omnipotence of love. That is to say, he would be able to *do all that an agent who loves can be conceived to do.* It would be in accordance with the thought of God as good, in the ordinary meaning of 'good', that he should prefer a world with free personal beings in it to one without, and that he should seek to overcome their evil doing by the redemption which love can effect rather than by destroying them. I think a solution of the problem of evil along such lines is possible.

I appreciate that, if such lines are followed, problems arise. For instance, what about natural, as distinct from moral, evils? I confess that I have no clear answer to this question but I think that, so to say, the onus of proof is on the other side. It needs to be shown – and I doubt if it can – that a good God would, as such, never have created free personal beings, for all the positive value which their existence would have added to his creation, rather than allow them to suffer natural evils such as famine and pestilence. Natural evils remains a difficulty for the theist who takes the line which I have taken, but not, I think, an utterly damning one.

Another difficulty has to do with the notion of free will. It has been argued that for any personal being to have free will in the ordinary meaning of 'free will' it is only necessary that the causes of his actions should not arise, so to speak, outside himself. It is not necessary that his actions should be uncaused, only that they should be caused by motives which he would *recognize* as his own. Now, if this is so, then God could (logically) have given men free will, in the ordinary sense of 'free will', but ensured that in the case of each what I have called 'the motives which he would recognize as his own' were *good* motives. In which case men would never have exercised their free will in doing what was evil and hence moral evils and their consequences would never have occurred. If God could have achieved this result and did not do so, then how can he be good in any ordinary sense of 'good'? This is a cogent argument but not, I think, triumphant. It is an essential tenet of theism that God stands related to men as the divine self over against several individual human selves. Now, it would be contrary to the ordinary meaning of 'self' to conceive of anyone as a self, if all his motives are pre-determined by some other self. Therefore it is not compatible with theism to suppose that the divine self, God, could (logically) have pre-determined all the motives of all human selves to be good and these latter remained selves.

If this way which I have taken is plausible it saves the meaning of 'good' from erosion into unintelligibility where God is concerned.

The other two beliefs which I said that I would consider are (i) that God *acts* in the world and (ii) that under certain circumstances God, *meets* or encounters men in the world. These two beliefs are implicit in the whole of theism. The God of theism, and in particular the Christian God, is a God who acts in the world as benign providence; and who meets or encounters men as, to use H. H. Farmer's expressions, 'ultimate demand' and 'final succour'. The charge of unintelligibility arises on both counts because theists, besides believing these things about God also believe that he is an immaterial or spiritual being who has no physical body. Philosophical critics of theism hold that it does not make sense to say that a being without a physical body can act in the world or meet with men. I will take two examples of such criticism, one from Professor Paul Edwards and the other from Professor R. W. Hepburn, and then I will comment upon them.

Edwards thinks it unintelligible to speak of God as acting when he has no physical body. He writes :

I have no doubt that when most people think about God and his alleged activities, here or in the hereafter, they vaguely think of him as possessing some kind of rather large body. Now, if we are told that there is a God who is, say, just and good and kind and loving and powerful and wise and if, (a) it is made clear that these words are used in one of their ordinary senses, and (b) God is not asserted to be a disembodied mind, then it seems plain to me that *to that extent* a series of meaningful assertions has been made. And this is so whether we are told that God's justice, mercy, etc. are 'limitless' or merely that God is superior to all human beings in these respects. However, it seems to me all these words lose their meaning if we are told that God does not possess a body. Anyone who thinks otherwise without realizing this, I think, is supplying a body in the background of his images. For what would it be like to be, say, just, without a body? To be just, a person has to *act* justly – he has to behave in certain ways. This is not reductive materialism. It is simple empirical truth about what we mean by 'just'. But how is it possible to perform these acts, to behave in the required ways, without a body? Similar remarks apply to the other divine attributes.[23]

Two issues, both of which seem to be touched on here, must be clearly differentiated, namely the psychological and the logical issues. We are not concerned with the former. It may as a matter of psychological fact be the case, as Edwards says, that people 'vaguely think of [God] as possessing some kind of rather large body' or that they 'without realizing [it] . . . [supply] a body in the background of [their] images', when they talk about God acting. But that is beside the point for our purposes. What does, or does not, go on in people's minds when they talk about God is a question for the experimental psychologist not the philosopher as such. Our concern is with the logical issue : what does the word 'acts' *mean* when 'used in one of [its] ordinary senses'? Is it true, as Edwards avers, that the words 'acts justly' (etc.) *'lose their meaning if we are told that God does not possess a body'*? The problem here is not what anyone happens to think or to imagine at any given time, but what it does, or does not, make sense to *say*.

Edwards's point with which we must deal, is about the meaning of words. It is to the effect that it is nonsense to say 'God acts' where 'God' is defined as 'a disembodied mind' and 'acts' is used in 'one of [its] ordinary senses'. To this we shall return in a moment.

Hepburn thinks it unintelligible to speak of God meeting with men when he has no physical body.

He begins by pointing out that personal relationships can become less and less dependent upon 'use of bodily features, sounds and appearances' and offers these examples:

(a) Someone is noticing very carefully all my hand and arm movements, the expression in my eyes, the modulations of my voice etc. in order to impersonate me. He watches me as he might watch a thing in order to discover how it works.

(b) A friend observes my gestures and changes of expression and listens to what I say. He does so in order to find out what I am thinking or feeling. He treats me as a person whose ideas or feelings he wishes to understand or to share.

(c) Someone I love is sitting with me in the dark. We cannot see or feel each other and we say nothing at all, yet we are deeply conscious of each other's presence and it is important to us to bc together.[24]

In these examples bodily movements seem to become progressively less essential to the encounter as we move from (a) to (c). The question which they raise, as Hepburn points out, is: *can a point be reached at which an encounter would not depend at all upon bodily movement?* The relevance of that question to our present discussion is, of course, that if the answer to it is yes, then we can make sense of the claim that God, who has no physical body, nevertheless meets with or encounters men. Hepburn for his part thinks that the answer is no. He makes two points in support of that opinion: (i) even in a case like encounter (c) above, our awareness of another person is logically parasitic upon our recollections of his bodily movements on past occasions, that is on gestures which we have seen him use, on words we have heard him speak, or things which we have watched him do; (ii) however intimately I may know somebody, my knowledge of his character or personality may always be increased by something new which he says or does, i.e. by his bodily movements. And Hepburn argues that the hope of a personal relationship entirely independent of bodily movement could (logically) not be fulfilled for the following reason :

> I might imagine that the ideal here would be a state where I did not have to see John flush, hear him slam doors, and shout, to know that he was angry : but simply knew it as John knows it himself. I should feel the ascent of blood to the head, the kinaesthetic feelings that go with cry-uttering and door-slamming, the tension and temptation to lose control. But how could this be distinguished from temporarily *becoming John*? This would be not to *encounter* some other personality, but to *assume* another personality. Or, if that sounds too fantastic, one could describe the situation in quite another way : by saying that instead of encountering an angry John (which was my original aim), I now merely become angry myself – a very different thing.[25]

In becoming John, I would render it logically impossible for me to have a relationship with John.

Turning his attention now to the particular case of God, Hepburn notes that some religious thinkers have compared a man's encounter with God to his encounter with another human will. Farmer, for instance, describes an essentially personal relationship as 'an awareness of the other [person's] will as standing over against our own in a certain polarity or tension'. In an I-thou relationship, Farmer holds, we encounter another person's will both as something in which we can trust (succour) and as something which lays claims upon us (demand). He finds some counterpart to this in our experience of unconditional values; that is, those moral claims to tell the truth, show benevolence, etc. which to the man of sensitive conscience admit of no exception. Will, he thinks, is the core of personality and in these unconditional values God encounters man as will. The ultimacy and absoluteness of the claim which unconditional values lay upon us are an indication that they have their source in that which is other than themselves and which, Farmer thinks, we are entitled to take to be God's will. He concedes that our awareness of will in another human being is given through impressions which certain of the other's bodily movements make on us. But he thinks that this condition need not be fulfilled in the case of the divine will.[26] To all of which Hepburn replies :

My anxiety about this is that the transition from human to divine encounters (whether or not valid) has been made to look deceptively smooth. We learn the use of the word 'will' by being shown people persisting in difficult tasks, ignoring distractions, grunting and perspiring with effort, and so on. We remember ourselves clearing our desks of holiday snapshots, keeping our pen moving though the wrist ached, muttering to ourselves 'However long it takes me, I'll finish it tonight'. What is very doubtful indeed is whether anyone could conceivably be in a position to say, 'I am sure X is "willing", but this is not revealed through his uttering a command or by signs of tension on his face or hands, or by any resolute behaviour. Nor did he predict or promise or otherwise give me reason to believe that he would exercise his will at this hour of the day'. The point at stake here is not that Farmer is necessarily wrong when he stresses the importance of will in personal relations. The misleading move is the statement, 'will means person'. This is true (and trivial) if it means 'once you are entitled to claim contact with someone's will, you are entitled to claim contact with that person'. For instance, I have heard the resolute commands, seen the clenching of fists, noted the absence of wavering. This is indeed the Sergeant-major and no wraith. But it by no means follows that if I have an experience that I want to call 'experiencing a will' (a sense as of a will over against me), I am entitled to say, 'I am therefore in contact with a person (although the usual manifestations are lacking)'.[27]

On such grounds then Hepburn claims that the ordinary sense of 'meet' will not permit us to say that though God has no physical body he can (logically) meet with men. In his view meeting someone, even if it is not logically identical with, is nevertheless logically dependent upon, the awareness of the other being's bodily movements past or present. If God has no physical body, then of course he cannot engage in bodily movements. It follows, according to Hepburn's line of argument, that we cannot therefore be said to meet with God nor he with us.

It is important to grasp the precise point which is being made by Edwards and Hepburn. They are maintaining that it is a *necessary* condition of a being acting in the world or meeting with men that the being concerned should have a physical body. A necessary, not a sufficient, condition. A is a sufficient condition of B, if, given A, B must exist or occur; A is a necessary condition of B, if, given B, A must exist or occur, (or in each case, 'must have existed or occurred'). Edwards and Hepburn are *not* saying that if God has a physical body then it follows logically that he is a being who acts in the world or meets with men. They *are* saying that if he is a being who acts in the world or meets with men, then it is logically necessary that he should have a physical body.

We may pause for a moment to see why they cannot say the former : i.e. that having a physical body is a sufficient condition of a being's acting in the world or meeting with men. It is because neither of the words 'act' or 'meet' – at least as applied to *conscious* beings and God is conceived within theism as a conscious being – can be 'cashed' entirely in terms of bodily conditions or movements. Let me try to make this clear by two examples.

Take first the remark 'Smith kicked Jones'. This reports an action performed by Smith. When Smith kicked Jones certain movements of, and changes within, Smith's physical body took place. These constituted a causally-connected series of spatio-temporal events culminating in the impact of Smith's foot on Jones' shin. When this series of events is described, does it follow logically from the description that Smith kicked Jones? There seems good reason to think not. What if Smith was off-balance and collided with Jones? What if he was lifting his foot in order to tie his shoelace and Jones's shin got in the way? On either of these suppositions, the bodily movements involved could (logically) have been the same as those involved in Smith's kicking Jones. Or so it would appear. It may be, of course, that if the descriptions of the causally-connected spatio-temporal events were filled out, some difference would appear between, for example, the description in the case where Smith was off-balance and collided with Jones and that in the case where Smith kicked Jones. But, it is to say the least, not immediately apparent that this would be so. However complete we made the description of the bodily movements involved where action is said to have taken place, I think we should find on reflection that it was *logically compatible with* more than one answer to the question : what was the agent concerned *doing*? If this is so then no description of bodily movements or conditions can (logically) serve as the sufficient condition for any particular action being said to have occurred.

If the question is raised 'How then can we know what action has occurred?', the answer seems clearly to be : when we know the agent's intention. 'What were you doing?' we ask Smith. 'I was kicking Jones' he says. If we had no reason to think (i) that he is trying to deceive us or (ii) that he does not understand the meaning of the words which he is using, then we would normally take his reply to answer the question with finality. We may remonstrate with him and say 'Oh come, surely you weren't doing that!' But if he persists in affirming that he was, there can be no appeal against this insistence. As Professor S. Hampshire has pointed out, given the fulfilment of conditions (i) and (ii) immediately above, an agent can never be accused of not knowing what he is doing without it being implied in the accusation that the 'action' in question is not intentional.[28] I put 'action' in quotation marks here because, although that word is sometimes used of unintentional behaviour, its normal use implies intention. When it is said by Christians that God acts in the world, what is meant is certainly that God acts intentionally. All I have been concerned to bring out so far is that the word 'acts' in 'God acts in the world' cannot be reduced to any description of bodily movement.

Let me bring out the same point with regard to the word 'met'. 'Smith met Jones'. A moment's reflection will show that the word 'met' here cannot be 'cashed' solely in terms of movement of, or changes in, the bodies of Smith or Jones or both. It may be that they could (logically) not have met, unless certain spatio-temporal events had occurred, e.g. their hands touched, sounds were made by, or heard by, either or both of them, and so on. But suppose that Smith had been hypnotized into saying 'Hello!' when he saw Jones and that is all he said and then passed on, would it be a normal use of the word 'met' to say that he had met Jones? I think not. Meeting – at least in the sense of personal encounter which is the only sense in which we are interested here – must be intentional. Unless a person who encounters another person is aware of and intends to do what he is doing, it would not be accurate to say that he had met the other person. So, since theists conceive of God's encounter with men as personal, bodily movement cannot be its sufficient condition.

In both these examples, the element added to bodily movement (or condition) in the meaning of the words 'act' and 'meet' is intention. It is intention which cannot (logically) be reduced to bodily movement. This can be shown in the following way. We noted that we know a man's intention when we know his answer to 'What are you doing?' or 'What have you been doing?' But if we knew that the answer which someone gave to this question was one which he had been hypnotized to give, or in any other way physically or psychologically conditioned by someone else into giving, then we should not accept that answer as a genuine statement of intention. It is never a sufficient condition of a statement being a statement of intention that any set of bodily movements, however numerous or complex, can be said to have occurred.

No theist, of course, wishes to say that bodily movement (or condition) is a sufficient condition of God acting or meeting with men. But it is important in a discussion such as that which I am here conducting to take possibilities one at a time in order to get the issues clear. Having got rid of the possibility that bodily movement is a sufficient condition of intentional action or encounter, we are in a better position to see clearly what is involved in the claim that it is a *necessary* condition. Edwards and Hepburn both claim, as we saw above, that the possession of a physical body is a *necessary* condition of any being, divine or human, acting in the world or meeting with men. The possibility that this is correct is a much more difficult matter for a theist to deal with and I am not at all sure that I can dispose of that possibility successfully.

It should be noted that this difficulty is not simply that of unpacking the notions of action or encounter without some reference to bodily movement (or condition). Added to that is the problem of how a being who acts or meets with other beings is to be *identified* if he has no physical body. There is not only the problem that bodily movement seems to be a necessary condition of the intelligibility of the verbs 'to act' or 'to meet', but that the possession of a physical body seems *prima facie* to be a necessary condition of any subject of these verbs being identified as such. 'Smith kicks Jones'. 'Smith meets Jones'. We can make sense of each remark only if there is some way of knowing who is being referred to by the name 'Smith'. This can be known because Smith has a physical body which can be located in space and time and thus identified. He may not be logically identical with his physical body – his possession of a physical body may be only a necessary condition of our being able to know who he is – but if it is the latter, then we could not identify him without his body, and so could not make sense of talk about him if he possessed none. So, if *ex hypothesi* God has no physical body, how are we to make sense of talk about him?

Drawing these issues together, there are two main questions which have to be faced : (i) how can God, if he has no physical body, intervene in the course of spatio-temporal events in the ways in which he must (logically) intervene if he is to be said to act in the world or to meet with men?; and (ii) what is to take the place in the case of God of that identification of the subject of the verbs 'to act' or 'to meet' by means of the spatio-temporal location of the subject's physical body? Of all the issues which I consider in this book, it seems to me that this is the point at which the shoe pinches hardest for anyone who wishes to offer a philosophical defence of religious belief in general and theism in particular. It is the very essence of the latter that God, an identifiable being, acts in the world and meets with men. Contemporary attempts to circumvent the problem about the intelligibility of such beliefs by substituting for God the notion of the ground of being or the gracious neighbour, and for God's activity and presence in the world, the notions of human freedom or alongsideness, succeed only at the price of making theism logically indistinguishable from humanism. A price, which for me at least, is too high. If I have been right in my fundamental contention throughout this book that the concept of god, i.e. of some form of transcendent consciousness and agency, is constitutive of religion, and so of theism, then it is absolutely imperative that I offer some plausible answer to the two main questions formulated immediately above. In order to answer either of them it is necessary to find some logical substitute in God's case for a physical body. Can this be done?

I want to hazard the suggestion that spatio-temporal events may serve as a substitute for a physical body in the case of God. I will apply this suggestion to the two main questions in reverse order, taking as an example of the kind of spatio-temporal event (or sequence of events) which I have in mind the deliverance of the Israelites from Egypt as this is recorded in the Old Testament.

If it is said 'God delivered them', can God who performed this act be identified as follows? There are two elements to the belief that God delivered Israel from Egypt : (a) the succession of events which constituted Israel's escape from Egypt, namely the plagues, Pharoah's initial release of the Israelites, the dividing of the Red Sea when he subsequently pursued them, etc.; and (b) the relational idea, as Professor W. A. Christian has called it, of 'an agent who ordered or arranged' these events.[29] If (a) and (b) are now put together, we have spatio-temporal events which 'point to' God and thus he can (logically) now be identified as that to which they 'point'. The difficulty in all this is, of course, that 'point' has to be written within quotation marks since it is not being used in its normal sense. How can one (literally) point to that which is beyond time and space as God, by definition, is? Perhaps this difficulty can be surmounted because all we are trying to make sense of is the notion of a logical subject of sentences attributing activity or encounter to God and, in order to do so, we only need some way of tying in the concept of God (though defined as non-spatial and non-temporal) *intelligibly* with other concepts which we wish to use, such as those of acting or meeting. And the empirically observable evidence of Israel's flight from Egypt, for instance, *is* tied in even with the notion of a not empirically observable God by the concept of agency.

This is made perhaps the more acceptable as a logical move, when we bear in mind that the concept of agency cannot (logically) be identified with that of bodily movement. There is always a logical gap between an agent as such and what may be called his situation.[30] Suppose Smith's situation is that he is bankrupt. It makes sense to ask Smith 'What are you going to do about your bankruptcy?' The idea of Smith, the agent, 'stepping back' so to speak from his situation and forming some intention as to how he will deal with it makes perfectly good sense. Now, the point to take is that exactly the same will be true if Smith's situation is that he has a broken leg or is suffering from kleptomania, for examples. That is to say, Smith's body and indeed Smith's psyche can be conceived as part of Smith's situation from which as agent he is logically distinct. He, as agent, is not to be identified with his broken leg or his compulsive psychological mechanism any more than with his bankruptcy. There is, that is to say, some kind of Cartesian parallelism in the last analysis between mind and body even in the case of human agents. Mind and body cannot (logically) be reduced either to other or both to some unifying concept. If an agent is logically distinct from his body and if the latter can be regarded as part of his situation, then why not a like parallelism between certain intentional acts of God and certain spatio-temporal events in the world? On the one hand *God wills* the deliverance of Israel from Egypt; on the other hand, *the waters part* before the Israelites as they flee.

In the case of a human agent we normally know what to attribute to his agency because we observe a causal connection between movements of his physical body and spatio-temporal events occurring in the world. We know that Smith kicked Jones because we saw Smith's foot come into contact with Jones's shin. This is not, as we said, a sufficient condition of saying that Smith kicked Jones; but normally it would be a necessary condition of saying so that someone had observed Smith's foot come into physical contact with Jones's shin. Our problem is that such observations cannot be made in the case of God because God has no body. However, we sometimes speak of a human agent doing something when we have not observed any movements of his body in this connection. We attribute what has happened to his agency because we believe it to be the kind of thing that he would have done. A letter comes through the post containing a cheque for fifty pounds which we urgently need and we say to ourselves 'It's good old Uncle Fred coming to the rescue as usual'. True, it is not impossible in principle for anyone to have observed Uncle Fred writing the cheque as it would have been impossible in principle for anyone to have observed God parting the waters before Israel. That difference may be damning against the case which I am trying to make for God as a bodiless agent. However, the fact that agency can never be reduced to bodily movement seems to allow that to attribute agency to Uncle Fred, where all that we can observe are certain spatio-temporal events taken to be the consequences of his agency, is not a logically different move from attributing agency to him, where certain movements of his body can also be observed. The movements of Uncle Fred's hand as he writes the cheque are *not* identical with his drawing the cheque any more than its arrival through our letter-box is identical with his sending it. We say that he drew it and we say that he sent it : in both cases we are referring to that which is logically distinct from any movement of Uncle Fred's body. It is true that we could not (logically) say that he had drawn the cheque if there had been no movement of the pen in his hand on paper, just as we could not say that he had sent it if there had been no delivering of it through our letter-box. It may be, that is to say, that some spatio-temporal events must (logically) occur, where agency occurs. But this does not mean of course that the agency is not logically distinct from these events. Note that I am *not* suggesting that bodiless agency means agency in the absence of some spatio-temporal event(s). On the contrary, when God acts or meets with men, something spatio-temporal always occurs. But, to revert to my example, does it make all the difference that the hand which drew the cheque was Uncle Fred's and the hand which put it through the letter-box was the postman's? What I have been suggesting is that it does not : that Uncle Fred's agency was logically distinct from the hand movement in both cases *and therefore it would not be entirely unintelligible* to attribute something which goes on in the world to an agent even though one could not identify *anything in the world* as his hand. If this is intelligible, then we *can* make sense of the notion of a bodiless agent and so of the belief that God acts in the world and meets with men. It then makes sense to speak of certain occurrences in the world as God's actions simply on the ground that they are characteristic of God as we take him to be. Of course, all kinds of questions would remain. What *do* we take God to be? Have we any good grounds for taking him to be that? Which events in the world do we attribute to him and which not – and why? And so on. But all such questions are beside the present point. I am only concerned here with whether or not sense can be made of the belief that a conscious being who has no body acts in the world and meets with men. I have, very tentatively, suggested a way in which I think that might be done.

As I have already indicated I think that concept of rationality which I have been considering in this section raises the most crucial questions concerning the philosophical respectability of religious belief. My aim has been to show that, judged by the criterion that to be rational is to use language intelligibly, religious belief – and in particular some form of Christian theism – can survive as rational. A god who is good and who acts in the world and meets with men is a conception of which as a theist I must be able to make some sense. If I have gone *any way* to showing that I can I am more than satisfied.

Pascal's Wager

The fourth conception of rationality which I shall consider is that which lies behind 'Pascal's Wager', so called because it occurs in Pascal's *Pensées*. Recently Pascal's argument has been restated thus by Prof. R. G. Swinburne: 'The rational man is the man who pursues a policy if and only if he judges that the expected gain . . . from it exceeds the expected gain (positive or negative) from not pursuing the policy'. The expression 'expected gain' here is defined by Swinburne as follows:

> The expected gain from a policy is the sum of the values of each possible outcome of the policy, each multiplied by the probability of that outcome.[31]

Take an example which Swinburne uses. Suppose a man has to decide between betting and not betting on a horse. The probability that it will win he estimates at two in ten, and that it will lose, at eight in ten. The bookies offer six to one against. He is able to stake £1.00. The expected gain of betting is:

$$£6.00 \times 0.2 - £1.00 \times 0.8 = £0.40$$

and the expected gain of not betting is:

$$£0.00 \times 0.2 - £0.00 \times 0.8 = £0.00$$

£0.40 is a greater gain than £0.00, and on these odds a rational man as such will stake his £1.00, provided of course that the situation is not complicated by the fact that for him to lose £1.00 would be as *undesirable* as it would be desirable for him to gain £6.00. In this latter case the expected gain of betting would be in effect:

$$£1.00 \times 0.2 - £1.00 \times 0.8 = - £0.60$$

against the expected gain of not betting as above, that is £0.00. In such case a rational man as such would *not* bet.

Pascal applied this conception of rationality to religious belief and Swinburne attempts to rehabilitate that application of it. Religious belief promises an infinite gain to those who embrace it. Should one trust this promise and embrace religious belief? It may cost something to do so. Let us call what it is actually going to cost X. X then, is a finite gain from which one excludes oneself if one embraces religious belief : it is all those things which one will have to go without if one becomes a believer. So, if one's trust in the promise of an infinite gain from religious belief *is* disappointed, one will have sacrificed X for nothing. But if this trust is *not* disappointed, one will have sacrificed X for the sake of an infinite gain. Now, however *low* the probability that one will *not* be disappointed that probability times an infinite gain will amount to *more* than the highest conceivable probability that one *will* be disappointed times X. In general terms :

'Probability that you will not be disappointed (however *low*) ✕ *Infinite* Gain' is a *greater product* than 'probability that you will be disappointed (however *high*) ✕ a finite gain'.

By the criterion of rationality which we are here considering, the rational man as such will back the chance of winning the infinite gain from becoming a religious believer, provided of course that it is not as undesirable for him to lose X as it would be desirable for him to win this infinite gain. But the proviso here is necessarily fulfilled because it could *not* (logically) be as undesirable to lose any finite gain as it would be desirable to win any infinite gain.

This argument seems to me to have much to commend it but certain questions arise in connection with it, as Swinburne rightly points out and to these I will briefly refer.

What is the 'infinite gain', which religious belief promises? Pascal thought of it as everlasting bliss – heaven as against hell – but it need not mean that literally. Provided a man thinks that the gain which religious belief would bring is infinitely desirable, the argument works. It is the task of advocates of any religion to show the difference which belief in it makes to those who embrace it. Presumably they themselves believe the gain to be infinite. It is up to them to give some plausible explanation as to why and how it is. With the decline of what theists would now consider crude ideas of everlasting life in heaven and hell, that task may well have become more difficult. But we should not assume it to be impossible. It may make sense to say, as for example a writer such as Malcolm Muggeridge seems to wish to say, that the gain in one's psychological condition, or in the orientation and satisfaction of one's practical life, which comes through religion, is infinite here and now.

A second question is: what does it mean to speak of *embracing* religious belief? One cannot *make* oneself believe things. However, there is reason to think that one *can put oneself in the way* of acquiring religious belief. If it can be shown – as perhaps it can – that there is a certain degree of probability that people who engage in, for instance, Christian worship and service, even when they are not believers to start with, tend to become believers as a result of the effect which such worship and service have upon them, then one can put oneself in the way of acquiring religious belief. The above argument will still work if we have to say, not that the rational man will embrace belief, but that he will, as a rational man, put himself in the way of acquiring belief for the sake of the infinite gain which will accrue to him should he be fortunate enough to become a believer.

But the question arises, in the light of what has just been said: is it morally right to put oneself in the way of belief, if one thinks that there is a low degree of probability that such belief is true? I have said that however *low* the probability that trust in religion will not be disappointed, the fact that if it is not disappointed, there will be an infinite gain, requires a rational man to put himself in the way of embracing it. But is it morally right to try to acquire beliefs, the truth of which one thinks has low probability? There are many who would say that it is not. And they would advance this as an argument against proceeding in accordance with Pascal's wager. R. G. Swinburne counters this objection by pointing out that there is nothing immoral in choosing to believe one of two exhaustive alternatives between which one cannot decide by rational assessment of the evidence. Even if one thinks it improbable that religious belief is true, the fact, if it is a fact, that one can never prove it to be either true or false, may remove all moral objection to proceeding in accordance with Pascal's wager.

Open-Mindedness

The fifth conception of rationality which I shall consider is, in a word, open-mindedness. The case for this conception of rationality is most persuasively argued in a book entitled '*The Retreat to Commitment*' (London, 1964) by the American philosopher, Professor W. W. Bartley III. He calls the conception of rationality for which he argues in that book 'comprehensively critical rationalism' and he defines one who evinces such rationality thus (in the first italicized portion Bartley italicizes 'all', the rest of the italics are mine) :

> A rationalist [is] to be characterized as *one who holds all his beliefs, including his most fundamental standards and his basic philosophical position itself, open to criticism*; who never cuts off an argument by resorting to faith or irrational commitment to justify some belief which has been under severe critical fire. I shall call this conception *comprehensively critical rationalism*.[32]

Bartley contrasts this conception of rationality with two others which, he says, are unacceptable. One of these he calls 'comprehensive rationalism' : this is the view that there can be standards of rationality which are demonstrably self-justifying. The other he calls 'critical rationalism' : this is the view that rationality simply is what it is and needs no justification. The former conception he rejects because the quest for justification seems to involve an infinite regress : one standard has to be justified by reference to another and so *ad infinitum*. The latter conception of rationality he finds objectionable because it lays rationality open to the charge that in the last analysis it is based on an irrational commitment.

Bartley's aim was to arrive at a conception of rationalism which required no justification beyond itself, yet rendered it logically possible for a rationalist to be rational even where his adherence to the basic standards of rationalism was concerned. This is what he believed that he had provided in comprehensively critical rationalism as just defined.

There has been of late considerable controversy amongst philosophers as to whether or not it is possible to hold one's rationalism open to criticism as Bartley says that a rationalist must. 'Possible' here may mean either psychologically or logically possible.

Bartley seems to think that we can, if we so wish, as a matter of empirical psychological fact, hold even our deepest assurances with a degree of detachment sufficient to abandon them if good reason for doing so comes to light. It is, to say the least, doubtful whether this is true. Even the most sceptical of thinkers feels absolutely certain that a very great number of his beliefs are true; and it is perhaps facile to suggest that he could abandon all these in the ordinary way of thinking. If he had to surrender a large proportion of these assurances, might this not be like discovering that he was subject to bouts of insanity – an experience which completely undermined his confidence in his reasoning powers and threw all his ordinary ways of thinking into chaos? However, I do not want to make much of this psychological point because the logical question is much more important.

Is it *logically* possible to do what Bartley says that a rationalist must? Bartley supports his claim that it is by challenging anyone who rejects his theory of rationality to show that comprehensively critical rationalism – i.e. a rationalist's 'basic philosophical position' – is *un*criticizable. His opponents need to be able to show this, Bartley thinks, if they are going to substantiate their view that it is impossible for a critical rationalist to be critically rational about his rationalism. Bartley is confident that his opponents cannot meet this challenge.

Controversy about Bartley's theory of rationality has centred largely around this challenge. Professor J. W. W. Watkins has argued that Bartley is not really putting his theory at risk by his challenge because the latter cannot possibly be met.

> If the critic [sc. of comprehensive critical rationalism] comes nowhere near to meeting the challenge, Bartley wins; and if the critic *does* come near to meeting the challenge, the critic loses, since his nearly successful criticism establishes criticizability.[33]

A challenge which cannot be met is no challenge. A theory which nothing could conceivably falsify is uninteresting and without significance. This, Watkins thinks, is the case with Bartley's challenge and with the theory, i.e. comprehensively critical rationalism, which it purports to put at hazard.

Against Watkins, some philosophers have contended that Bartley's theory of rationality is like any other theory in that:

> ... it can be conclusively shown to be criticizable (refutable) only after the event – when it has clearly been successfully criticized (refuted).

They point out that:

> ... a reinforcement of the criticizability of CCR (i.e. comprehensively critical rationalism) need not be a reinforcement of

CCR in the sense of a heightened inducement to hold CCR; on the contrary an admissible criticism of CCR might force one to reject CCR.

They would claim that it makes no sense to speak of the successful criticism (i.e. refutation) of a theory as *confirming* it. In this they must surely be right.

Watkins for his part could perhaps agree but say that it is just this fact which Bartley overlooks and in overlooking it renders comprehensively critical rationalism meaningless. But this in turn might be countered with the reply that the vacuousness of Bartley's challenge, as Watkins interprets it, creates a presumption that Bartley must have intended by his challenge something other than Watkins takes him to have intended. Watkins's opponents offer this as an account of Bartley's intention :

> Bartley's challenge was not to attempt to show CCR to be un-criticizable by showing all its standards to be uncriticizable – as Watkins rightly shows, this cannot be done – but rather to refute CCR, show it to be inconsistent, by showing at least one of its standards to be uncriticizable. The vulnerability of CCR to attack is, thus, independent of the fact that every attack establishes the criticizability of the programme as a whole.[34]

The controversy continues and I confess that I cannot yet see with certainty who has the better of it. But for what my opinion is worth I think that it is unfair to Bartley to dismiss his argument as though it resolved itself into nothing but a vacuous challenge. He is surely correct in fastening upon open-mindedness as an essential element in what we ordinarily mean by rationality. He is entitled to raise the question 'Is there *anything* which we cannot be open-minded about?' and to support his view that there is not by asking for examples which prove otherwise.

There is, however, on the one hand, a *difficulty* which I find in Bartley's position and, on the other, a *question* which it prompts me to ask. I will say a little about each.

The *difficulty* which I find in Bartley's position resides in his belief that a rationalist could (logically) *as such* give up rationalism. Bartley says :

> ... A comprehensively critical rationalist who was not *committed* to the belief that his position was the correct one could be argued, or argue himself, out of his rationalism.[35]

A rationalist might discover, for instance, that certain things have to be accepted if there is to be argument at all. For example, that true premises will lead to true conclusions. So he might find that he must either (a) give up argument or (b) give up comprehensively critical rationalism. It is conceivable that, as a comprehensively critical rationalist, he should choose the latter course. He could (logically) thus be led by rational procedures to give up rationalism.

Now, it is one thing to say that a rationalist as such could give up every standard to which he, as a matter of empirical fact, adheres. But it is another to say that he could give up rationalism itself. If I gave up rationalism *for some good reason* would I have given it up?

Bartley says that for a rationalist to give up rationalism is like a democrat voting for the abolition of democracy.

> Just as it is possible for a democracy, through democratic processes to commit suicide (e.g. through a majority vote to abolish democracy in favour of totalitarianism), so a comprehensively critical rationalist who was not *committed* to the belief that his position was the correct one, could be argued or argue himself, out of his rationalism.[36]

There is certainly nothing incoherent in the idea of democrats using their voting powers to end democracy. But in so far as a rationalist is someone who has reasons for what he does, is it coherent to suppose that a rationalist should have reasons for giving up rationalism? Would not that be self-contradictory? A rationalist is not simply someone who is prepared to give up the beliefs which he holds. He is someone who is prepared to give up his beliefs, *if, and only if, there is good reason to do so.* Would it make sense to say that anyone had good reason to stop reasoning? I am inclined to say that it would not. But though that is my conclusion, I still think that it is very important to take Bartley's point that to be rational is to be open-minded – that is, as open-minded as it is logically possible to be.

The *question* which Bartley's account of rationalism prompts

me to ask is : can a religious believer – and in particular a Christian
theist – evince a degree of open-mindedness which qualifies him
for the description 'rational'? Bartley is at pains to emphasize the
difference between the open-mindedness, which he takes to constitute rationalism, and Christian belief. He says :

> ... Theologians have argued that not only to abandon
> allegiance to Christ, but even to subject that allegiance to criti-
> cism, is to forsake Christianity. But for a comprehensively
> critical rationalist, continued subjection to criticism of his
> allegiance to rationality is explicitly *part* of his rationalism.[37]

I wish to claim that the difference is not as great as Bartley makes
it out to be. The view of religious belief for which I have argued in
this book indisputably allows for a good deal of open-mindedness.
In Chapter 1, I presented religious belief as not so much the acceptance of a creed but the exploration of a universe of discourse. At
the end of my account of the logical structure of religious belief
I emphasized that this account of it permits, indeed welcomes,
new religious explanations and experiences and the giving up of
old ones in so far as they are incompatible with the new. A
rationalist as such when he gives up or changes a belief does so for
what he considers good reasons. A rationalist *in religion* will necessarily be someone who does so for what he considers good *religious*
reasons. I suggest that *within* religion it is possible to hold *all* the
beliefs, which as a matter of empirical fact one holds, open to
abandonment or revision if one has, or thinks one has, good religious reasons for doing so. Even within one form of religious belief, such as Christian theism, it is possible to be rational in this
sense.

Bartley speaks as if Christianity consisted fundamentally of the
acceptance of certain dogmas concerning the Person or the Work
of Christ, which dogmas constitute, in his words, 'allegiance to
Christ'. But I think it possible to interpret Christianity differently.
True it involves allegiance to Christ. But the latter does not mean –
or need not – what Bartley takes it to mean. Allegiance to Christ,
in a perfectly acceptable Christian interpretation of that phrase
means giving the concept of God content from what is observable
in Christ. This process is dynamic. Not only does recent Christian
theologizing show this to be the case but the whole history of
Christianity's doctrinal development does so. The latter is the

story of conceptions of Gods' nature and activity subject to continual change and revision by what men have learned or believe themselves to have learned from reflection upon the life, teaching and death of Jesus. A Christian as such is free to abandon or revise any particular view of *what* is revealed about God in Christ and still remain a Christian. The opinion that he is not has indeed often been held within the Church but that is simply one conception of what is revealed in Christ and, in the view of many Christians like myself, a mistaken one. A Christian can (logically) hold *all* his particular beliefs open to criticism.

But what, to recall Bartley's definition of a comprehensively critical rationalist, of the Christian's 'basic philosophical position itself' (cf. p. 180)?

It is *not* logically possible to be a Christian and abandon one's commitment to give God content from Christ. There could not (logically) be *Christian* reasons for doing so. But is this some sort of defect in Christianity? Surely not. One could not have moral reasons for giving up morality or scientific reasons for giving up science, any more than Christian reasons for giving up Christianity. Then are they all non-rational? Certainly not, if I am right in my view that one could not have good reasons for giving up rationalism.

Christianity is essentially rational although only *Christian* good reasons count within it, where 'Christian good reason' means something like 'a reason for saying something in terms of God which derives from the basic belief that "God" is to be given content from what is observed in Christ'. Reasons do not subsist *in vacuo*. They must always be moves within some language-game or other and the basic presuppositions of the game will determine in the last analysis what counts as a good reason within it and what does not. If being rational means *more* than simply having good reasons for what one says or does – if it means, as in this sub-section we take it to mean, being open-minded, always ready to respond to some new reason, always subjecting the reasons one has hitherto accepted to critical re-examination – nevertheless the fact remains that what counts as a reason is determined by the language-game or form of life in which it has to play its part.

There may be all kinds of reasons for giving up Christianity – one may consider it immoral or unscientific, or whatever. But I cannot see that one must give it up because a Christian is *necessarily* less open-minded in his Christianity than a moralist in his moralizing or a scientist in his researches. A Christian is not necessarily so.

Conclusion

I said at the beginning of this chapter that the word 'rational' has a constant emotive meaning of approval as well as varied descriptive meanings. I approve of all the kinds of thinking or activity, which I have listed in this chapter as possible conceptions of rationality, namely, suiting beliefs to the evidence, avoiding self-contradiction, using language intelligibly, pursuing a policy only if one judges the expected gain from doing so to exceed the expected gain from not doing, and holding all one's beliefs open to criticism. I believe that, as a Christian, one can practice them all.

Proportioning belief to the evidence is possible for a religious believer provided it is borne in mind that what counts as evidence is always determined by the language-game within which it is offered.

While it is true that many religious believers have gloried in contradictions or used language in ways so far removed from the normal as to constitute unintelligibility, I hold that neither of these misdemeanours is necessarily involved in Christian belief. A Christian can say all that *qua* Christian he may be required to say about God without wallowing in self-contradictions or twisting the ordinary meanings of words such as 'goodness', 'action', 'encounter' to breaking-point.

It is possible that the gain which Christian belief brings to a believer should be 'infinite' in some sense of that word which will make Pascal's Wager work. If a rational man is one who would back a long shot provided that the odds against were infinite, then it is arguable that *qua* rational he should stake belief on Christianity.

Although so much Christianity has been, and no doubt still is, dogmatic in the worst sense of the word, I contend that Christianity is not necessarily so. Like any other language-game it has tacit presuppositions : being one form of religious belief, it is constituted by the concept of god and, being Christian, it is further constituted by Christ as the key to the concept of God. But within that logical framework it is, I would maintain, possible for a Christian to be open-minded in his allegiance to Christ. This latter phrase 'in his allegiance to Christ' does not mean that there are certain tenets of the faith which a Christian *qua* Christian must always slant his inquiries or conclusions to confirm. I acknowledge that this kind of Christianity-is-right-after-all apologetic occurs and can be depressingly, even nauseatingly, dishonest or one-sided. I am certainly not claiming such an apologetic to be a rational activity. What I have in mind is quite different. By being open-minded *in one's allegiance to Christ* I mean holding all one's be-liefs open to abandonment or revision *for reasons which rest on* : (a) particular claims that there is empirical evidence that some-thing or other is observable in Christ, and (b) the general principle that content must be given to the concept of God from what is observable in Christ.

Much 'Radical Christianity' would qualify as a move, or set of moves, within the Christian language-game as I here interpret it. Where I quarrel, when I do, with such Radical Christianity it is *not* because I think that it is unchristian, but simply muddle-head-ed. Its reasoning, that is to say, is Christian reasoning but some of its conclusions seem to me immediately open to criticism. How-ever, the fact that such thinking *is* Christian – and this particularly where it is most 'way out' to the minds of orthodox or traditional believers – is the point which I wish to emphasize. What Radical Christians observe, or think they observe, *in Christ* is a legiti-mate *candidate* for the content of the concept of God within Christianity. It is the kind of move which they make – and the *legitimacy* of it – which constitutes what I mean by the open-mindedness which is possible for a Christian. If being rational is holding one's beliefs open to criticism I maintain that it is as possible to do this within Christianity as within any other universe of discourse.[38]

Conclusion

In the Introduction I said that philosophy enables us both to define and to evaluate religious belief, to understand what it is and to form a judgment about it.

In the preceding pages I have tried to do both these things. Throughout this book I have been endeavouring to define the logical structure of religious belief and to defend what I chose to call in the Introduction its intellectual respectability.

How successfully I have achieved these objectives the reader will have decided for himself. But in conclusion there is one claim which I venture to make.

It is this. In my attempt to say what religious belief is and to assess its intellectual respectability, I have used the expressions, 'religious belief' and 'intellectual respectability', in perfectly normal ways. I have not stipulated a meaning for either which runs against their ordinary use.

Authors who set out to defend religion often re-define the notions either of religious belief or of intellectual respectability, or of both, to suit their own convenience. For example, I think that Braithwaite and Tillich re-define 'religious belief' to suit their convenience (above pp. 130, 135); and that Torrance re-defines intellectual respectability to suit his (see above, pp. 160). I would claim that I have not succumbed to either temptation.

I define religious belief as a language-game constituted by the concept of god and I think that this fits in with what religious belief is normally taken to be.

To test this claim, recall some of the points which I have made in this book about the logical structure of religious belief and consider how true or otherwise they are to that aspect of religious belief commonly called faith. I have argued that commitment to the concept of god is essential to religion. I have shown how this concept constitutes religious explanations and experiences as such. Concerning this concept of god there is a question, 'Does god really exist?' which, I have contended, is both (a) meaningful and (b) elusive to an indisputable answer. This question, I said, calls for an ultimate ontological choice.

The concept of faith, as commonly understood by religious believers, seems to me to fit in with these points perfectly. Faith is a commitment to something ultimate. It means interpreting experience in certain ways – e.g. seeing the hand of god in whatever happens – and entering into certain characteristic experiences – e.g. finding the peace of god whatever happens. This is exactly in line with what I have said about the concept of god constituting religious belief. Again : faith is (a) an affirmation that god really exists in (b) a situation where such affirmation could (logically) be doubted. Now, unless the question 'Does god really exist?' were meaningful, an affirmative answer to it would not be meaningful; and if any answer to that question were indisputable, then, given such answer, faith would not be logically possible. It is, therefore, a necessary condition of the occurrence of faith, as commonly understood, that both my contentions about the question 'Does god really exist?' – (a) that it is meaningful and (b) elusive to an indisputable answer – should be true.

Within religious belief, as commonly conceived, there is room for change and development. A believer's faith may increase or diminish. He may learn from other believers. His thought of god may be enriched by what he learns of the world about him; his trust in god, deepened by what he experiences of good, or ill, fortune. All this scope for development and change within religious belief seems to me to be allowed for in the account of its logical structure which I have offered. Questions and answers in terms of god may become more, or less, important to a man and this is what constitutes the logical possibility of the increase or diminution of faith. The content which is given to the concept of god is open to very diverse formulation and re-formulation, which allows for what can properly be called learning from other believers, or from the world about one, or from one's experience of life. Believers sometimes speak of the life of faith as an exploration into god. What I have done is to indicate the logical implications of such a description.

I can think of no point at which my definition of religious belief need – or indeed will – have struck believers as odd. To conceive of the logical structure of religious belief as I have done is, I would therefore claim, to give an account of it which is not only philosophically attractive but which fits perfectly what is normally meant by religious belief.

So far as my consideration of the intellectual respectability of religious belief is concerned, I would claim that I have throughout avoided special pleading on its behalf. This explains why so much of my book has consisted of the adverse criticism of arguments which have been put up to support religious belief.

Where, for example, evidence of the kind which is used to support a scientific hypothesis is invoked to substantiate belief in god, I have insisted that such evidence should be assessed exactly as it would be in a scientific context. In so far as the argument from design, to take one case, implied that the existence of god can be treated as a scientific hypothesis, I insisted, following Hume and countless others, that its proponents should not be allowed to count only the evidence which favoured their purpose. Or again, in so far as this argument purported to be an argument from analogy, I insisted that it conform to the normal conditions for that kind of argument.

When discussing the question of rationality, I was at pains to avoid any move which rested on the contention that god is 'above logic'. Contradictions in religion are as self-stultifying as in any other context. Religious language in so far as its meaning is parasitic upon the meaning of language as used in non-religious contexts – and so it is to a considerable extent as I have tried to show – must for its intelligibility conform to the rules for its use which apply in non-religious contexts. We cannot, for example, cavalierly dismiss the problem as to how god acts in the world without a body simply by pointing out that he is god. Or again, since rationality implies open-mindedness, religious belief must allow for it to the same extent as do other universes of discourse, which are indisputably rational. None of this have I denied.

When pointing out that religious belief is logically dependent upon an ultimate ontological choice I recognized that its claim to intellectual respectability depends upon the fact that other universes of discourse do this as well. The logical features of the question 'Does god really exist?' are no different from those of the questions 'Do physical objects really exist?' or 'Does moral obligation really exist?' I have avoided special pleading for religious belief which would make its ultimate presupposition as such of a different logical character from the constitutive concept of any other universe of discourse. This was essential, of course, to an argument intended to show that it is as intellectually respectable to be religious as to be scientific or moral.

Notes

CHAPTER I

1. Micah, vi. 8.
2. Op. cit. 4.22 (my italics).
3. Op. cit. 2.021 (my italics).
4. Op. cit. 2.18.
5. *Ludwig Wittgenstein: A Memoir* (London, 1958) p. 69.
6. *Philosophical Investigations* (Oxford, 1958) 40.
7. Op. cit. 47.
8. Op. cit. 88.
9. Op. cit. 421.
10. Op. cit. 7 (italics mine).
11. Op. cit. 2.
12. Op. cit. p. 223e.
13. *The Philosophy of Wittgenstein* (Englewood Cliffs, N.J., 1964) p. 243.
14. Op. cit. 563.
15. Op. cit. 109.
16. *The Blue and Brown Books* (Oxford, 1960) p. 26.
17. Op. cit. p. 48.
18. Cf. Op. cit. p. 43.
19. See Op. cit. pp. 56 and 54.
20. Cf. G. Ryle, *The Concept of Mind* (London, 1949) pp. 16-18; cf. his *Dilemmas* (Cambridge, 1960).
21. Cf. A. Flew, 'Theology and Falsification', in *New Essays in Philosophical Theology*, edited by A. Flew and A. MacIntyre (London, 1955).
22. *Philosophical Investigations* (Oxford, 1958) p. 179e.
23. Op. cit. p. 55.
24. Op. cit. p. 56.
25. Op. cit. p. 57.
26. Op. cit. 54.
27. Pp. 101 ff.
28. Op. cit. p. 55.
29. Cf. R. M. Hare, 'Theology and Falsification, B' in Flew and MacIntyre, op. cit.; D. D. Evans, *The Logic of Self-Involve-*

ment (London, 1963); and P. van Buren, *The Secular Meaning of the Gospel* (London, 1963).

30. See M. Hesse's remarks on my contribution to *Talk of God*, edited by G. N. A. Vesy (London, 1969) in her review article, *Philosophy*, 1969.
31. P. Bertocci's review of my contribution to *We Believe in God*, edited by R. E. Davies (London, 1968) in *Religious Studies 1969*.

CHAPTER 2

1. *Proslogium*, preface, translated by S. N. Deane, *Anselm: Basic Writings* (La Salle, III, 1961) p. 2.
2. Aliquid quo nihil maius cogitari possit. Variants in Anselm are : aliquid quo maius nihil cogitari potest; id quo maius cogitari nequit; aliquid quo maius cogitari non valet.
3. Op. cit. Chap. II, Deane, p. 8.
4. Op. cit. Chap. III, Deane, p. 8.
5. Deane, pp. 150–1.
6. Deane, p. 162.
7. Deane, p. 158.
8. Eg. J. Hick, 'A Critique of the Second Argument' in *The Many-Faced Argument*, edited by J. Hick and A. C. McGill (London, 1968).
9. Deane, p. 160.
10. Chap. VI, Deane, pp. 48-9.
11. *Dialogues Concerning Natural Religion*, second edition by N. Kemp-Smith (London, 1947) p. 189.
12. *Critique of Pure Reason*, translated by N. Kemp-Smith : reprinted in *The Ontological Argument*, edited by A. Plantinga (London, 1968) p. 59. This latter volume contains a useful collection of extracts from classical authors and papers by contemporary philosophers on the ontological argument.
13. *Mind*, 1948 : Plantinga, op. cit. pp. 119-20.
14. Findlay is not now so confident of this line of argument : see his *Language, Mind and Value* (1963) quoted in Plantinga, op. cit. p. 121, and his *The Transcendence of the Cave* (London, 1967) pp. 89-90.
15. C. Hartshorne, *Man's Vision of God* (London, 1941) : in Plantinga, op. cit. p. 135.
16. 'Anselm's Ontological Argument', *Philosophical Review*, 1960, reprinted in Plantinga, op. cit. p. 145.
17. Op. cit. pp. 170-1.
18. For a very brief but trenchant criticism of Anselm see M. Roth 'A Note on Anselm's Ontological Argument', *Mind*, 1970; for

a recent study see J. Barnes's, *The Ontological Argument* in my series *New Studies in the Philosophy of Religion* (Macmillan).
19. Cf. L. Wittgenstein, *Tractatus Logico-Philosophicus* (London, 1922) 5.6.

CHAPTER 3

1. A. Kenny's translation in his *The Five Ways* (London, 1969) p. 46. The reference in 'just as was shown in the case of efficient causes' is to Aquinas's Second Way.
2. T. Gilby's translation in his *Aquinas Philosophical Texts* (London, 1951) p. 39.
3. Cf. Kenny, op. cit. p. 51.
4. Op. cit. p. 53.
5. Cf. Kenny, op. cit. p. 56.
6. Op. cit. p. 8.
7. Cf. Kenny, op. cit. p. 48.
8. *Aquinas* (London, 1955) pp. 118-19.
9. 'The Existence of God – A debate between Bertrand Russell and Father F. C. Copleston, S.J.' broadcast by the B.B.C. in 1948, reprinted in B. Russell, *Why I Am Not a Christian* (London, 1957) pp. 153-4.
10. Op. cit. p. 65.
11. Cf. Kenny, op. cit. p. 83.
12. 7.2c Some italics mine. Cf. Kenny, op. cit. pp. 91-2.
13. *Aquinas* p. 116.
14. J. Burnet, *Greek Philosophy* (London, 1914) p. 81.
15. Kenny's translation, op. cit. p. 96.
16. *Review*, edited by D. D. Raphael (Oxford, 1940) p. 285.
17. Op. cit. (Fontana edition, London, 1958) pp. 122-8.
18. Op. cit. p. 101.
19. Op. cit. p. 131.
20. *Dialogues Concerning Natural Religion*, second edition by N. Kemp-Smith (London, 1947) p. 204.
21. Op. cit. pp. 239-40.
22. Op. cit. p. 149.
23. 'The Argument from Design', *Philosophy*, 1957; see also his monograph *The Argument from Design* in the series which I edit *New Studies in the Philosophy of Religion* (Macmillan).
24. Op. cit. pp. 179-81.
25. Cf. K. R. Popper, *The Logic of Scientific Discovery* (London, 1959) p. 253.
26. Cf. A. J. Ayer, *The Problem of Knowledge* (London, 1956, Pelican) pp. 127-8.

27. J. Wilson, *Philosophy and Religion* (London, 1961) p. 84.
28. *Systematic Theology,* vol 1 (London, 1953) p. 114.
29. Ibid.
30. Ibid.
31. Op. cit. Chapter v.
32. Some such interpretation appears in W. H. Walsh's 'Kant's Moral Theology', *Proceedings of the British Academy* XLIX (1963).
33. See his *The Theological Foundation of Ethics* (London, 1961) p. 89.
34. *The Moral Argument for Christian Theism* (London, 1965) p. 80.
35. See A. N. Prior, *Logic and the Basis of Ethics* (Oxford, 1949).
36. Op. cit. p. 10.
37. See W. D. Ross, *The Right and the Good* (Oxford, 1930) and *Foundations of Ethics* (Oxford, 1939); H. A. Prichard, *Moral Obligation* (Oxford, 1949).
38. See my *Modern Moral Philosophy* (London, 1970) Chapter II.
39. *The Language of Morals* (Oxford, 1952) pp. 118-19.
40. On the different kinds of evaluative use see P. H. Nowell-Smith, *Ethics* (London, 1954) p. 98.
41. *Philosophical Investigations* (Oxford, 1958) 664 and 109, cf. my *Ludwig Wittgenstein* (London, 1968) p. 55.
42. See my *Ethical Intuitionism* (London, 1967), *Reason and Right* (London, 1970), and *Modern Moral Philosophy.*
43. See P. Foot's papers in section IV of my *The Is-Ought Question* (London, 1969); and also G. J. Warnock, *Contemporary Moral Philosophy* (London, 1967) and *The Object of Morality* (London, 1971).
44. Op. cit. p. 20.
45. Op. cit. p. 54.
46. See *Ethics and Language* (New Haven and London, 1944) and *Facts and Values* (New Haven, 1963).
47. See *The Language of Morals* (Oxford, 1952) and *Freedom and Reason* (Oxford, 1963).

CHAPTER 4

1. 'Is it a Religious Belief that God exists?' In *Faith and the Philosophers,* edited by J. Hick (London, 1964) p. 108.
2. 'Belief-In', *Mind,* 1970.
3. For an explanation of 'performative' see J. L. Austin, 'Performative Utterances' in his *Philosophical Papers* (Oxford, 1961) and also his *How To Do Things With Words* (Oxford, 1962).

4. Op. cit. p. 407.
5. Op. cit. p. 452.
6. Cf. D. D. Evans, *The Logic of Self-Involvement* (London, 1963).
7. Cf. Op. cit. p. 437.
8. Op. cit. pp. 107-8.
9. 'On Believing that God Exists', *Southern Journal of Philosophy* 1967, p. 168.
10. 'Faith, Scepticism and Religious Understanding' in *Religion and Understanding,* edited by D. Z. Phillips (Oxford, 1967) p. 72.
11. Op. cit. p. 71.
12. Quoted by C. A. Coulson in *Science and Christian Belief* (London, 1955) pp. 136-7.
13. Op. cit. pp. 74-5.
14. Amongst those who have held a similar view is T. R. Miles, *Religion and the Scientific Outlook* (London, 1959), Chap. 4 on 'the "absolute existence" mistake'.
15. Op. cit. pp. 66-7.
16. Op. cit. p. 69.
17. 'Wittgensteinian Fideism', *Philosophy,* 1967 p. 208.
18. Op. cit. pp. 208-9.
19. Op. cit. p. 207.

CHAPTER 5
1. *Philosophical Investigations* (Oxford, 1958) 23.
2. *Religion in Britain and Northern Ireland* (London, 1970).
3. *Faith and the Philosophers,* edited by J. H. Hick (London, 1964) p. 129.
4. Op. cit. p. 132.
5. Ibid.
6. Op. cit., second edition, p. 38.
7. I leave aside here the question whether or not the criterion of meaningfulness is empirical verifiability or falsifiability. See section iii.
8. Op. cit. p. 9.
9. Op. cit. p. 39.
10. Op. cit. p. 41.
11. *New Essays in Philosophical Theology,* edited by A. Flew and A. MacIntyre (London, 1955) p. 99.
12. Op. cit. p. 311.
13. Op. cit. pp. 325-6.
14. Op. cit. p. 360.
15. Op. cit. pp. 326-7.
16. Op. cit. ibid.
17. p. 327.

18. Op. cit. p. 360.
19. Op cit. p. 285. Cf. R. Bultmann, *Kerygma and Myth* (London,
20. Cf. p. 124.
21. Op. cit. Reprinted in *Christian Ethics and Contemporary Philosophy*, edited by I. T. Ramsey (London, 1966) p. 59.
22. Op. cit., Ramsey, p. 66.
23. Op. cit., Ramsey, p. 71.
24. *The Secular Meaning of the Gospel* (London, 1963) pp. 99 and 145.
25. Op. cit. p. 128.
26. Op. cit. p. 126.
27. Op. cit. p. 132.
28. Cf. my article 'Discernment Situations : Some Philosophical Problems' in *Scottish Journal of Theology*, 1966.
29. *Systematic Theology*, vol ɪ (London, 1953) p. 234.
30. Cf. P. Tillich, *The Courage To Be* (London, 1952) *passim*.
31. Cf. *Systematic Theology*, vol ɪ, p. 303.
32. Op. cit. pp. 239-42.
33. Op. cit. p. 163.
34. Op. cit. p. 260.
35. *The Courage To Be*, p. 177.
36. Op. cit. p. 179.
37. For a fuller critique of Logical Positivism see my *Modern Moral Philosophy* (London, 1970) pp. 32-7.
38. Cf. K. R. Popper, *The Logic of Scientific Discovery* (London, 1959) pp. 35-6.
39. I discuss this development more fully in my *Modern Moral Philosophy*, pp. 44-63.
40. *Philosophical Investigations* 23.
41. *How To Do Things With Words* (Oxford, 1962) p. 98.

CHAPTER 6
1. Cf. C. L. Stevenson, *Ethics and Language* (New Haven and London, 1944), Chapter ɪɪɪ.
2. Op. cit. edited by L. A. Selby-Bigg (Oxford, 1902) p. 110.
3. Op. cit. p. 125.
4. View taken by Lampe in *The Resurrection*, by G. W. H. Lampe and D. M. MacKinnon (London, 1966).
5. View taken by P. van Buren in his *The Secular Meaning of the Gospel* (London, 1963).
6. *Lectures on Religious Belief* (Oxford, 1966) p. 61.
7. By. K. Buhler, *Sprachtheorie* (Leipzig, 1934) and K. R. Popper, *Conjectures and Refutations* (London, 1962). On this cf. W. W. Bartley, *Morality and Religion*, pp. 30-3.

8. Reprinted in *Religious Experience and Truth: a Symposium*, edited by S. Hook (London, 1962).
9. Op. cit. p. 303.
10. Op. cit. p. 315.
11. Op. cit. p. 316.
12. First published, 1917; Pelican edition (London, 1959) p. 74.
13. E.g. P. G. Forsyth, *The Person and Place of Christ*, fourth edition (London, 1930) p. 70.
14. On this subject-matter cf. *inter alia* A. I. Melden, *Free Action* (London, 1961), and *Freedom and the Will*, edited by D. F. Pears (London, 1963), which give some indication of how the matter is discussed among philosophers today.
15. Op. cit. p. 228.
16. See in particular his paper, 'Paradox and Discovery' in his collection called *Paradox and Discovery* (Oxford, 1965).
17. Op. cit. p. 134.
18. Op. cit. p. 124.
19. *Theological Science* (London, 1969) pp. 279-80.
20. Cf. A. Flew's paper 'Theology and Falsification', in *New Essays in Philosophical Theology*, edited by A. Flew and A. MacIntyre (London, 1955).
21. Op. cit. p. 68.
22. Op. cit. p. 79.
23. 'Some Notes on Anthropomorphic Theology', in Hook, op. cit., pp. 242-3.
24. R. W. Hepburn, *Christianity and Paradox* (London, 1958) pp. 32-3.
25. Op. cit. pp. 36-7.
26. Op. cit. pp. 40-1.
27. Op. cit. pp. 40-1.
28. *Thought and Action* (London, 1960) pp. 94-5.
29. *Meaning and Truth in Religion* (New Jersey, 1964) pp. 28-9.
30. Cf. Hampshire, op. cit. Chapter I.
31. 'The Christian Wager', *Religious Studies* 1969, pp. 217-18.
32. Op cit. p. 146.
33. 'Comprehensively Critical Rationalism', *Philosophy* 1969, p. 60.
34. See J. Agassi, I. C. Jarvie and Tom Settle, 'The Grounds of Reason', *Philosophy* 1971.
35. Op. cit. p. 149.
36. Ibid.
37. Op. cit. p. 150.
38. I discuss some of the issues raised in this chapter in contributions to *Second Order*, 1973 and *Religious Studies*, 1973.

Index of Names

Adams, J. C., 64
Anaxagoras, 56, 58
Anselm, xii, 27-40, 42
Aquinas, 41-56, 58
Aristotle, 52, 113-14
Augustine, 8
Austin, J. L., 20, 91, 142
Ayer, A. J., 116-18, 129

Barry, F. R., 128
Bartley, W. W., 179-86
Bonhoeffer, D., 116, 120-6, 128
Braithwaite, R. B., 127-31, 132, 133, 188
Bultmann, R., 124-5
Buren, P. van, 21, 131-3

Christian, W. A., 174
Copleston, F. C., 47-8, 55
Coulson, C. A., 57-8
Cox, H., 127, 133-7

Descartes, 27

Edwards, P., 165-7, 169-70, 172-3
Einstein, A., 139, 159
Evans, D. D., 21

Farmer, H. H., 165, 168
Findlay, J. N., 32, 33-9
Flew, A. G. N., 118-19
Foot, Mrs P., 83

Gaunilon, 29-31

Hampshire, S., 171

Hare, R. M., 21, 82, 86
Hartshorne, C., 27, 35-9
Hepburn, R. W., 165-70, 172-3
Hick, J. H., 32
Hume, D., 33-4, 58-61, 144-8

Jeans, J., 57

Kant, 33-4, 74-7
Kenny, A., 43, 46, 50, 53
Kierkegaard, 96

Laplace, 65
Leibniz, 27
Leverrier, 64

MacIntosh, J. J., 90
MacIntyre, A. C., 113-15, 138-40
Maclagan, W. G., 78, 83, 85-8
McPherson, T., 60
Malcolm, N., xii, 4, 27, 32, 38-9, 91-4
Moore, G. E., 78-9, 84, 102-4
Muggeridge, M., 178

Newton, I., 63, 139, 155
Nielsen, K., 99-101

Occam, 65
Otto, R., 67, 155-6, 161
Owen, H. P., 78, 84-5

Pascal, 177-9
Paul, St, 22, 67
Phillips, D. Z., 94-9
Pitcher, G., 7

Popper, K. R., 17, 63
Price, H. H., 90-1
Price, R., 57, 58
Prichard, H. A, 79

Ramsey, I. T., 163
Ross, W. D., 79
Russell, B., 95-6

Sartre, J-P., 19
Stevenson, C. L., 86
Swinburne, R. G., 177-9

Tillich, P., 72-3, 127, 133-7, 153-6, 161, 188
Torrance, T. F., 160-1, 188

Walsh, W. H., 195
Warnock, G. J., 83
Watkins, J. W. W., 181-2
Whitehead, A. N., 158
Wisdom, J., 159-61
Wittgenstein, xi, xii, 3-14, 18-20, 21, 24, 82, 106, 142, 149
Wordsworth, W., 67